We Have Never Been Postmodern

We Have Never Been Postmodern

Theory at the Speed of Light

Steve Redhead

Edinburgh University Press

Edinburgh University Press Ltd
22 George Square, Edinburgh

www.euppublishing.com

Typeset in 11/13 Ehrhardt MT
by Servis Filmsetting Ltd, Stockport, Cheshire, and
printed and bound in Great Britain by
CPI Antony Rowe, Chippenham and Eastbourne

A CIP record for this book is available from the British Library

ISBN 978 0 7486 4344 8 (hardback)

Contents

Acknowledgements

Many of the ideas in this book have had outings in different settings. They have been tested off and online in small circulation publications and websites, in podcasts, photostories and mini lectures, as well as in front of many gatherings of students, writers and academics at events around the world. Thanks to all who have published earlier and very much abbreviated versions of some of these Chapters. Thanks also to all the readers, viewers and listeners who have responded to my experiments in public and my gratitude for their critical appreciation to all the live audiences who hosted me in their mobile city cultures on various continents – Amsterdam and Belgrade; Perth and Melbourne; Auckland and Wellington; Brighton, Liverpool and Manchester; Chicago and San Francisco; and Montreal, Toronto and Vancouver. Thanks, finally, to Vicki Donald, my editor at Edinburgh University Press, for all her work on and support with the book.

'What I called claustropolis has replaced cosmopolis'
Paul Virilio, in conversation with Sylvere Lotringer
(Virilio and Lotringer 2008, p. 211)

For Tara
With All My Love

CHAPTER 1

After Postmodernity?

As the end-of-the-century party dreamed up by Jean Baudrillard (Redhead 1990) finally closed and pre-millennial tension gave way to a post-millennial hangover (Redhead 1997b) new cultural, economic and social theories have emerged at the speed of light to describe supermobile modernities, globalised markets and international mobile city cultures. The world experienced more than a decade of globalisation, modernisation and mobility but in the wake of economic, political and environmental crises these processes seem to be on the verge of being reversed: welcome to deglobalisation, immobility and demodernisation with millions of displaced people wandering the globe (or the universe) in the uncertain future which lies ahead in the long twenty-first century imagined by Paul Virilio and Raymond Depardon (Virilio and Depardon 2008b; Virilio 2009b, 2010a, 2010b). But these changes, as many have warned in the past, are inevitably 'uneven developments' in a 'new old world' (Anderson 2009) that we as world citizens now inhabit. Prediction of trends and the shape and contours of what I call in this book the 'post-future' is notoriously difficult.

What can we say with some certainty about such trends? Cosmopolitanism, long the dominant characteristic in sociology, has it appears become claustropolitanism, or is certainly in the process of 'becoming claustropolitan'. We can all be in favour of cosmopolitan values, but a cosmopolitan sociology looks to have run its course. For these new 'new times' (Hall and Jacques 1989), often engaging the same 'old enemies' (Clarke 1991), with all the fast changing 'new' media technologies that underpin the upheavals, this book offers a hypothesis/slogan/mantra: *we have never been postmodern*. Such a slogan, plundered from my own casual use of the phrase over a number of years (Redhead 2008) echoes, ironically and playfully in pseudo-postmodern style, the statement made famous by Bruno Latour, one of the less quoted French social theorists, that 'we have never been modern' (Latour 1993). However, the book's claim that we have never been postmodern is no paean to the idea that there is no modernity or that modernity is itself coming to an end (Sim 2010). Conversely, the argument is that modernity is *all* that there is. There is, however, what this book envisages as the non-postmodern condition or non-postmodernity. In other words, in this argument, there is only what can be called 'the modern condition' or post-postmodernity, where the debates about the postmodern have left us reluctant to adhere to old certainties or resurrect the gurus of the past to explain the future. There is, still, then, in my version of the sociological imagination a possible position in contemporary social and cultural theory which claims there is only modernity, nothing after it or beyond it, but which reflexively is able to take into account the debates about postmodernism, postmodernity and the 'post' as a cultural condition and assess the effects of such debates on our search for new thinking. In this book the ubiquitous 'post'- prefix is seen to be always, already part of the modern, not an era *after*; or as Orchestral Manouevres in the Dark (OMD) put it in album title, what we have here is the culture and 'the history of modern'. Bruno Latour has written of 'non-modernity'. Opposing this idea, but in keeping with the jokey, artful taking up of Latour's notions, this book dares to conceive instead of 'non-postmodernity', a world which it claims is replete with what it sees as Mobile Accelerated Nonpostmodern Culture (MANC). The pages of *We Have Never Been Postmodern: Theory at the Speed of Light* probe the exciting possibilities of accelerated culture and non-postmodernity, profiling various cutting edge studies of the social formations of our time, and some of their most iconic figures, along the way.

In this misperceived postmodern condition, nevertheless, it is possible to say that we *have* been neo-liberal, an era which however long it takes finally to expire (and it may be decades) is in its death throes. That does not amount to arguing that postmodernity and postmodernism was somehow the 'cultural logic of late capitalism' (Jameson 1991) or that the postmodern was 'conservative' (Boyne and Rattansi 1990: 35; Perryman 1994: 240–60) or that neo-liberalism is necessarily over right now, but it does mean that neo-liberalism can be periodised and that some some kind of great transformation, what Richard Florida has called the 'Great Reset' (Florida 2010), is occurring once again. It is instructive to look at the history of what has been widely labelled, almost every day, for at least a decade, the 'new media' – old of course as soon as it is invented in accelerated culture – in this regard. The internet and world wide web have been characterised as moving from an earlier static and top down phase of Web 1.0 to today's Web 2.0 where interactivity and mass participation are rife, with a Web 3.0 or even 4.0 on the not too distant horizon. There has been one major dot.com boom and bust, with more on the horizon. Capitalism itself has been described by financial journalist Anatole Kaletsky as entering a comparable age, a veritable 'capitalism 4.0' (Kaletsky 2010), following at least three previous economic, political and social upheavals of seismic proportions in the world in the last two centuries. The question of our time, in a near-past racked by catastrophic global market meltdown minutes away from empty automatic teller machines (Seldon and Lodge 2010) and a 'new barbarism' (Levy 2008), has become 'capitalism or barbarism?' – rather than the 1960s question 'socialism or barbarism'? The historian Eric Hobsbawm, whose own life (Hobsbawm 2002) spanned so much of the twentieth century, has argued in writing about globalisation, democracy and terrorism that, coming after the era he had labelled the 'age of extremes' (Hobsbawm 1994) in 'the short twentieth century' from 1914 to 1991, there is now unfolding before our eyes, quite manifestly, a 'new era which has emerged from the old' (Hobsbawm 2007: 1) and which will be sustained in 'the new century' (Hobsbawm 1999). Furthermore, Jonathan Rutherford (Rutherford 2008: 8), looking at contemporary changes in the practices and cultures of capitalism, has proclaimed that:

> We are living through an age of transition. The new co-exists with the old. We can identify political, economic and cultural elements of this change, but we do not yet have a way of describing the kind of society we are living in. The great explanatory frameworks of political economy and sociology inherited from the industrial modernity of the nineteenth century leave too much unsaid. Theories of the moment tend to skip from one modern phenomenon to another. They are like stones skimming across the surface of water. We lack a story of these times.

This so-called 'new era' has also been characterised variously as the 'age of fallibility' (Soros 2006), the 'age of access' (Rifkin 2000), the 'age of uncertainty' (Bauman 2007a), the 'age of turbulence' (Greenspan 2007) and the 'age of instability' (Smith 2010) and there is no let up today in the rush to characterise in a pithy, poignant, pregnant phrase, the culture of the period we are seen to be entering. We have been here before. Many attempts have been made at capturing such a story in the last two decades. Starting in the 1990s, Anthony Giddens, who later went on to become Tony Blair's favourite sociologist (Giddens 2002, 2003, 2007; Seldon 2004, 2007; Radice 2004: 415–16; Rentoul 2001), has often claimed that we are in a 'period of evident transition' and offered the view that we are now 'living in a post-traditional society' (Beck, Giddens and Lash 1998: 56–109). 'Alternative modernities', on the other hand, as Lawrence Grossberg has dubbed them, are seen as a product of a contemporary 'struggle over modernity' (Grossberg 2006: 12–19). As the fierce conflict over precisely which capitalism will take over the globe develops apace, it seems that we are consumed (again) by the question of which modernities we will inhabit in the near future. A fast modernity to displace the open access online journal *Fast Capitalism* editor Ben Agger's original couplet of slow modernity / fast capitalism? A cold modernity for a world in what Paul Virilio has called a 'cold panic' (Virilio 2005a)? A dangerous modernity (Redhead 2004b) to go along with the rise of Naomi Klein's 'disaster capitalism' (Klein 2007), a sign of the sociologies of the future where 'trajectories of the catastrophic', or in this book's claustropolitan sociology language 'post-catastrophe', will materialise more and more? The French urban theorist of speed, technology and modernity Paul Virilio, although categorically no postmodernist, has spoken of the 'postmodern period' and the 'atheism of postmodernity' as well as the 'profane art of modernity' (Virilio 2007a). Followers of Virilio, whose urgent, futuristic, poetic, provocative and sometimes reactionary ideas are always, already in the background throughout this book, have even suggested a subsequent displacement, or replacement, of the postmodern condition by a social formation they say is the 'dromocratic condition', based on Virilio's idea of dromocracy – the society of speed or of the 'race'. Many other contemporary social theorists have turned away from their erstwhile interests in the postmodern in the 1980s and 1990s. Scott Lash, for instance, has acknowledged that he does not 'particularly like the term postmodern' (Gane 2004) and one time guru of postmodernity, Zygmunt Bauman (Bauman 1991, 1993, 1995, 1998, 1999; Blackshaw 2005; Bauman and Tester 2001) has conceded that for some time he has been distancing himself from the concept, preferring his own original idea of 'liquid modernity' (Gane 2004) and committing himself to a thorough going sociological rethinking of the modern (Bauman 2001, 2002, 2004a, 2004b, 2007b, 2008, 2010a, 2010b). This reconceptualisation of modernity and modernisation is reflected in contemporary debates about 'what it means to be modern' as has been argued in relation to modern terror groups such as Al Qaeda whose origins are for a writer like John Gray (Gray 2003, 2007, 2009b) squarely in modernity rather than 'tradition'. Further, the central issue has become what it is to experience an attempted 'demodernisation', say in 'post-war' Iraq (Graham 2004; Žižek 2004), Afghanistan or Pakistan or how 'remodernisation' can take place in the case of what Francis Fukuyama (Fukuyama 2004, 2006) and other neo-conservatives have called state building in 'failed states' (such as Rwanda, Somalia, Yemen, Democratic Republic of Congo, Haiti and Sudan) and what critical geographer Stephen Graham (Graham 2004, 2010) has prophesied as 'the new military urbanism' which threatens to spread 'claustropolis' everywhere around the globe over the coming century. The theorisation of imperialism and colonialism, especially post-empire and post-colonialism (Gilroy 2004), is a continued imperative for us all whether or not postmodern theorists (Boyne and Rattansi 1990) have been able accurately to describe the 'rise of the West' in these global processes.

So the time is ripe for a rethinking of modernity; and social theory. Notions of conditions *after* modernity are, I argue, not ultimately persuasive. What is argued further, though, in this book is that there are only *modernities*, conflicting and overlapping. 'New' modernities sit alongside 'old' modernities. A 'new mobilities paradigm' amongst researchers at CeMoRe (Centre for Mobilities Research Centre) at the University of Lancaster in the UK has pioneered work on cosmopolitan sociology and mobilities – in other words, 'cosmobilities' research. This influential mobilities paradigm (Urry 2000, 2002, 2003, 2007) has threatened to shake up cosmopolitan sociology as a modernist, or postmodernist, project. Modernities, and their mobility, provide the conceptual key to looking at the contemporary condition afresh. There are different modernities, different ways of being modern. Anthony Giddens conceives of what 'other people call the post-modern' as the 'radicalising of modernity' (Giddens and Pierson 1998: 116). Ulrich Beck, who has talked of the 'modernisation of modernity' (Gane 2004: 143–66), has suggested, helpfully, that there are not only different paths to modernity but also different modernities, and that we live in an 'age of entangled modernities'. Global modernities have been identified in social and cultural theory in the 1990s but now in the second decade of the twenty-first century they are sorely in need of a radical reconceptualisation. The sociology of society, of modernity, has threatened to become the sociology of mobility. These contemporary modernities are mobile. The city cultures, for instance, of the twenty-first century are mobile city cultures. These are modern mobilities. Modernity is always, it appears, on the point of arriving. In Paul Virilio's frequently used original French language nugget, *ce qui arrive!*

The periodisation of transition within modernity has been fraught with difficulty as has the periodisation of the process from tradition to modernity. Early to late modernity, old to new modernity, heavy to light modernity, solid to liquid modernity, first to second modernity, condensed to diffuse modernity, systemic to network-like modernity, original modernity to reflexive modernity and modernity to present-day modernity are just some of the myriad conceptualisations of the transitions within modernity that have been suggested in recent contemporary social and cultural theory throughout the world. On top of that there is the much hinted at transition from modernity to postmodernity. Then we have claims at various times in the last three decades that there needs to be new social theory 'after postmodernism' or beyond postmodernity (Woodiwiss 1990; Gane 2004). But we are never quite sure when these transitions have taken place. Phases or stages or eras of modernity are being constantly theorised but the question of when did the new condition appear, when did the 'present' phase or stage or era occur, is left strangely unanswered. Much of social and cultural theory today, innovative and stimulating as it often seems, is speculative sociology without periodisation, an apparently endless reflection on a problem earlier designated as the shift from Fordism to post-Fordism, or old times to New Times, or old (manufacturing) economy to new (knowledge) economy. For instance, Zygmunt Bauman talked at the turn of the millennium of 'the present phase of modernity', what he has christened 'liquid modernity' (Bauman 2000, 2007a) with its attendant offshoots such as 'liquid love' (Bauman 2003), 'liquid life' (Bauman 2005), 'liquid fear' (Bauman 2006) and the 'liquid modern world' (Bauman 2010b). In Ulrich Beck's case (Boyne 2001; Beck, Giddens and Lash 1994; Beck and Beck-Gernsheim 2002; Beck and Wilms 2004; Beck 1992, 1999, 2005, 2006) the idea of 'first' to 'second modernity' has become a strongly argued case. But as readers of such theoretical speculation we remain unsure when it was that the move from the earlier phase actually happened, indeed if it ever did. What Bauman saw as solid modernity must have metamorphosed into liquid modernity at some point for the argument to work. Was solid modernity the state we were in during the 1970s, 1980s and 1990s? Or even the 1870s, 1880s, 1890s? Bauman, to give him his due, does recognise, significantly, that *all* modernity is that which 'melts into air' as Marx and Engels, exemplary theorists of earlier modernity in many ways, though, ultimately, flawed theorists of capitalism, put it over a century and a half ago when writing *The Communist Manifesto* in 1848 (Marx and Engels 1998). 'All that is solid melts into air' is always the principle definition of the modern condition as Marshall Berman astutely pointed out a quarter of a century ago (Berman 2010). The 'melting of solids' is not just a phase of modernity, it is the constant, permanent present, what can be seen throughout the pages of this book, and earlier texts, as 'accelerated culture'. I would argue that the problems in contemporary humanities and social science debates often lie in this lack of periodisation and a rigorous theory of transformation from one period to another. The user generated content movement, open source or Web 2.0 as it has also been called, which includes the 'knowledge economy' of WikiLeaks, MySpace, YouTube, Facebook, Academia.edu, Twitter and Wikipedia engaging hundreds of millions of users worldwide, alongside millions of other webpages, has been interpreted as signalling a 'new media' revolution – from passive consumerism to mass creativity in one fell swoop as Charles Leadbeater has envisaged its trajectory (Leadbeater 1999, 2002, 2008). The flattening of expertise and authority, the attack on professionalism and the rise of the cult of the amateur that these changes herald has often been seen as examplifying the onset of the postmodern, instancing postmodernism and postmodernity. In fact it is more a sign of anti-statist libertarianism, of the right and left, as much as it is evidence of a transition to the postmodern. Often, too, the language of postmodernism and postmodernity have been confused with what is in effect a critical discourse of French post-structuralism, led by Jacques Lacan, Michel Foucault and Jacques Derrida itself emerging out of battles with Enlightenment thinkers (including contemporary theorists such as, for example, Jurgen Habermas) and becoming for a while the normalised intellectual and cultural analysis of/in many different countries (Anderson 1983; Easthope 1988).

This book is a contribution to debates in the humanities and social sciences which are attempting to rethink modernity *after* neo-liberalism (whenever that era may come to its end), and the body of theory which has emerged to start to help with this rethink. Were we, though, once postmodern? Theorists like Jean-Francois Lyotard (Lyotard 1984, 1991) and Fredric Jameson (Jameson 1991, 1998) became associated in the 1970s, 1980s and 1990s with the idea that there had, sometime in the late twentieth century, been a period of transition, morphing into a 'postmodern condition', which itself had a long and complex historical trajectory. For example, Perry Anderson (Anderson 1998) has noted that the 'idea of postmodernity' dates back to at least the 1930s. Jean-Francois Lyotard, author of several highly influential texts on postmodernity, aesthetics, politics, the avant-garde and the sublime (Lyotard 1984, 1988, 1991; Lyotard and Thebaud 1985), once associated with the leftist grouping in France in the 1960s which, translated into English, was emblazoned with the epithet 'Socialism or Barbarism', imagined, in the 1970s and 1980s in the course of his 'report on scientific knowledge', that there had been developing an 'incredulity' towards grand and meta-narratives (often exemplified by, for instance, science, Marxism, feminism, liberalism and so on) so profound that he labelled it a 'postmodern condition'. But then everything, seemingly overnight, became postmodern enough to necessitate dictionaries of postmodernism (Sim 2005), even though postmodernism was written off itself as just another grand or meta narrative. Everywhere, for a time, there was 'PoMo' – postmodern art (Ferguson 1990), postmodern sociology (Lash 1990; Featherstone 2007), postmodern cinema (Denzin

1991), postmodern architecture (Jameson 1991), postmodern criminology (Morrison 1995) and postmodern jurisprudence (Morrison 1997; Douzinas and Warrington with McVeigh, 1991; Frug 1992; Leonard 1995); there were even postmodern pop charts. Always, as soon as these postmodern formations proclaimed their emergence over the last thirty or forty years, they were declared to be dead on arrival (DOA) in various channels of official media discourse of the day. Today, it is proclaimed, such an era or structure of feeling is well and truly over – it is said that we are living, today, somehow or other, *after* postmodernity. Surmodern, supermodern, intermodern and post-postmodern; altermodernity, liquid modernity and autmodernity; and pseudomodernism, hypermodernism and digimodernism have variously been put forward as alternative terms for those no longer satisfied by the idea of the postmodern, postmodernity and postmodernism. There is, as Terry Eagleton has pointed out (Reisz 2010), even a return of 'grand narratives', once condemned to the dustbin of history by postmodern theory, especially in the debates about resurgent global religious belief (Ruthven 2002) and the general idea that 'God' or 'He' is 'back', and a concomitant 'new aetheism' (Hitchens 2007; Cottee and Cushman 2007), often with 'a materialist core' (Žižek 2006b), to counter such beliefs.

For an imaginary graduate seminar on the subject of whether we have, or have not, been postmodern, there is a whole sub-literature for students around the world to read in order to signpost where we have been and where we are heading, published, and republished, over a quarter of a century: Bryan Turner's edited collection of essays *Theories of Modernity and Postmodernity* (Turner 1990), Keith Tester's *Life and Times of Postmodernity* (Tester 1993), Steve Connor's *Postmodernist Culture* (Connor 1997), Jonathan Bignell's *Postmodern Media Culture* (Bignell 2000), Martin McQuillan's edited essays collection *Post-Theory: New Directions in Criticism* (McQuillan 2000), Jim McGuigan's *Modernity and Postmodern Culture* (McGuigan 2002), Gary Hall's *Culture in Bits: The Monstrous Future of Theory* (Hall 2002), Paul Bowman's edited essays volume *Interrogating Cultural Studies* (Bowman 2003), Nicholas Gane's interviews with key social theorists in *The Future of Social Theory* (Gane 2004), John Hutnyk's *Bad Marxism: Capitalism and Cultural Studies* (Hutnyk 2004), Gilles Lipovetsky's *Hypermodern Times* (Lipovetsky 2005) Gary Hall and Clare Birchall's *New Cultural Studies: Adventures in Theory* (Hall and Birchall 2006), Paul Bowman's *Post-Marxism versus Cultural Studies* (Bowman 2007), Alan Kirby's *Digimodernism: How New Technologies Dismantle the Postmodern and Reconfigure our Culture* (Kirby 2009), Jean Baudrillard's posthumous *Why Hasn't Everything Already*

Disappeared? (Baudrillard 2009), Stuart Sim's *The End of Modernity* (Sim 2010) and Josh Toth's *The Passing of Postmodernism: A Spectroanalysis of the Contemporary* (Toth 2010) all highlight aspects of these debates in social, economic, political and cultural theory. 'Postmodernism' in these debates is frequently associated, for a good or ill, with a culture without history, or where history has stopped, as if nothing done a couple of minutes ago was of any 'authentic' value. Multiple alternative definitions of the 'postmodern' abound in these debates as will be seen throughout the pages of this book: for instance, postmodernism as the breakdown of the binary division of art and commerce; postmodernism as the breakdown of the binary division of law and culture; postmodernism as the breakdown of the binary division of high and low culture; postmodernism as the breakdown of fiction and 'reality'; postmodernism as the general breakdown of hierarchies – social, cultural and political; postmodernism as cultural plagiarism; postmodernism as moral relativism; and so on and so forth. Much of this literature works on the basis that we were once postmodern but now we are not – in some cases such a condition is celebrated for allowing 'real' politics, ethics and social action to come back into our culture. Slavoz Žižek, who has been described as 'the most dangerous philosopher in the West', as well as 'an academic rock star' and 'the Elvis of Cultural Theory' (Žižek 2007), has frequently placed postmodern or postmodernism or postmodernity in inverted commas in his many books and other writings, arguing ultimately for a revived Leninist communism after postmodernism, or a communism beyond postmodernity (Žižek 2002a, 2002b, 2005, 2006a, 2006b, 2008a, 2008b, 2009, 2010). Others argue for a new, twenty-first century defence of the ideas of the Enlightenment which have been seen to be widely called into question by postmodernism for many decades (Taylor 2010). This book goes further than these many engaging and stimulating debates to claim that we are not in any sense 'after postmodernity'. There never has been a postmodern era – only modernity. And such notions of the modern, modernism and modernity can be thought of as 'militant', 'socialist' or 'revolutionary' (Hatherley 2008) as they once were in the not too distant past; for example in the twentieth century when what Owen Hatherley calls 'left modernisms' (Hatherley 2008: 12–13) emerged, 'modernisms' which can still be seen as 'useful', offering a 'sense of possibility' that 'decades of being told 'There is No Alternative'' has almost beaten out of us'.

This book is of its time, and hopefully timely. It reactivates key tropes and signposts in contemporary theory and may help to reboot the endeavours of scholars in various sub-disciplines in the social sciences and the humanities. It offers, tentatively, some resources for what it calls a claustropolitan sociology of the future, some fragments of 'theory at the speed of light' where we are, maybe definitely, 'beyond societies' and finally, at last, free from all the debates about modernity versus postmodernity. The contentions being made in the book have profound consequences for the contemporary version of what C. Wright Mills half a century ago called the 'sociological imagination'. Especially the notion that the postmodern is not an era after modernity in a teleological, linear fashion but that it is always already part of modernity. The individual chapters in the book all explore and operationalise original concepts developed for this putative claustropolitan sociology project: namely, post-cultural state, post-space, post-pop, pastmodernism, post-sports, post-politics, post-catastrophe, post-theory, post-future – all part of ways of seeing a new sociological object, mobile accelerated nonpostmodern culture (MANC). They produce, as a result, concrete studies of fragments of contemporary culture, and some of its outstanding theorists, in the course of this abstract exploration. I have elsewhere (Redhead 1997a, 1997b, 2000, 2004b, 2008) introduced the concepts of post-youth, post-subculture, accelerated culture and non-postmodernity as better alternatives to explain and explore what seemed always to be presented extensively and rather randomly as 'postmodern culture'. While open to different and competing conceptualisations for the world we now inhabit, this book claims that there never was an era of postmodernity in the first place. But that does not mean we might be 'before postmodernity' in the same way as some have argued (Ali 2010), due to communism's 'first' failure in the twentieth century, we might be, in a very long historical process, 'before communism' . For those still waiting for this long historical process to unfold, what Louis Althusser and others have referred to as the lonely hour of the last instance, the divisions between scientific and other materialisms, humanism and anti-humanism, and utopianism and anti-utopianism, remain as stark as ever they were. One thing is for sure, we are not *after* postmodernity.

CHAPTER 2

Post-Cultural State

Just look at it! The statism we are in now! But, as students carrying placards protesting at the fee hikes by the David Cameron led coalition government in the UK proclaimed, 'It's the knowledge economy, stupid!' When Tony Blair and Gordon Brown began New Labour's path to power in 1994 they were seen as part of a new 'postmodern political culture' (Perryman 1994) which offered all kinds of possibilities, especially in the area of 'creative industries'. The concept of the 'post-cultural state' is introduced here into the international debate about the theory and practice of creative industries (Kong and O'Connor 2009; McKinlay and Smith 2009; Bilton 2007) in the context of this apparent postmodern political culture. This creative industries debate has become part of the so-called 'new', or 'knowledge', economy – the 'new capitalism' even (Doogan 2009). Although often the cause of deep scepticism (there is even a business magazine called *The New Economy*) it is a crucial step in the understanding of culture and the economy in the new century. The entire globe is supposedly in an era after the 'crash', or as Gordon Brown, former prime minister of the UK who was prepared to put the global economy through 'whatever it takes' (Richards 2010) put it, in a book length justification for 'better globalisation', 'beyond the crash' (Brown 2010). But globalisation itself, and global culture (Featherstone 1990), are themselves constantly 'in question', having just as much justification to be seen as beginning in the late nineteenth century as the late twentieth century (Hirst and Thompson 1996) or early twenty-first.

In the mode it is employed here, the post-cultural state recalls, playfully, the phrase 'the new industrial state' once used, in another era, by J.K. Galbraith. It has a double meaning. It refers to the new cultural condition we find ourselves in, and the way in which the modern state has governed, or intervened in, culture through law and other means of governance or regulation. It should be remembered, as Peter Fitzpatrick has shown in *Modernism and the Grounds of Law* (Fitzpatrick 2001), that law takes impetus and identity from modern society; law, truly, is crucial for modernity. The use of the term post-cultural state involves close examination of the 'vanishing line between law and popular culture' as Richard Sherwin (Sherwin 2000) has called it, when legal culture and popular culture (Redhead 1995) dissolve into each other in a process which has been labelled 'postmodernisation' of law 'in the Age of Images' (Sherwin 2000: 3–15). In this process, the modern nation state, as it did in the UK for a while, sometimes becomes a part of the 'popular cultural' sphere. Such processes can be seen clearly in a rethinking of the story of the creation and development of 'creative industries' policy (Andersen and Oakley 2008) especially in the Department of Culture, Media and Sport (DCMS) in the thirteen-year-long New Labour government of Tony Blair and Gordon Brown which ended in 2010. Brown and Blair conducted an experiment which is often cited approvingly in the creative industries debates around the world, especially in Oceania and Asia (Leo and Lee 2004). The post-cultural state, in my argument, involves the social engineering of a more widespread 'new individualism' where citizens are to be remade as creative entrepreneurs. It is argued here that debates about creative industries should be resituated within the wider framework of the agenda of cosmopolitan sociology and its (still problematic) analyses of modernity, the state and culture – the selfsame flawed framework that leads this book to call instead for a claustropolitan sociology of the future.

As the question 'what would new thinking for social, political and cultural theory after the crash look like?' (Cruddas and Rutherford 2009) is forced on the agenda of various 'new social movements' as well as more mainstream parties, the nature of the role and function of the state in the twenty-first century global society looms large once again. Will we revive the thinkers, and thought, of the past? Will the economic and political thought of Karl Marx and Friedrich Engels 'change the world' once again as Eric Hobsbawm has imagined in his nineties (Hobsbawm 2011)? Maybe the commodity exchange 'general theory of law and marxism' of Soviet legal theorist E.B. Pashukanis (Naves 2009, 2000) will suddenly become fashionable as we hurtle back to the conditions of the 1930s in what has been called a 'new depression' (Jacques 2009a, 2009c, 2009d), a concept so pertinent that singer Loudon Wainwright III even recorded his 'Ten Songs for the New Depression'. Or is it time to draw a line under the past and start anew? Will there be a Government 2.0 or State 2.0 to go along with Web 2.0 as neo-liberalism, finally, bites the dust? The 'economic 9/11', as Nick Clegg, the leader of the Liberal Democrats in the UK coalition government with the Tories (Laws 2010), has described the spectacular financial collapse at the culmination of the year long global 'credit crunch' (Brummer 2008; Turner 2008; Tett 2009; Smith 2010). The meltdown that occurred on the world's stock markets between August 2007 and October 2008, has, it is said by commentators of various political persuasions, effectively ended the neo-liberal era, which can itself be dated to the mid -1970s. In Britain's case, the oil price hike of 1973, the International Monetary Fund intervention in the Wilson/Callaghan Labour government of 1974–9, the election victory in May 1979 of Margaret Thatcher's Conservatives constituted the beginnings of this era. It was Margaret Thatcher, as prime minister in the 1980s, who famously stated 'there is no such thing as society'. As her successor, several times removed, and seen to be in a conservative tradition 'after Blair' (O'Hara 2007), David Cameron's public refutation of this 'dry Tory' position in his attempt to construct a progressive, or compassionate, conservatism (Jones 2008), and even adopt the 'left' 'Red Toryism' proposed by Phillip Blond (Cruddas and Rutherford 2008; Blond 2009a and b, 2010) with its much trumpeted commitment to voluntarism, localism, civil association and social enterprise, was supposed to signpost a new era. 'There is such a thing as society – it's just not the same thing as the state,' argued Cameron, then leader of the opposition Conservative Party, in November 2005 in a speech to the National Council for Voluntary Organisations. He also said in 2009 in the Annual Hugo Young lecture in London, before he succeeded Gordon Brown's doomed three-year Labour government (Rawnsley 2010; Seldon and Lodge 2010; Radice 2010; Richards 2010; Mandelson 2010), and became prime minister of the UK, that:

> our alternative to big government is not no government – some reheated version of ideological laissez-faire. Our alternative to big government is the big society. But the big society is not just going to spring to life on its own: we need strong and concerted government action to make it happen. We need to use the state to remake society.

For some commentators, in some cases having been through 'new times' debates before, the times are 'entirely new, tumultuous and dangerous' (Jacques 2009b). Now it is, almost overnight, said to be a world that is 'post-American', 'post-liberal', 'post-New Labour', 'post-modern' (again) and 'post-free market', whilst hyper neo-liberal policies are being pursued at home and abroad (Seldon and Lodge 2010). There are other commentators who, while agreeing that the end of the 'neo-liberal' age is nigh, have claimed that we are in a 'new conjuncture' and that 're-regulated capitalism' will have widespread cultural and social effects and consequences for 'progressive politics' (Cruddas and Rutherford 2009). The state, which was seen merely as 'enabling' by New Labour in the 1990s, has been rethought as 'the smart strategic state' (Kettle 2008) by the likes of New Labour's original co-architect Peter Mandelson (Rawnsley 2000; Mandelson 2010) and 'the sheltering state' by yet others (Blond 2009a and b). David Cameron's policy pronouncements before he became prime minister point to a basic philosophical rhetoric of a shrunken, minimalist state, the way for which was rigorously paved by legal and political theorists such as Iredell Jenkins (Jenkins 1980) and Robert Nozick (Nozick 2001) in the 1970s and 1980s and subsequently taken up enthusiastically by the Tea (Taxed Enough Already) Party and Palinite movements in the late 2000s in the USA in the presidency of Barack Obama. But the reframing of the state's role pervades all efforts to move beyond the contemporary laissez-faire philosophy and the dominance of the free market. The question of the state is, crucially, brought back in establishing 'the state we're in' (Hutton 1995, 1997, 1999, 2002, 2010).

In the important discussions of the so-called global 'weightless' knowledge economy there have been various new conceptual tools created to analyse the phenomenon. For some commentators the idea of there being a 'new' economy at all is itself a fantasy, and a dangerously debilitating one at that. What I argue here is that whether or not there is something new in the 'knowledge economy' that radically differentiates it from previous economic eras, the state and culture are involving themselves in modernity in new formations, and that this process deserves taking seriously, theoretically and politically. The best way to see this process is in the relationship between the state and creative industries. I am interested here in the form in which the relationship between state and culture fits into more general social theorising about modernity. The case study chosen here, the example of the creative industries policy of the UK government Department of Culture, Media and Sport, which from 1997 onwards spawned the label 'creative industries' (Andersen and Oakley 2008; Bilton 2007), is instructive, particularly in view of the fact that this specifically New Labour experiment in state, modernity and culture has been applied, more or less approvingly, internationally over the past decade. In 2010 one of the right wing think tanks seeking to advise the Liberal Democrat-Conservative coalition government actually recommended the complete demolition of the Department of Culture, Media and Sport as part of the 'shrinking of the state' argument. In the event, the coalition government comprehensive spending review implemented deep cuts in the department and restricted its role in regulation and promotion of issues like school sport and local provision of leisure and the arts. Literally, the recommendation was that the UK state, become after, or beyond, the cultural moment, a process speeded up by the public sector cutbacks following the coalition government's comprehensive spending review. The historical emergence of 'creative industries' as a realm of endeavour and as a 'project' (Radice 2010) for the 'new individualism' in state intervention on modernity by the Blair/Brown government from 1997 to 2010 (Seldon 2004, 2007; Rentoul 2001; Radice 2004, 2010) seemed, finally, over. What was regarded by some as a 'failure of style over substance' had apparently ended (Bayley 1998).

The post-cultural state, too, must be seen in the context of a retheorisation of modernity and postmodernity by various social and cultural theorists all over the globe. For instance Zygmunt Bauman has put forward the idea of there being a recent change in modernity to what he calls 'liquid modernity' (Bauman 2000) whilst Ulrich Beck, proponent of both a 'cosmopolitan sociology' (Beck 1999; Boyne 2001) and a 'cosmopolitics' (Beck 2005) has argued for both the idea of a 'new modernity', which he has termed 'risk society' and 'world risk society' (Beck 1992, 1999, 2006), and, furthermore, the idea of a 'second modernity' that has recently displaced the age of simple 'first modernity'. First modernity, in Beck's theorisation, appeared to reign until some unspecified period in the late twentieth century. Second modernity for Beck is distinguished by 'relexivity', where what is taking place today is the modernisation of modern society. This condition is qualitatively different from the postmodernity that earlier social and cultural theorists put forward in the 1980s and 1990s. For Scott Lash (Lash 2003) this second modernity is moreover a 'non-linear modernity'. It is characterised explicitly by Lash as signifying 'an information age' where as far as critical thought is concerned there is 'no longer an outside place to stand' and where power becomes almost solely a question of intellectual property. In the so-called 'information age', it seems from this mode of argument, ownership and property relations have been replaced and the 'culture industry' (Adorno 1991) of Theodor Adorno and the Frankfurt School has imploded into the 'social' in the form of pervasive culture and information technology industries (Wynne 1992).

I want to set these debates about modernity in the context of the development of what can be called here the post-cultural state. Some insight into the post-cultural state is gleaned from the creative industries debates which have for some time been impacting on government departments, and media, communications and arts faculties in universities, all over the world. Definitions of 'cultural' and 'creative' industries vary widely (O'Connor, 2002, 2004; Bilton 2007) but 'culture' in this sense, at the very least, means industries and practices like design, architecture, multimedia, film, broadcasting, publishing and fashion, as well as information software and video games. As some leading international academic commentators (Cunningham 2002a; Andersen and Oakley 2008) have pointed out, cultural industries as a phrase is essentially an older notion with creative industries emerging as an international label in the mid-1990s, essentially through the preparations of the Blair/Brown Labour Party in the UK, first in opposition after the death of John Smith and then in government from 1997 to 2010 (Andersen and Oakley 2008; Kong and O'Connor 2009). Major arguments have taken place over the area covered by the two seemingly similar labels, cultural and creative industries. It may be, too, as again participants in the debates have claimed, that cultural industries policy has more connection with the nation state formation as such and creative industries strategy more affinity with the global and the local international order of governance. In countries like Canada and Australia that has meant more intervention through state governments than federal, for example. Further, for at least two decades, the notion of cultural industries has sat side by side with city cultures and urban regeneration, which in turn has included the problematic idea of cultural regeneration (O'Connor 2002, 2004; Žižek 2010; Kong and O'Connor 2009) of cities, with cultural and leisure precincts or quarters becoming the major focus for boosterism and economic impact, dragging more diverse cultural pursuits such as sporting industries, galleries and museums, and gardens in their wake. Cities throughout the world have begun to 'brand' themselves through culture as the notion of the 'creative city' has emerged and expanded globally (Landry 2000; Kong and O'Connor 2009).

These debates have raised fundamental questions about the very existence and purpose of certain disciplines in the academy especially in the humanities and social sciences as well as the function and purpose of the modern nation state as an enabling state (Botsman and Latham 2001), sometimes called the 'new managerial state' (Clarke and Newman 1997), and its role in the formation and sustainability of creative futures in the 'new economy' (Arthurs 2002; May 2002; Hodsoll 2002; Andersen and Oakley 2008). As Stuart Cunningham (Cunningham 2002a), then director of the Creative Industries Research and Applications Centre at Queensland University of Technology in Brisbane, succinctly put it in the early 2000s (Cunningham 2002b): 'We can no longer afford to understand the social and creative disciplines as commercially irrelevant, merely civilizing activities.' Such statements became highly quotable by various governments in the world wishing to dynamise their economies through creative industries strategies and harness their universities to the task. Further, Cunningham's view was, importantly, that these disciplines 'must be recognized as one of the vanguards of the new economy'. Again, such statements are widely quoted, and sometimes acted upon in policy terms. It is generally assumed in these debates that the idea of the 'new economy' is a fait accompli.

It is possible to set these kinds of viewpoints in a different context, without necessarily accepting the transition from an 'old' to a 'new' economy, by examining something that is definitely new (or post): namely, the 'post-cultural state'. In some ways this term complements the notion of 'cultural capitalism' (Bewes and Gilbert 2001; Perryman 1994; Perryman and Coddington 1998) that had been put forward by some contemporary theorists who have looked at the 'postmodern' political possibilities after the regimes of the likes of Tony Blair, Gordon Brown and followers of a 'third way' (Perri 6 1998; Hargreaves and Christie 1998; Giddens 2002, 2003, 2007) in governance. In the 1980s and 1990s postmodernist theorists, or at least theorists of postmodernism, stressed what Fredric Jameson (Jameson 1998) once called the 'cultural turn': that is, the tendency for everything to become 'cultural' (Du Gay and Pryke 2002). For Scott Lash (Lash 2002) at that time the 'logic of the social' was being 'displaced by that of the cultural' as society moves to 'another modernity' (Lash 1999), from an age of industrial capital to an age of informational capital or 'global information society'. The role, and even the long-term existence, of the nation state is called into question in these theoretical battles, at least in terms of power and sovereignty. As the modern nation state, and indeed the local state (state governments in Australia and Canada for example), sought to find a new role in the wake of two decades of dominance on the international scene by the pervasive philosophy of neo-liberalism (with all its concomitant implications of minimal statism), the 'cultural' emerged as an economic imperative. The regulation of 'culture' by the state has a very long history (Hunt 1996a), which cannot be fully interrogated here because of space, and is undoubtedly entangled with the transition from 'police' to a more modern form of liberal governance (Hunt 1996b). Such necessary study, which has also spawned the sub-discipline of 'non-modern' sociology, is now massively informed by the posthumous release of Michel Foucault's copious lectures at the College de France from the 1970s when he was Professor of the History of Systems of Thought (Foucault 2004, 2008, 2009). Importantly though, the modern, territorial, sovereign state that had originally emerged in the sixteenth century (Hirst 2001) may well have been seriously undermined by the globalising neo-liberalism (Gray 2009a, 2009b) of the last few decades, and the question 'what should happen to the state?' now being put back onto the agenda is a testament to the importance of these questions. Nevertheless the modern nation state, from all the evidence, still plays a major role in economic life. The debate about creative industries, and the nature and scope of state intervention in them, is a classic case in point. What precise role should be played by the post-cultural state is a matter that is constantly at stake as can be seen in the serious think tank suggestions for the complete demise of the Department of Culture, Media and Sport in the UK. In the 1980s, and especially the 1990s, cultural industries, largely made up of the arts and sport, became a province for governmental agency in a post-industrial, de-industrialising world. Relabelling of industries (and the national and local state) as 'cultural' has also taken place on a wide international scale. To push the arguments forward Anthony Giddens (Giddens 1994), eventually a guru of the social sciences for New Labour and the New Democrats like Bill Clinton especially on 'the politics of climate change' (Giddens 2009), suggested a problematic move 'beyond left and right' to analyse some of the current confusions around the economics and politics of culture and the relation of the 'creative' industries to such considerations. In the words of Giddens (Giddens 1999) much of the backdrop to all this was a 'runaway world' where globalisation was 'reshaping our world' bringing in changes from Adelaide to Ankara, Aldershot to Assisi – changes which to Giddens and other cosmopolitan sociologists were 'broadly positive'. This perspective involves more than a redesignation of the interventionist (more or less social democratic mode) or non-interventionist, laissez faire (more or less neo-liberal mode) debate, sometimes couched as regulation versus economic liberalism. As can be seen in the emergence of the label creative industries in the UK, the state has involved itself in the creative industries through the 'project' of refashioning culture and society right from the beginning of the Blair/Brown partnership – beginning in something of a coup d'etat within the British Labour Party rebranded as the project of New Labour and its concomitant social engineering of a new individualism gathered pace (Radice 2010; Seldon 2004).

The new, weightless, or knowledge economy, celebrated by writers like Charles Leadbeater (Leadbeater 1999) is by no means an accepted truth, although more widely accepted than in the 1990s when it was first declaimed. The terrain is an arena of struggle, a veritable battleground of ideas and practices, and rightly so. For its most celebrated supporters (Leadbeater 2002, 2008) the 'new' knowledge economy has been 'driven by new factors of production and sources of competitive advantage' like 'innovation, design, branding and know-how' which are at work in this 'new era' in all industries. Others see the information economy as only relevant in the technologically advanced economies. Some commentators claim that the old economy was already, at least by the early 1990s, post-manufacturing and therefore substantially knowledge based and dominated by the service sector and communications technologies. For some critics though the issue is, indeed, is there a 'new economy' at all? The question, too, can be asked, is there a post-cultural state? Is there a 'smart' or 'creative' state (federal or national) in the same way that countries and cities have been termed 'smart' or 'creative'? It can certainly be argued that the move has been from the strategically 'cultural' to the 'creative' in the sense that the focus is less the public arts and broadcast era media and more the general application of creativity in all areas of industrial endeavour. But the emergence of the post-cultural state is traceable in a way that the transition to a supposed 'weightless' new economy is not. The role of the modern nation state has undergone something of a transformation in the years since the early 1970s, and cultural industries ideas that were developed around the national and local state (O'Connor 2002, 2004) have in some ways given way to more free floating creative industries strategies as the 1990s melted into the noughties, and eventually the tens. The question of the modern cultural state and its role in creating what I call here 'sustainable creative futures', both the universities and the cultural entrepreneurs that develop the creativity and the industries which produce it, has become central. The legal issues around copyright, patent, design and trademark have also been given a renewed boost since that is where the economic dynamism of creative industries strategies can be found. But, still, alarmist commentators can be found proclaiming dire warnings, suggesting that the economies which become over reliant on creativity – in other words on the knowledge economy – risk bankruptcy. Governments, buying a creative industries strategy off the peg as it were, therefore had to beware.

'Post-cultural state' is my label for the form in which the cultural state comes to the fore. The main examples here are drawn from the UK but have far more widespread international import and implication (Kong and O'Connor 2009; Leo and Lee 2004), especially because so much reliance has been placed on this specific model, or international experiment. The self-styled 'New Labour' governments of Tony Blair and Gordon Brown (Seldon 2004, 2007; Seldon and Lodge 2010), often said by the participants, with some pride, to be based around a more wide ranging self-important 'project' (Radice 2010), are a convenient starting point for exploration. The label 'creative industries' emerged from within the ranks of New Labour in the first Blair term, which lasted from May 1997 until June 2001. The Blair government example had been 'a beacon' for many interested in cultural policy, even though some of its severest critics have regarded the UK government as having indulged in a 'national accounting gimmick' to promote the creative industries' role in the future of the

British economy (Andersen and Oakley 2008).

Since its first general election victory in 1997 the New Labour party of Tony Blair has been frequently equated with New Right thinking rather than New Left. New Labour is distinguishable though from some of the politics of the New Right, neo-liberalism and free market experiments that dominated the 1980s and early 1990s but in many ways leaned to the centre-right media on a daily basis as the diaries now published after the event manifestly reveal (Campbell 2010, 2011). However, there were centre-left strategies, too, including cultural policy, in an emergent, supposedly third way, politics which former director of the London School of Economics Anthony Giddens frequently proclaimed (and politicians like Bill Clinton, Gerhard Schroeder and Tony Blair officially signed up to). Because they explicitly did not encompass social democracy of the post-war type (Giddens 2001, 2003, 2007) they were frequently interpreted as part of a 'postmodern politics' (Perryman 1994) which 'progressive' supporters of the Conservatives/Labour/Liberal-Democrats could support.

Manifestly, questions of 'culture', and especially popular culture, have been massively changed by the economic, social and political thrust of the New Right since the late 1970s. It is only now that social and cultural theorists are fully grasping what that process might mean in terms of the limits, extents and possibilities of state intervention, and moreover political shifts in the governance of culture around the globe in the decades to come. Particularly in a field like Culture, Media and Sport (as in the United Kingdom 1997 New Labour rechristened the Tory Department of National Heritage, itself only in existence since 1992) the question becomes what can actually be achieved through state and other means of regulation and intervention in economic and cultural fields (McGuigan 1998, 2009; Greenhalgh 1998) in a world ruled by neo-liberal policies since the 1970s. In particular, for cosmopolitan sociologists like Ulrich Beck and Elizabeth Beck-Gernsheim (Beck and Beck-Gernsheim 2002) a 'new individualism' was seen to be becoming a widespread, normalised cultural condition, partly as a result of more than thirty years of neo-liberalism and partly due to a globalisation of culture on an unprecedented scale. This new individualism also simultaneously undermines attempts to restore a social engineering function for the state and law. For some commentators (Wheeler 2002) third way thinking has eschewed the regulatory function of the state in favour of co-operation and partnership even in the area of corporate behaviour. What is clear is that the 'collective' culture of the past is increasingly being eroded and new forms of collectivism and communitarianism (White 2009) are difficult to sustain. If many of the tenets of what was previously seen to be neo-liberal thinking on the economy are seen by pollsters to be accepted by majorities of voters, the cultural changes are in a more libertarian, anti-statist, direction though these are formed by 'right' libertarianism as much as 'left'.

What though did this mean for the Blair/Brown project of new individualism in a country like Britain? After all, the Blair/Brown project was one of social (sometimes moral, or even religious) engineering of its citizenry after nearly twenty years of the regimes of Thatcher and Major (Campbell 2010, 2011; Seldon 2004, 2007). Did New Labour herald a 'New Culture'? Or was 'Blairism' merely an extension of the much vaunted so-called 'Thatcherism' – a 'Blatcherism' to compare with the 'Butskellism' of the 1950s – of the 1980s? 'Enterprise', 'freedom' and 'individualism' had been keywords of the Thatcher and Major years; what would replace them – if anything – in the new era? Especially, what cultural revolution had taken place in the rise and fall the of the New Right, and what might 'New Labour Culture' look like? Enterprise Culture was as much in evidence in 'culture' as in any other sphere of economic activity in the 1980s, 1990s and 2000s. The 'new economy' debates of the 1990s and 2000s gave entrepreneurialism a new dynamism, cultural workers in this self-labelled knowledge economy seemingly especially privileged. Some commentators saw the 'gains' made by the Thatcher and Major governments as especially pronounced in the 'business' of the arts. For them the message to New Labour on taking office was 'culture is booming, just don't blow it' parodying the Tories' 1997 election slogan 'Britain is booming, don't let Labour blow it'. The restrictions perceived to be associated with Labour's 1970s (interventionist, corporatist, union-oriented) regime for these critics had been wiped away – deregulated – between 1979 and 1997. The crisp conclusion being proffered was that people were better off – culturally – than they were in 1979 when Margaret Thatcher was first elected as prime minister. New Labour was, in this version of the story of our times, generously bequeathed a lasting cultural legacy to go along with the supposed economic boom created by Tory Chancellor Kenneth Clarke which failed to win his party a fifth term in office. For its own part New Labour's resurrection of D-ream's 1995 dance pop hit 'Things Can Only Get Better' (O'Farrell 1998; Harris 2003) as its election theme tune suggested, rhetorically, a cultural continuity rather than a radical and ultimately decisive break with the recent past. It also underlined, in a rather hamfisted way, Labour's 'New'ness, keying in several years too late to 1990s "clubcultures" ' (Redhead 1997a). According to the writer and Blairite policy analyst Charles Leadbeater (Leadbeater 2008) in a pamphlet for the then influential think tank Demos (Leadbeater 1997):

clubbing is . . . the most popular past-time amongst a highly individualistic 'young generation', foreshadowing a more widespread principle of 'mutuality' in 'club culture' (from sports clubs to local history clubs) which might help to renew civic culture.

The idea of 'collective' or 'mutual' culture arising from the individualistic and hedonistic clubcultures of the mid-late 1990s is an intriguing one (Redhead 1997a). The transition, however, is by no means as easily achieved politically as it was with other examples of New Labour and popular culture such as the saga of 'Diana's death' in 1998 (Campbell 2010) and the collective grief expressed for Blair's 'People's Princess'. Tony Blair frequently seemed to hark back to a liberalism before the Labour Party in Britain was formed early in the twentieth century. However his 'third way' pamphlet for the Fabian Society (Blair 1998) in its rhetoric at least echoed much of the 'beyond left and right', 'renewal of social democracy', argument outlined in Anthony Giddens' books on the same subject (Giddens 1998, 2000, 2002, 2007; Giddens and Hutton 2000; Hutton, 2002), initially also incorporating the idea of a 'stakeholder society' (Hutton 1999). It also sought to distinguish New Labour from the New Right without comprehensively forging a 'third way' between neoliberalism and conventional post-war social democracy. A platform for future development of such a twenty-first century objective was undoubtedly suggested but to many observers little was put in place in either of Blair's administrations to suggest that this could be achieved. Creative industries was, though, one of the sites where such strategic thinking was indeed applied.

But how might all of this 'post-social democracy' (Diamond and Liddle 2009) impact on culture, and indeed the creative industries in regimes adopting or aping New Labour? New Labour's connection to culture, popular and otherwise, is a complex story. To playwright Tom Stoppard New Labour' s first five years showed a persistently grudging attitude to 'the arts' in general and critic Robert Hewison dismissed them as 'a pretty philistine lot'. Nevertheless in the 2002 spending review announced by Chancellor Gordon Brown arts funding was increased from £297 million to £412 million in 2005 to 2006, a record level for arts spending. But the issue was more than just state funding for the arts. For these opponents of New Labour the problem was not just finance but to some extent the down market aspect of the culture New Labour were prepared to celebrate. Others bemoaned the lack of feeling for the popular even amongst the populism of New Labour. For Mark Perryman (Perryman 1994, 1996; Perryman and Coddington 1998) New Labour, at least initially, was guilty of an arrogant dismissal of popular culture: 'it has little or no sense of culture', he claimed even before New Labour took office (Redhead 2000: xi–xxviii, 137–50). Certainly in 1997 Jack Cunningham, shadow secretary of state for national heritage in the previous parliament, seemed defensive on films and plays he had or hadn't seen, such as the film of Irvine Welsh's novel *Trainspotting* (Redhead 2000). Tony Blair himself, though, campaigned in the 1997 British general election as a 'modern man', by which he meant he was from 'the rock'n'roll generation, colour TV and the Beatles'. He even played in his own rock band – the Ugly Rumours – in his Oxford University days in the early 1970s. This contrasted with the more 'traditional' jazz fandom of his deputy, John Prescott, whose preference for late nights at Ronnie Scott's club in London mirrored Tory Kenneth Clarke's. The fact that the first out gay MP in the House of Commons, Chris Smith, was picked by Tony Blair to take over the reins of the Department of National Heritage once the election was won, and that the choice of first minister for sport was the late former Greater London Council member and lifelong Chelsea fan Tony Banks, suggested to some commentators that Blair's sense of 'modernity' extended further than mere rhetoric. This was confirmed during the 1997 election itself in an interview for Channel 4 with comedian and writer David Baddiel, whose anthem 'Football's Coming Home' (officially entitled 'Three Lions', music courtesy of Ian Broudie from The Lightning Seeds, and the theme tune of the Euro 96 soccer tournament) co-written with fellow lyricist and soccer fan Frank Skinner was adapted by New Labour at its pre-election conference as 'Labour's Coming Home'. Soccer fandom, rather than the more conservative cricket culture that his predecessor John Major so publicly adopted, seemed to be a talisman of 'modern man'. Martin Kettle confided to *Guardian* readers after the 1997 general election that the new prime minister was probably not quite so keen on soccer in the mid-1980s when the sport was much less politically correct in the wake of the Heysel disaster in Brussels in 1985. Or as Irvine Welsh (Redhead 2000) put it, when exactly did Tony Blair become a lifelong Newcastle United soccer fan? Under David Cameron, supposedly an Aston Villa supporter since a young boy, there is little need to affect a love for football or to speak 'mockney' (Harris 2011).

Overall, though, the connections between New Labour and the cultural sphere seemed, initially, to recall the previous time a 'new' young Labour prime minister took office after a long period of Tory misrule: the time was 1964 and the prime minister Harold Wilson. In that era the Beatles were, initially, a symbol of the enterprise of Wilson's 'New Britain'. The year 1964's slogan 'Let's Go With Labour' hinted at the promise of a cultural rebirth which by Wilson's large 1966 general election victory had already begun to pay political and economic dividends. Harold Wilson's cultural envoy Jenny Lee, as minister for the arts, was remembered in the debates about culture in the wake of Tony Blair's own triumph. It was suggested that New Labour needed a new 'Jenny Lee'. Tony Blair himself made a keynote speech during the 1997 campaign outlining arts and cultural industries policy and introducing the idea of a 'NESTA' (National Endowment for Science, Technology and the Arts) talent fund for individuals. The National Trust for Talent and Creativity, proposed in 'The People's Lottery' white paper following the 1997 election, aimed to create an environment fostering talent and innovation. This included financial support for creative individuals, grants and loans to help develop ideas for products and services, placement schemes for talented individuals and master classes and summer schools. In July 2000 the new Department for Culture, Media and Sport announced the 'Creative Partnership' initiative which was the culmination of the proposals bringing together schools, arts and other creative organisations to provide enhanced opportunities for school leavers especially in deprived areas, encouraging opportunities to work in what the Blair government had regularly begun to call at the drop of a hat the 'creative industries'. In April 2000 the Department for Culture, Media and Sport (in conjunction with the Design Council and the Arts Council for England) produced *Your Creative Future*, the first ever careers guide booklet on 'creative industries' which was put out as a web version in October 2000. It provided detailed information on the range of jobs available within the creative industries and how to get into those jobs. In March 2001 the department also launched a Creative Industries Higher Education Forum, which sought to draw together the experience of people in the creative industries and in the higher education sector to ensure that students had the knowledge and skills necessary to obtain employment in the creative industries.

The generation that some have labelled 'Freedom's Children' took the political rhetoric of the 1980s at face value, at least in Britain. Such other politicisation as did take place emanated from the state proclaiming the curtailing of the freedom (or 'right') to 'party' and Freedom's Children's reaction to such intervention. Laws such as the Licensing Act 1988, Football Spectators Act 1989, Entertainments (Increased Penalties) Act 1990 and Criminal Justice and Public Order Act 1994 certainly proclaimed the curtailing of freedoms. These laws, together with the Public Entertainments Licences (Drug Misuse) Act 1997 (which only came into force when New Labour took office although it was a Private Member's Bill introduced by Barry Legg MP in the dying days of the Major administration) seemed to fly in the face of the 'old' individualism espoused by the Conservative Party led by Margaret Thatcher and John Major, most in evidence in the naked greed and conspicuous consumption of the financial services sector, especially in the City of London. 'Freedom's Children' in fact forged a different individualism which was needed simply to survive in a merciless deregulated economic and social environment – a veritable 'hedonism in hard times' (Redhead 1997a). It was this 'hedonistic individualism', which, manifested in all kinds of youth cultures, was damned legislatively by the Tories and allowed New Labour to claim a wide mandate at the general election in 1997. The mid-1990s, though, was a watershed. The creative industries such as design, film and fiction co-existed with youth culture in a way not witnessed before. A 'creative modernity', a new creative individualism, was on the horizon, with specific industries in the lead. By the millennium, after Blair's first term, Charles Leadbeater was able to argue that cultural workers in the contemporary cultural industries were the prime example of cultural entrepreneurship and that creative industries and the new individualism, or what Ulrich Beck and Elizabeth Beck-Gernsheim have identified as a deep and widening international process of 'individualisation' (Beck and Beck-Gernsheim 2002), had come together particularly in relation to the young people (essentially under thirty-five) who he has labelled 'the independents' (Leadbeater and Oakley 1999) and 'Britain's new cultural entrepreneurs' (Andersen and Oakley 2008). Leadbeater (Leadbeater 2002: 214) has said that:

> The ethic of creative, productive individualism is being fed from both ends of society. Young people, especially those working in cultural and creative industries, regard work as an expression of themselves: they are working creatively, as well as earning a living. They want to negotiate an accommodation between creativity and commerce. Working for commercial clients is a price they are prepared to pay for a measure of independence and as an outlet for creativity. These young entrepreneurs in cultural industries are creative and collaborative individualists par excellence.

This idea became pervasive. 'Please don't think the idea of name-checking Richard Florida is redundant for poor old east Lancashire . . . artists are already moving to Bacup, and Ramsbottom is already a desirable suburb for young creatives in Manchester', stated the late owner of Factory Records and Hacienda club Tony Wilson in a report on the Pennines and creative industries in 2005 (Carter 2005). As a management consultant on the creative industries Florida in a number of influential works (Florida 2002, 2005a, 2005b, 2008, 2010) became a guru for cities and countries wishing to take up creative industries strategies.

In Gordon Brown's first post 1997 election budget as chancellor of the exchequer – the first by Labour since Denis Healey's finale in March 1979 – it was precisely the creative industries which underpinned contemporary youth culture that New Labour promoted (Harris 2003). Brown argued that 'Britain is increasingly leading the world in those industries which most obviously depend on the skills and talents of their workers – communications, design, architecture, fashion, music and film' recognising that these are the creative industries most attractive to youth and most likely to have potential for future expansion of employment and mobility. Some commentators in the creative industries debate have pointed out that young people, in the wake of deindustrialisation and decline in the need of manufacturing industry for manual workers, have turned to the creative industries, offering attractive lifestyles as well as monetary rewards. Add sport to this list and the New Labour idea for renaming the Department of National Heritage (created by the Tories in 1992) the Department for Culture, Media and Sport made good sense. The new department had policy responsibility for museums, galleries and libraries, the built heritage, the arts, sport, education, broadcasting and the media and tourism, as well as the creative industries, the Millennium and the National Lottery. Later in 2001 new responsibilities also included liquor, gambling, horse racing, censorship and video classification, the Queen's golden jubilee and the 2002 Commonwealth Games in Manchester. The belief behind such inclusiveness was seen to be that the activities of all these sectors 'brings us pleasure and broadens our horizons'. Since it believed 'culture and creativity are vital to our national life' the department aimed to 'improve the quality of life through increased access to and participation in all its areas of responsibility' (Smith 1998: 20–2). In his account of 'Blair's Hundred Days' (the perceived honeymoon period of the New labour administration) the later to be discredited lobbyist Derek Draper (Draper 1997: 173) has argued that 'Heritage became History' on Monday, 14 July 14 1997:

> First it was called the Office of Arts and Libraries, and was headed by Norman St John Stevas. Then it became the Department of National Heritage and had David Mellor for a boss. From today, it is to be known as the Department of Culture, Media and Sport, and Chris Smith is supremo. Like the old DNH – which was also known as the Department of Nobody Home – the new version will cover everything from the media to football. The difference is one of presentation. Whereas the old model was backward-looking and stuffy the new one will look forward . . . at long last the deification of heritage is history.

For Chris Smith, the first secretary of state of the new department, the name change the new department represented 'much more than a change of name'. 'It is a change of direction,' he argued, 'a recognition that cultural and leisure activities are of growing significance, not only to individuals but . . . also of rapidly growing economic importance.' Smith further claimed that the creative industries are 'the basic fuel' of the 'hugely successful international tourist industry, and the heart of a series of activities in which Britain is genuinely a world leader – from music, theatre, TV and software to rising industries such as fashion, advertising, product design and architecture' (Smith 1998: 50; all succeeding unattributed political quotes come from pp. 1–33 and 48–55).

For Smith the 'new modernity' of so-called 'Cool Britannia' (Harris 2003; Andersen and Oakley 2008) was here to stay, a proposition (though he clearly noted it as a flawed label which was inappropriate) that was to rebound on him when he was later dropped from the Department of Culture, Media and Sport after New Labour's second election victory in June 2001. What he was actually emphasising though was creativity and innovation in the areas covered by his department and to underline this new approach Smith, whilst secretary of state, wrote a book called *Creative Britain* (Smith 1998) a label which echoed in part the Creative Nation national cultural policy (in the document *Creative Nation: Commonwealth Cultural Policy*) of Australian Commonwealth government Labour prime minister Paul Keating earlier in the decade, and joined new initiatives in the 1990s such as the change of name of the New Zealand Arts Council to Creative New Zealand. The magazine of the International Designers Network, *idn*, ran a series on 'creative countries' starting with the United Kingdom, as a kind of tribute to this labelling, and in particular to Britain's prominence in the process. The cover of Smith's book boasted two 'Brit-artist' Damien Hirst paintings: 'beautiful, all round, lovely day, big toys for big kids, Frank and Lorna, when we are no longer children' on the front cover and 'beautiful snail crunching under the boot painting' on the back jacket. The connection between the creative industries and the legacy of modern visual art was writ large (McNamara 2002; Gibson 2001). The book itself was a collection of Smith's speeches in the area of culture along with specially written chapters. An appendix to the book, 'A Summary Map of the Creative Industries' can be regarded as the first departmental mapping document. The title was significant, too. Smith in his first year in the job developed the idea of 'creative industries', a refinement of the older notion of cultural industries (Hesmondalgh 2002; McKinlay and Smith 2009). Chris Smith pronounced that 'employment in the cultural industries has consistently grown against a background of almost no change in the rest of the economy' and claimed that 'the continuing strength of our "creative industries" opens up the prospect of Britain enjoying immense competitive advantage in the decades ahead, as economic activity becomes even more global and even more competitive'. The 'creative industries' for Smith went 'much wider than any conventional definition of the arts, but they are all dependent on the talent and skill of individuals, which means that all of them are ultimately fed by the quality of our artistic and cultural environment'. In his view it was part of 'the Government's role to ensure that environment is rich and stimulating'. These creative industries, according to Smith were 'a dynamic new sector of today's economy, and make an impact on our everyday lives'. New Labour wanted to ensure that they continued to thrive which is why Tony Blair had asked him 'to set up and chair a task force, which will include representatives of the Government and some our most successful creative entrepreneurs – people like Richard Branson, David Puttnam and Paul Smith'. The reason for choosing such celebrities was, Smith claimed, that they 'are the people who understand how to build and develop creative business'. As if to emphasise the shift from traditional manufacturing industry to the new, creative economy in Britain in the 1990s, David Puttnam had himself claimed that 'rock musicians contribute more to the balance of payments than the steel industry' (Heartfield 2000). Other commentators claimed (Rifkin 2000) that cultural production, with information and services, would soon eclipse manufacturing and agriculture.

By retelling the story of the birth of the creative industries label in the United Kingdom as a part of the 'project' of new individualism, I have begun to pose new questions about postmodern politics, the post-millennial state, modernity and culture which are explored throughout this book. Debates about the modernisation of modernity which I have regurgitated here have tended to shy away from persistently pertinent questions of government by the nation state, often relegating the nation state to the role of bystander; literally a 'minimal state'. Reading Ulrich Beck and some of the other cosmopolitan sociology theorists of modernity it seems as if the nation state really is being eclipsed as the theorists of globalisation claimed initially in their early formulations of the 1990s. But the important questions about the role of the state do in fact remain and are highlighted impressively by the intertwining of the state and culture which have been excavated in the focus here on the post-cultural state and its connection to the rethinking of modernity. The double meaning of the post-cultural state as both cultural condition and regime of governance or state formation helps to underline some of the issues that are missing in some current theorisation about state, culture and modernity. New individualism as a project within creative industries strategies helps to identify the missing links.

Chris Smith, as secretary of state for culture, media and sport between 1997 and 2001, helped to usher in the new Blair/Brown era. However, this was as we have seen, a more wide ranging project of remaking of citizens as creative entrepreneurs. Chris Smith, launching the updated UK mapping document in 2001 stated that 'original creativity' is the lifeblood of creative industries as these businesses seek a competitive advantage, a state he did not see as contradicted by a society looking to solve new problems in new ways and to improve the quality of life for its citizens. Government and culture are crucially intertwined here (Gibson 2001) as creativity and, by implication, creative modernity are part of new 'technologies of the self', part of liberal governmentality's formation of self-regulating citizens (Hunt 1996a, 1996b). Smith stressed that he wanted: 'our creative industries in particular to continue to seize the opportunities of a fast-changing world to innovate, to be flexible, to be swift, to strive to fulfill potential'.

To emphasise its pervasiveness in what he confidently regarded as the new knowledge economy Smith defined the business of culture widely. Creative industries' influence was 'all around us' in Smith's view:

> the work of our creative industries is all around us. The shoes and clothes we wear, the buildings we live and work in, the computer software we use for business and pleasure, the music we listen to, books and TV programmes we enjoy at leisure.

All businesses, in any case, for Smith should be 'creative' and recognise 'creativity not as a luxury add on but as an essential ingredient for success'. Moreover, creative industries have a responsibility in Smith's view to 'lead' other new industrial productivity. He argued while in government that 'our creative industries to continue to take the lead to do what they do best – to think "outside the box", to be flexible and quick to seize the opportunities'. He also expressed confidence that they 'will continue to grow building further on the astonishing success they have enjoyed over the last few years'.

'Modernity' for New Labour was explicitly seen as a 'project' of individualism, an intervention into the history of 'modern', even when it became tangled up in debates over 'Cool Britannia' (Harris 2003) a label first thought up by Viv Stanshall's Bonzo Dog Doo Dah Band in the 1960s. Chris Smith did also suggest in his statements in the early days of the new department of DCMS that 'Cool Britannia' can be an entirely inappropriate label if it suggests 'tradition' is bad, but also that registering an 'exciting new modernity' and 'creativity' is very important and that government action remains significant in the whole field of culture, media and sport. Some of the participants in the debates about creative industries have lamented how definitions of the creative sector itself have got in the way of more important analytical questions. But there is no doubt that the definitions have been very widespread and often contradictory. The creative industries have been defined in various different ways (Flew 2003; Florida 2002, 2008, 2010; Caves 2000; McKinlay and Smith 2009) including the whole gamut of the 'culture of services' in the 'new knowledge economy'. For some commentators it is the digital 'content' produced that marks the industries like film production, pay television, book publishing, game publishing, e-commerce, even health and education as 'creative'. For some writers, like John Howkins (Howkins 2001), the creative industries comprise the four areas of industry covered by intellectual property law. The four areas are design, trademark, copyright and patent. Creativity in this sense is a massive part of the whole economy, much wider than the previous idea of the 'culture industry' or cultural industries, and further, much wider than the idea of the business of the arts, dominated as it is by grant funding models. Howkins' idea allows science and engineering a major presence in the creative industries. For Chris Smith, speaking as secretary of state in the first Blair/Brown government, creative industries were 'those industries which have their origin in individual creativity, skill and talent and which have a potential for wealth creation through the generation and exploitation of intellectual property' but importantly he also recognised the 'close economic relationships with other sectors such as tourism, hospitality, museums and galleries, heritage and sport'. That was the significance of the second task force in Smith's Department of Cultural Media and Sport, to complement other groups such as the Football Task Force. The Interdepartmental Creative Industries Taskforce, to give it its official title, also included Eric Salama director of marketing services group WPP as well as Alan McGee then of Creation Records and later owner of Poptones label, designer Paul Smith, entrepreneur Richard Branson and film maker David Puttnam. Tony Blair instructed Chris Smith to set it up as a forum for 'cultural' advice to New Labour and to look at how Britain could boost its creative industries. A further group, to look at the music industry, was organised by Chris Smith in early 1998 which carried on, giving advice to government, as the Music Industry Forum. Including Simply Red's New Labour supporting Mick Hucknall, and led by then arts minister Mark Fisher, the panel was asked to look at music teaching in schools, to develop an analysis of the current and possible future health of the music industry, to identify areas where its commercial performance could be improved and to consider copyright protection issues in the light of the then multi-million pound bootleg compact disc market, later to be virtually eclipsed by the global downloading boom.

For some New Labour supporters like the QC Geoffrey Robertson such initiatives still did not go far enough: the barrister's plea was that the arts needed a fully fledged Royal Commission which would produce a 'complete cultural Domesday Book'. The then newly created Culture, Media and Sport department came up instead with a significant document based on research into the creative industries in Britain. This was the Creative Industries Task Force Mapping Document published in 1998 at the Department for Culture, Media and Sport's headquarters at Cockspur Street in central London. It looked specifically at the economic value and potential of creative industries. The need was to raise awareness of the industries themselves, the contribution they made to the economy and the problems they faced in developing an even greater role. In March 2001, this time launched at the Channel 4 building in London, Chris Smith unveiled an updated Creative Industries Task Force Mapping Document stressing that now the term 'creative industries' was more widely used and understood and that in a knowledge economy the importance of these industries to national wealth was vital. In June 2001 Smith was replaced as secretary of state by Tessa Jowell and he returned to the back benches in the wake of the second landslide election victory for Blair's New Labour and his own role in the farce of the scandal over the national soccer stadium at Wembley. The creative industries, though, in the first Blair term, for Smith were a 'real success story' and a key element in today's knowledge economy or, as some have termed it, the creative economy (Howkins 2001; Florida 2005a, 2008, 2010; Kong and O'Connor 2009), where it is said that it is ideas that make money (Leadbeater 2008; Andersen and Oakley 2008).

Once the work of the Creative Industries Task Force was published in the mapping documents by the Department for Culture, Media and Sport the Ministerial Creative Industries Strategy Group helped to ensure a co-ordinated response to the needs of the creative industries from across government departments and devolved administrations in Scotland, Wales and Northern Ireland. At the time of the publication of the updated Creative Industries mapping document in 2001 the strategy group comprised Chris Smith as secretary of state; Janet Anderson minister of state in the Department for the Environment, Transport and the Regions; Kim Howells from the Department of Trade and Industry (later to join the DCMS as minister for tourism, film and broadcasting after the election in 2001 and to gain notoriety for blaming gang violence on gangsta rap and criticising Brit-art); Patricia Hewitt from the Department of Trade and

Industry; Stephen Timms from the Treasury; and representatives from
the Foreign and Commonwealth Office, the Department of Employment
and Education, the Northern Ireland Assembly, the National Assembly
for Wales and the Scottish Executive. Policy co-ordination was then
achieved across a number of aspects of the state apparatus. In England
the Regional Development Agencies (abolished by the Conservative-
Liberal Democrat coalition government in 2010) explicitly recognised the
growing importance of the creative industries and set about exploiting
their potential. The Department for Culture, Media and Sport regularly
boosted the cultural and creative development of the regions with various
initiatives. Local authorities adopted drives to put culture at the heart of
local authority decision making. In Scotland Scottish Enterprise identified
the creative industries as a key cluster for development. In Wales it was
proposed to establish Wales Creating as an umbrella body to develop and
support the creative industries and in Northern Ireland a document called
Unlocking Creativity was published to develop a strategy for young people
to gain employment in creative industries and beyond.

Announcing the 2001 document to a fanfare of publicity Smith argued
that it showed creative industries in Britain were moving from the
'fringes to the centre stage', from the periphery to the mainstream. The
creative industries were defined to include advertising, architecture, arts
and antiques markets, crafts, design, designer fashion, film and video,
interactive leisure software, music, performing arts, publishing, software,
television and radio. According to the 2001 document they collectively
produced £112.5 billion of revenue, export earnings of £10.3 billion,
employed 1.3 million people and produced 5 per cent of GDP. In the year
1997–8 output in these industries grew by 16 per cent compared to 6 per
cent in the general economy. In Chris Smith's view expressed when he
was secretary of state 'the most successful economies of the twenty-first
century will be creative ones'. Creativity will bring a 'key commercial
advantage' claimed Smith, who urged that everybody take 'up that challenge across all elements of society':

> I want a society in which every child has experienced creative and cultural
> activity, has access to training to develop their creative talents and has the
> opportunity – for those who want it – to work in the creative industries.

By May 2009 the Department for Culture, Media and Sport, then
headed by Andy Burnham, in the document *Lifting People, Lifting Places*
estimated that total creative employment increased from 1.6 million in
1997 to 2 million in 2007, a growth rate double that of the UK economy as
a whole:

Creative industries are an ever growing part of the economy and a source of comparative advantage and exports. The creative industries, excluding Crafts and Design, accounted for 6.4% of Gross Value Added (GVA) in 2006. They grew by an average of four per cent per annum between 1997 and 2006. This compares to an average of three per cent for the whole economy over this period. Exports of services by the creative industries amounted to 16 billion pounds in 2006, equating to four per cent of all goods and services exported. Knowledge and creativity have always played a significant role in the economy. Creative industries perform well against the five drivers of productivity, particularly innovation and skills. Analysis of the UK innovation survey 2002–2004 shows that 78% of creative industry firms are active innovators – higher then in any other major industry sector. The UK is in a strong position. Although we are facing increased competition from growing overseas markets, there is a real opportunity for the creative industries to benefit from those markets and grow further still.

No wonder then, given all of the frenetic activity around the culture business, especially in the capital city of London, that the *New Yorker* magazine celebrated the 'London Renaissance' and the 'Culture of Blairism' in the Blair years. Blair's own rhetoric certainly tended to celebrate a 'new individualism' and a view of economic success emanating from enterprise. For Blair, writing in **The Guardian** on the eve of hosting a Downing Street reception for people in the fashion, architecture, product design, graphics, animation and film industries,'the new entrepreneurs' were the 'wealth creators' and 'deserve our backing'. Geoffrey Robinson, a minister at the time, characterised the relationship as 'Labour and the luvvies'. The 'cultural entrepreneurs' were, as far as the New Labour prime minister was concerned, 'ambassadors for New Britain' because they 'embody strong British characteristics as valuable to us today as they have ever been: know-how, creativity, innovation, risk-taking and most of all, originality'. For Blair 'all the things that put us ahead of the game one hundred and fifty years ago are once again giving us a competitive edge'.

Critics might object that such statements from the project of modernity and new individualism would not have been out of place in the 1980s, or in the early 1990s, before New Labour, and also before proclamations of the existence of a new knowledge economy. For example, fashion designers were feted as entrepreneurs 'batting for Britain' just as much by Margaret Thatcher as by Tony Blair. Moreover, many die hards today still hold to views about art and culture developed as long ago as the 1950s and continue to argue that the arts are not helped by government ministers rolling them up into one economic and industrial category (Tusa 2003) of 'creative industries' and 'cultural entrepreneurship'. Furthermore, the economic impact studies conducted in the 1980s (Myerscough 1988; Wynne 1992; Zeitlin and Hirst 1989; Landry 2000) pointed to 'the culture industry' as an engine of city and regional regeneration through creative entrepreneurship a long time before the 'creative industries' label began to be used. As a result, over at least a decade, the arts and cultural industries (including sport) became increasingly central to cities, through urban regeneration, cultural tourism, city imaging and employment creation. The important planning of 'creative clusters' of creative industries in certain parts of particular international cities called 'cultural districts' (Tepper 2002; Kong and O'Connor 2009) or 'cultural quarters', recalls debates in the 1980s about 'reversing industrial decline' (Zeitlin and Hirst 1989; Wynne 1992) and the need for 'local industrial strategies'. There is now an established creative clusters network internationally which links people working throughout the globe in the development of creative industries designed to help them 'communicate and share resources with one another' through the website www.creativeclusters.co.uk. In March 2009 a national network of creative entrepreneurs, opinion formers and other prominent figures from the creative industries in the UK was formed and launched at 11 Downing Street. Called 'New Deal of the Mind', it was dedicated to helping the 'creative economy drive the recovery' after the crash of 2008 and directly references in its name President Roosevelt's 1930s New Deal which set up work creation programmes for artists, writers and musicians in the USA in the depression years. The document *Do It Yourself: Cultural and Creative Self-Employment in Hard Times – A New Deal of the Mind Report for the Arts Council England* outlined its purpose. Once New Labour left office there was a more general anxiety about the sustainability of the creative clusters – for instance the think tank the Social Market Foundation (SMF) published a report *Disconnect: Social Mobility and Creative Industries* which looked at the problems for networking after the crash. In theory, the new businesses of the creative industries, often micro or small and medium sized enterprises, could locate anywhere; in practice they seem to need to 'cluster' geographically as in previous economic formation of industrial districts. The digital version of industrial districts also seems to need 'place' although the question still rings out: are clusters determined by people already being in the area, or are people attracted to those already formed clusters? These debates were mostly taking place in an era before the new knowledge economy was identified by its disciples and seen to be producing a 'creative sector' (Healy 2002; Andersen and Oakley 2008) and becoming part of a new post-millenial economics of competition which was to end in a global crash (Porter 2002; Florida

2010; Cruddas and Rutherford 2009). University humanities, arts and social science departments all over the world began to redesign themselves in the wake of the demands of the new knowledge economy (many have relabelled departments and faculties with the phrase Creative Industries) and even constructed creative industries precincts where academia and the creative industries have come together and combined with government, retail and property companies either to research the creative industries or to actively participate in them. This is all well and good, especially for the better established experiments which are based on well thought out plans, but many of these initiatives are not wholly new and frequently involve a fair amount of window dressing – effectively relabelling cultural industries work as 'creative'.

As I have argued here what is new in the supposedly postmodern political culture of New Labour is the post-cultural state, both in the sense of post-cultural as a new cultural condition since the mid-1990s, and in the way that the modern state becomes 'cultural' in, for example, its social engineering project of the creative industries. I have shown, through an excavation of the experiment of the now threatened with extinction Department of Culture, Media and Sport in the New Labour government (particularly its first term between 1997 and 2001) that the Blair/Brownproject was a very specific one, in time and place, and although pregnant with political and theoretical possibilities for 'remaking' modernities, may not be something that can be easily exported around the world without considerable adaptation. Nevertheless, in various countries policy documents and mapping surveys have followed in the footsteps of the Blair/Brown example. In the coming claustropolitanism it will be more difficult to sustain creative industries strategies whether by nations or cities, but the post-cultural state is likely always to be with us. During Gordon Brown's regime as prime minister light entertainment guru Andrew Lloyd Webber had been invited to join the New Labour government as a 'cultural ambassador' (Seldon and Lodge 2010: 10), an invitation he ultimately declined, and under Tony Blair's leadership New Labour had courted 'Britpop' bands such as Blur and Oasis for the popular 'cultural state' he was attempting to build between 1994 and 2007 (Harris 2003). Post-Blair/Brown, as the 'arts' and 'artists' (like Gary Barlow of Take That) ally themselves with the Tories (Harris 2011) in more subtle and invidious ways, Cool Britannia has given way to 'uncool Britannia' and 'born to rule Britannia'.

CHAPTER 3

Post-Space

Since at least the mid-1990s there has been a rethinking in key contemporary social and cultural theorists' discourse of the notion of modernity (Gane 2004), and furthermore 'what it means to be modern', as John Gray has put it (Gray 2003, 2007, 2009a, 2009c, 2011). Moreover, a distinct move has taken place away from the once widespread embrace of the concepts and intellectual framework associated with postmodernity, postmodernism and the postmodern in general. The myriad texts on theories of modernity and postmodernity, for instance including theorists such as David Harvey and Fredric Jameson alongside others from various disciplinary persuasions (Hutcheon 1988; Harvey 1989; Jensen 1990; Turner 1990; Connor 1997; Jameson 1991; McGuigan 2002, 2009) from an earlier, though recent, era have rapidly been overtaken by events and influential postmodern theorists have been standing in line to confess the error of their ways or to offer theorisations of what they see as the 'new modernity' (Gane 2004; Bauman and Tester 2001; Beck and Willms 2004; Giddens and Pierson 1998). All of a sudden, it seemed, the future contours of social and cultural theory, like the global economic and political outlook, were uncertain and in a state of flux once again.

As a contribution to these debates in contemporary social and cultural theory, especially since the mid-1990s, where a rethinking of the notion of modernity was initially taking place, I want to concentrate on the notion of 'post-space', or alternatively 'post-architecture'. Post-space as a concept is itself a reframing of the struggles for meaning within, and over, postmodern architecture in relation to current critical theorists of postmodernism such as Fredric Jameson, Douglas Kellner and Slavoj Žižek (Jameson 1991, 2005; Best and Kellner 1991; Kellner 1994; Žižek 2010: 244–78). In these debates many contemporary social and cultural theorists have turned away from an erstwhile obsession with postmodernity, postmodernism and the idea of the postmodern in general without formulating an alternative theoretical direction. As one possible conceptual resource for retheorising modernity in this context, I want to consider the concept of critical modernity, or new modernity, as developed by Claude Parent, theoretical and architectural partner of French urban theorist par excellence Paul Virilio in the 1960s. Parent has been a significant figure, though little recognised as such outside France, in utopian architecture since the early 1950s. His work with and without Virilio has had wide influence. For example, Daniel Libeskind, who has found international fame for his design for buildings like the Jewish Museum in Berlin, the Wohl Centre at Bar-Ilan University in Israel, the ill-fated redesign of the World Trade Center site in New York and gravity defying towers in Milan in collaboration with fellow 'star' architect Zaha Hadid, has continued aspects of the theory of the oblique function of Parent and Virilio without explicitly and directly acknowledging this direction. For instance, Libeskind's design for the Imperial War Museum North in Salford, Greater Manchester incorporated disorienting sloping floors throughout and a 'typical Libeskind building' has been described by Slavoj Žižek as having 'tension between vertical and crooked lines' (Žižek 2010: 254) .

I want to look here at specific aspects of the life and work of Claude Parent and his partnerships with various luminaries such as Andre Bloc, Yves Klein and Nicolas Schoffer as well as Paul Virilio. Part of the purpose of this biographical detail is to introduce readers to the little known life and work of Claude Parent. However, I further look at the way in which the better known figure of Virilio and the lesser known Parent worked together on architectural commissions in the 1960s and how in 1963 they formed the group Architecture Principe and devised the function of the oblique, a theory of architectural space which was designed to end verticality and, to some extent, horizontality. Importantly, I want to show that Claude Parent, with and without partners, made a significant general contribution to retheorising modernity by conceptualising, and operationalising, what he called critical modernity, or new modernity, a concept which can be more broadly utilised in rethinking modernity. There is though a further, integrated purpose of this enterprise of intellectual biography. My archaeology of the 'post-space', 'post-architecture' of Virilio and Parent also assesses the significance of this work for the general body of contemporary social and cultural theory which is veering away from notions of postmodernity and could be said to be moving towards the terrain of a theory of critical modernity.

Claude Parent is a utopian modernist French architect, and creator with Paul Virilio of the theory of oblique architecture, or the theory of the function of the oblique. He has been a polemicist, writer and self-publicist extraordinaire as well as a professional architect for over six decades. He was born in 1923 in Paris, France. His educational studies in architecture were actually unfinished, having been preceded by scientific studies (mathematics and mechanics). Parent was twenty-six years old when in 1949, after a two year training course on historic buildings, he met Ionel Schein with whom he worked until the mid-1950s. Both Parent and Schein were described as children of Le Corbusier. In 1951 Parent met Andre Bloc, founder of *Art d'Aujourd'hui*, and the following year he paired up with sculptor Nicholas Schoffer, a meeting which proved to be a major starting point for utopian architecture in France in the 1950s and 1960s. But it is his partnership from 1963 with Paul Virilio, the self-styled critic of the art of technology, and its implications for Parent's theory of critical modernity, that is the main focus here.

I have introduced Parent by suggesting that there is a radical reassessment under way of notions of the postmodern. This process has generally been such an extensive rethinking in social and cultural theory that it could, by parodying Bruno Latour (Latour 1993), be claimed that 'we have never been postmodern'. Bruno Latour (Latour 1993) has written, too, of what he sees as the state of 'non-modernity'. As opposed to the thinking of Bruno Latour and others who contend that we have never been *modern*, it might be better conceiving of a state of 'non-postmodernity' (Redhead 2008) whilst utilising the concept of 'critical modernity'. The search has accelerated in recent years in this rethinking of modernity for conceptualisations which transcend previous theories of the modern condition but retain the term modernity or some variant of it; in a way to 'redeem modernity' (Jensen 1990). In order to replace the 'postmodern condition' widely purveyed by such theorists as Jean-Francois Lyotard from the late 1970s onwards (Lyotard 1984), some cultural and social theorists have turned, in the twenty-first century, to the relatively obscure theorist of speed, Paul Virilio (Armitage 2000, 2001; Gane 2003: 164–7), to propagate the idea of a 'dromocratic condition' (or a society of speed) which has already, in a sense, made the notion of the postmodern condition redundant. For instance, a call for papers for a conference entitled 'The Dromocratic Condition' at the University of Newcastle in the UK held in March 2005 explicitly put forward the idea for discussion of the possibility of the Virilio-influenced concept of the 'dromocratic condition' and its function of displacing Lyotard's notion of the postmodern condition in contemporary social and cultural theory. In truth, Virilio, a self-confessed high modernist, is better seen through the lens of his own self-description, a 'critic of the art of technology' (Redhead 2004a; 2004b), rather than any kind of theorist for a condition, or era, after modernity.

The idea of the 'dromocratic condition' alone is unlikely to be Virilio's lasting legacy.

However, Paul Virilio may yet have a place, albeit to one side, in some of these social and cultural theory debates about rethinking modernity. This is in my view linked to the resurgence of interest in the architecture and theoretical writing of his partner in post-space, Claude Parent. Partly this attention has been due to the association of Claude Parent, especially in the 1960s, with Paul Virilio himself. The duo conceptualised a new architectural order, a new spatial syntax, during the period 1963 to 1969 in what they came to call the theory of the oblique function or function of the oblique. The period of Parent's partnership with Virilio witnessed a growth in Virilio's work and thinking that has been almost hidden from history once his later work started to be read by an English speaking world and utilised by different kinds of theorists searching for the holy grail of the 'dromocratic condition' and 'accidentology' (Virilio 2007b). As an enterprise which might be called an 'archaeology of the post-future' using Parent and Virilio in general, concentrating on the Virilio of the 1950s and 1960s, and expecially his productive partnership with Parent, the contention here is that critical modernity is worth taking seriously. As Virilio's writings have multiplied and been subjected to greater forensic interrogation in the last decade, so has interest arisen at last, especially online, in the separate work of Claude Parent. Nevertheless, there is more to the history and biography of Claude Parent than simply being Paul Virilio's partner in the radical architectural project of the 1960s where they pursued an extreme utopian futurist vision of creating sloping cities on an incline. Certainly, in the ensuing years, the secular Claude Parent has been eclipsed, in the historiography of French public intellectuals, by the avowedly anarchistic, phenomenological and religious Paul Virilio. Yet it is important to keep in balance Parent's long-term contribution to architectural poetics in France, and to post-space studies in general. In the early years of the third millennium and a renewed interest in retheorising modernity the career of Claude Parent has found, very late in the day of his own life, a new topicality.

In the course of this rethinking of modernity in the context of the new significance of Claude Parent, the idea of critical modernity, which Parent introduced in his writing from the 1950s (Virilio 1996: 14–15), and its practical operation, needs to be resurrected and re-examined. It helps, when situated within a historical narrative of Parent's work, to assess Claude Parent's significance not just simply as a utopian and professional architect but as a putatative theorist of critical modernity. Critical modernity is a term applicable to the whole of his aesthetic oeuvre from the 1950s to the 2010s. The question of whether or not there is what has been described as a 'Parentian' aesthetic is a difficult one to answer, but a durable legacy of what he later called critical architecture (Parent and Virilio 1997: 15–17), as part of a new or critical modernity, was most certainly built up and sustained from the early part of Parent's career as an architect and polemicist to his role as the latter day elder statesman of French architecture honoured with a major retrospective exhibition of his work in Paris in 2010 (Migayou and Rambert 2010). What then does the term critical modernity signify? It should be pointed out at this juncture that I previously used the terms critical modernity, accelerated modernity and dangerous modernity in my introductory book on Paul Virilio as a 'theorist for an accelerated culture' (Redhead 2004a), a text which was complemented by a comprehensive reader of Virilio's works (Redhead 2004b). This trilogy of ideas was all introduced as concepts that help to situate Virilio in considering his contribution to a rethinking of modernity in the social and human sciences. They have the distinct advantage, too, of not designating an era of postmodernity. In other words, they imply that modernity is always, already impregnated with 'dangerous modernity' or 'accelerated modernity'. Modernity, in the argument of the book on Virilio as a theorist of accelerated culture, is seen as always dangerous and speeded-up: it is not envisaged that modernity undergoes transformation from an early modern condition to a later, accelerated or dangerous state. The phrase critical modernity in this work was derived from Claude Parent's use of the term and applied to the whole of Paul Virilio's theoretical enterprise from the 1950s to the present day. I will not discuss further here the concepts of accelerated and dangerous modernity, but the term critical modernity should be read as emerging in this context, and some of the archaeological study of Virilio and Parent in the earlier work (Redhead 2004a, 2004b) is developed here with a new emphasis on the singular contribution of Claude Parent.

Critical modernity, then, does not designate a late modern transformation: critical modernity is always, already within the modern. I want to consider first what Claude Parent means by critical modernity and what summary can be made of its meaning. To be 'for' critical modernity is to be in favour of relentless reviewing of processes and methods and a continual reinvention of vocabulary. It is to practise a positive questioning of modernism from within. It is to protest against industrial standardisation and mass construction, inherited from an earlier era of 'militant modernism' (Hatherley 2008). In his specific application of critical modernity in architecture Parent envisaged a sort of architecture of mobilities, or a mobile architecture, which involved, at least in the 1960s, the deliberate cultivation of disequilibrium and fluctuation as well as the preservation of both the built historical fabric and memory of a society. As with Paul Virilio's outlook, for Claude Parent critical modernity was intended to shake, and shock, people, and especially their bodies, out of passivity (Virilio and Lotringer 2002: 8–17), to put in their way environmental obstacles that would move citizens into action, as a mode of ensuring human mobility in the passifying, stultifying consumer society of the 1960s which radical figures of the time like Virilio and Parent saw around them.

The notion of critical architecture in critical modernity is a conceptualisation that Parent has played with over several decades without always referring to it in these terms. He has, however, used it retrospectively to try to make sense of his interventions into architectural practice and architectural poetics, alone and in association with others. For Claude Parent a critical modernity was the pair's most overriding theoretical focus when he and Paul Virilio were together as a working partnership in the 1960s, actively forging ahead of the conservative contemporary thinking in architecture in France, and more widely in the rest of Europe. They were embarked on creating a 'post-architecture'; Parent self-consciously considered that what he and Virilio were doing in the 1960s was nothing less than a cultural revolution in architecture. The questions they were posing in the course of developing the function of the oblique allowed them, in Parent's assessment thirty years later, to 'consider anew the modern architecture of the 1920s and 1930s' (Virilio 1996b: 14) and the 'limits of memory' (Parent and Virilio 1997: 15–17). Parent and Virilio, both theoretically and practically, were trying to give a new critical inflection to modernist architecture in the 1960s and distinguish it from work in the 1920s and 1930s and its standardising influences on urban planning in the 1960s. They considered themselves as being actively engaged in critical modernity with their strategies of 'positive questioning' of the 'modern movement' (Virilio 1996b: 14). It is important to note, nevertheless, that neither Claude Parent nor Paul Virilio was in any sense connected to movements associated with postmodernism, either in architecture specifically or more generally in social and cultural theory. Both Parent and Virilio remained 'high modernists', albeit ambivalently (Virilio and Lotringer 2002: 16), throughout their utopian architecture partnership in the 1960s. They remained uninfluenced by debates about postmodernism and postmodernity in the aftermath of their partnership when they went their separate ways for forty years from the late 1960s to the 2010s. I could conclude, cryptically, that 'they have never been postmodern'.

Part of Claude Parent's new topicality in the twenty-first century, for some commentators, is that in the words of the editor of a special issue of

an architecture journal devoted to Claude Parent the political and economic upheavals that have taken place since postmodernism have led to
a 'spatial turn', not only in architecture and urban discourse but also in
the field of cultural studies and social theory and this 'shift in paradigms'
has aroused particular interest in questions of post-space and bodily
movement which Parent had pioneered, and then pursued relentlessly
since the early 1950s (Bideau 2002: 1). Shortly before Parent's eightieth
birthday, the German architecture journal, *Werk, Bauen und Wohnen*,
published a special issue on Claude Parent (entitled 'Claude Parent und
die Folgen'). The issue attempted to assess the contemporary conceptual,
as well as historical, significance of Parent's aesthetic and indeed his entire
architectural and design oeuvre. The editorial introduction, by Andre
Bideau, charted 'the spatial turn' supposedly taking place after the reign
of postmodernism. The justification of the journal editor, Andre Bideau,
for Parent's work being relatively little known outside France, as opposed
to the fate of the writings of collaborators like Paul Virilio, was because, in
Bideau's view, it 'cannot be pigeonholed in any of the familiar categories
such as Brutalism, Structuralism, Metabolism or Pop'. Andre Bideau also
penned an assessment of Claude Parent, Paul Virilio and Architecture
Principe in the pages of the special issue, which ran alongside an article
on Parent by the specialist writer Frederic Migayou who would write the
catalogue of Parent's mammoth 2010 retrospective exhibition (Migayou
and Rambert 2010) and extracts from Parent and Virilio's contributions to
Architecture Principe manifestos.

It might also be said that the paradigmatic shifts, to the extent that
they have actually taken place, have cleared a space for looking again at
the concept of critical modernity in late 'late capitalist' (as Ernest Mandel
once called it) society. Looking back on the long-term significance of
the Parent and Virilio partnership some time after the post-millennial
blues had faded, Claude Parent claimed that the group he formed with
Virilio in the 1960s, Architecture Principe, anticipated today's architectural repositioning of the human body as a major feature of interest as
well as the rethinking of the 'body in movement' shown by, for example,
modern choreographers in the realm of dance (Parent 2001; Louppe
1994) and international academic journals like *Body and Society*. Claude
Parent's work, especially in the 1950s and 1960s, was prescient in many
different ways. For example, Claude Parent's drawings in the mid-1960s
anticipated the digital era of design in the fluidity of their dynamic, inde-
terminate form and the associated radical abandonment of the traditional
architectural orthogonal grid of verticality and horizontality in the function of the oblique houses and churches which he built. Because of 'digi-

modernist' (A. Kirby 2010) developments in recent years, today it can be conjectured that

> thanks to a revolution in digital modelling, architects are thinking outside the box, replacing straight lines with curves, right angles with bends, rectangles with sensuous silhouettes, plain, flat facades with shimmering folds and seams. Think Marilyn Monroe rather than Charlton Heston. (Callaghan 2010: 29)

Claude Parent in an overarching retrospective look at his career has argued the case for a movement of 'critical architecture' where a 'critical expression' seems to be 'the best of modernity's paths' (Parent and Virilio 1997: 17) and for a critical, or new, modernity which will 'free us from everything that is obsolete' (Virilio 1996b: 14). Architecturally, for Parent, this means that we 'must maintain significantly better relations with the historical built fabric than modernism has achieved to date' (Virilio 1996b: 15). The longer lasting contribution of Claude Parent may actually be the stress on a more general strategy related to critical modernity, a constant, if hidden, motif in his own architectural practice and writing, as well as in his partnership with Paul Virilio, where a critical, negating, or 'negative aesthetic' (Virilio 2005b) force is at work. Claude Parent has certainly shown us tropes and signposts on the way not only to a critical architecture but also what can be called 'an architecture of critical modernity'; in other words a spatial syntax, a map of the possible make-up of critical modernity. The background biographical context to the architecture and writings of Claude Parent himself is worthwhile exploring before reconstructing the partnerships he enjoyed with the likes of Andre Bloc, Yves Klein and Paul Virilio, and, finally, assessing Parent's overall importance in both architectural theory and in the social and cultural rethinking of modernity. What then precisely made Claude Parent a critical modernist in this context? Claude Parent was born in Neuilly-sur-Seine in north- western Paris on 26 February 1923. He studied at the Ecole des Beaux-Arts in the city in the 1940s and early 1950s. In a rather typical anti-establishment move he refused to complete his formal architectural training at the Ecole. Nevertheless, he obtained the right to appear among eight professionals registered without having a diploma. He was already a critical, modernist thinker and shadowed some of his famous colleague Le Corbusier's thinking in the Brutalist modern tradition before moving into his own utopian phase. Le Corbusier had become known by the 1950s for his 'breton brut' (literally, raw concrete) modernist architectural approach to building houses and churches. Parent even worked for Le Corbusier for a time in the early 1950s but always baulked at the idea that he was a 'post-Corbusian' architect in any way, though he often attracted the epithet from commentators during his long career. Claude Parent refers to Le Corbusier in interview and in his writings affectionately as 'Corb' and obviously admired some of his buildings and architectural style. An art exhibition on 'Corbu and Parent', which focused on the dialogue between the two enigmatic architects and featured largely unseen drawings and models, was held at a New York gallery in 2003 helping to reignite the international interest in the life and work of Claude Parent that culminated in the Paris retrospective of 2010 (Migayou and Rambert 2010). For his part, Paul Virilio told his long time friend and interviewer Sylvere Lotringer 'I am not a Corbusian. I don't like that culture. I love painting' (Virilio and Lotringer and 2002: 24). Parent, even so, did mark his career by being an artistic architect with concrete as his main material.

In 1949 at the age of twenty-six Claude Parent met another architect named Ionel Schein with whom he collaborated until the mid-1950s. Both were known as children of Le Corbusier. An even more significant meeting for Parent, however, occurred in 1952 when he came across the sculptor Nicolas Schoffer. Schoffer died in 1992 and Parent remembered him, in a heartfelt homage sent to Schoffer's family at the time of his death, as his first companion in architectural utopia. In the early 1950s Schoffer was a pioneer in importing Neo-Plasticism, Russian Constructivism and Bauhaus ideas into French sculpture. Modernism 'ce qui arrive', to borrow Paul Virilio's own favourite phrase. Schoffer's subsequent influence on the two young architects, Parent and Schein, was immense. Parent and his new friend, Schein, worked from 1952 to 1955 on translating Schoffer's sculptural language into architectural forms. While still students at the Ecole des Beaux-Arts their joint entry won the Maison Francaise competition with a design for a house, built at Ville d'Avray, whose plan was fractured in two by a wall. The concept of fracture was to be taken up by Parent many times in his subsequent writing which consistently promoted the idea of challenging form, and formalist architecture, with the notions of instability and disequilibrium. Also, in the same year of 1953, the two created a model for a radio and television station along 'Schofferian' lines. Parent and Schein soon went their separate architectural ways and Parent came to concentrate more on working with Schoffer directly. Parent and Schoffer's specific aim was to create an urban planning 'spatio-dynamics', a 'spatial dynamic architetcture', which included, in a foregrounding of later utopian cityscapes Parent planned with Paul Virilio in the 1960s, long housing units in bands, on two levels, supported by pylons, with helicopters buzzing around the buildings and cars circulating between the pylons. A functioning 'spatio-dynamic city' was in fact imagined as

reality by Schoffer and Parent. The practical application of such theoretical ideas, however, proved less than successful when plans for building a
supermarket and then two dwelling houses on 'spatio-dymamic' lines had
to be abandoned. The impracticality of building utopia was to haunt the
later Parent and Virilio association.

Claude Parent's partnerships were to be significant at all stages of his
life and work. The longest lasting of all was the association with the artist
and publisher Andre Bloc. After meeting Parent when he was a young
malcontent at the Ecole des Beaux-Arts, Andre Bloc worked with the
maturing Claude Parent for ten years. Parent has often paid tribute to
Bloc's huge influence, acknowledging that he instigated Parent's substantive education as an architect. In the early 1950s when this education was
beginning, Andre Bloc was (as he had been since the 1930s) editor of the
influential French architecture journal *L'Architecture d'aujourd'hui* and
consequently came into contact with a particular intellectual and artistic
milieu throughout the world. Bloc, also, was changing perspective in the
1950s; from architecture to painting and sculpture. Parent was to benefit
directly from these connections and changes. For example, the Group
Espace (whose number included Nicolas Schoffer) painters and sculp-
tors came to Parent's attention through Bloc's personal introduction and
Parent has cited their lasting influence on the eventual development of
what he has called a dynamic geometry, and the idea of spatial disequilibrium, a kind of setting in motion what is stable and immobile, which
would so endear him to Paul Virilio when they met in 1963. Bloc, too, took
to Claude Parent and allowed him to edit some sections of *L'Architecture
d'aujourd'hui*, a periodical that Parent would continue to work with for
the next forty years, and also Bloc's new emergent aesthetic review *L'Art
d'aujourd'hui*. The personal and professional collaboration with Andre
Bloc, though, went much further during the decade of the 1950s. The pair
of them, for instance, worked together on three chapels and numerous
houses, designed Andre Bloc's own personal summer home in Antibes in
1959, and later, in the early 1960s, produced the Maison de l'Iran at the
Cite Universitaire in Paris, one of the relatively few buildings that forms
part of Parent's most lasting legacy. Bloc's patronage as well as his propen-
sity to rethink spatial design in a more artistic fashion than architecture
had done previously, had given Claude Parent what he regarded as a 'true
education'.

Claude Parent was himself, by the early 1960s, a noted and somewhat
controversial figure in French architecture. Despite this notoriety, there
is relatively little written about Parent over the whole trajectory of his
life and career. Apart from one text in French (Ragon 1982) and one text

in Italian (Nicoletti 1998), the only full length books to be written about Claude Parent, there is surprisingly little secondary literature in any language considering both what he has himself done during his architectural practice and also the well known figures who have been associated with him. Amongst the sparse literature though there are articles in Spanish on aspects of his work published in *Nueva Forma* in Madrid in the 1970s. Parent, for his part, has been writing, fairly cryptically, about his own practice, and the ideas it contained, for decades in French in journals such as *L'Architecture d'aujourd'hui* and in *Architecture principe*. Parent has also published several untranslated books in French. Parent had become interested in architectural utopias in the 1950s and went on to develop certain links with other architectural utopists, as well as to forge numerous collaborations with contemporary conceptual artists. The broadening of his aesthetic ideas beyond the simply spatial, or the architectural in a technical sense, was a major shift in Parent's questioning of the sort of modernism on offer in the 1950s. By the late 1950s, he was associating with contemporary artistic figures like Jacques Polieri and Jean Tinguely and, most notably, the conceptual artist Yves Klein. Klein had moved to Paris in the mid-1950s. In the late 1950s Parent began working with Klein on his Air Architecture drawings. In Klein's conceptualisations compressed air was to be used to create transparent walls, roofs and furniture for domestic dwellings. As part of Klein's idea to return direct sensation to everyday life, the artist wanted to envisage a climate controlled environment where people could roam naked. In 1961, a year before Klein's sudden death, Parent further collaborated with Yves Klein on the design for fountains of water and fire, entitled Les Fontaines de Varsovie, for the Palais de Chaillot in Paris. Though Parent was not to know it at the time, the turn of the decade coincided with a downturn in artistic architectural collaborations in general. The 1950s, Parent's artistic incubation period, were pregnant with critical and utopian architectural ideas, in a way that the 1960s, for all their promise, were not. In many ways, Parent in the 1960s was to be out on a limb in his pursuit of the critical modernity in post-space.

The connection of Claude Parent to the 'Function of the Oblique', and with it to Paul Virilio, proved pivotal. Despite the stimulation of utopianism and the volatile Parisian artistic climate of the time, by the early 1960s Parent was becoming disillusioned with certain kinds of utopian architectural and artistic thinking. He wanted to push further out in his quest for what he envisaged as architecture of motion or architecture of disequilibrium. It was then that he met Paul Virilio, and there began a partnership which was to prove extremely fruitful for both parties. It went

on to produce the theory and practice of what they were to label the function of the oblique, or oblique function, a challenge to the orthogonal in
architecture, and an attempt to achieve the negation of the vertical. Claude
Parent and Paul Virilio had a mutual friend in Paris, the painter Michel
Carrade, so it was almost inevitable that they would get together sometime
in the French artistic melting pot of the early 1960s. In the subsequent
association, the younger Virilio (then only thirty-one years old) was to
collaborate closely with a figure already of some stature in Claude Parent.
Parent was initially the senior partner in the relationship, in all senses.
There is a story, apparently not apocryphal, which has it that the professional architect Parent had, eventually, to ban the interloper Virilio from
going into his architectural practice in Paris in the mid-1960s because
Virilio was so 'pessimistic' in his nature that he stopped Parent's employ-
ees from working! Nevertheless, initially at least, Virilio had skills to offer
Parent. As well as having obsessively photographed thousands of wartime
German bunkers in France by the early 1960s, Virilio had also trained as
a painter and an artist in stained glass. He had studied at the Ecole des
Metiers d'Art in Paris, the city where he was born and which remained his
home until the end of the century. At the time that he met Claude Parent
in 1963, Virilio was working, mainly in order to earn a living, as a painter,
and amongst other work, produced designs for Braque, at Varengeville
and Matisse, at Saint-Paul-de-Vence. Virilio has said that he has continued throughout his life to approach everything as a visual artist and has
gone so far as to admit that he always writes with images and confessed
that he could not write a book if he did not have images. It was this particular aesthetic perspective that was to pervade all that followed in Paul
Virilio's subsequent academic career. Virilio, like Nicolas Schoffer and
Yves Klein before him, was another in the long line of Claude Parent's collaborators in utopian architecture who had no formal architectural training at all. They were simply, but importantly, artists. As noted earlier in
this chapter, Paul Virilio has himself produced the pithy self-definition of
his work which accurately portrays this aesthetic identity – 'a critic of the
art of technology'. Claude Parent has always preferred just plain 'architect' as his epithet but in many ways he could be regarded, legitimately, as
much more of a secular social theorist than the avowedly religious Virilio.

Claude Parent has recalled in interview (Virilio 1996b: 49–57) that when
the two of them met initially in 1963, the future professor of architecture
Paul Virilio had no architectural training and that 'when Virilio came
to buy an apartment' in Paris where they both lived 'he was a painter of
stained glass'. Admiringly, Parent said that 'Virilio knew an extraordinary
amount about his craft'. But Virilio, according to Parent, 'also had a real

instinct for architecture – an instinct reflected in his impulsive decision to buy that apartment'. In fact, it was Claude Parent who was the architect of the apartment building! They shared a passion for fast Jaguar cars, Parent driving an E-type and Virilio preferring the S-type. But that real estate moment was how they originally paired up. For Parent it was his 'first big project' and when Paul Virilio initially saw the building it only consisted of two storeys of concrete. Nevertheless it was the basis of a professional architectural partnership, at least for a while, as Claude Parent and Paul Virilio subsequently began to work together furiously on architectural projects in France from 1963, carrying on commissioned work together until the late 1960s. The painter of stained glass and the critical modernist utopian architect proved to be something of a dream team of hip young gunslingers of post-space.

As their most lasting testament to the function of the oblique, Paul Virilio and Claude Parent built the church of Sainte-Bernadette du Banlay in Nevers in France between 1964 and 1966. This was the pair's first practical project based on their unique theory of the incline, which had itself developed from Virilio's ideas first generated around what he called 'bunker archaeology' and 'cryptic architecture' (Redhead 2004a, 2004b; Armitage 2000, 2001; Virilio 2009a; Gane 2003) and Claude Parent's notions of architectural movement and dynamic geometry. On the face of it the pair also seemed to plunder much of their muscular brutalism in the building of the church from late Le Corbusier but they have consistently, and independently, rejected any Corbusian or even post-Corbusian label. What is certain is that the theory of the function of the oblique had its origins in the concepts of the bunker through Virilio's 1950s studies (Redhead 2009) and of disequilibrium and motive instability (which had always intrigued Parent). Accordingly, Virilio and Parent set about imagining their first structure to be built on the theory of construction on an incline, on the idea of sloping surfaces, a concept that was meant to disturb and to provoke. The choice of the Sainte-Bernadette church in Nevers for the first oblique function project was a significant one for a less secular reason, too. Virilio often cites approvingly in his work the religious miracle at Lourdes in 1858 where a young girl, Bernadette Soubirous, supposedly had a vision of the Virgin Mary. It was in Nevers that Bernadette Soubirous died. For the centenary of her death, the Bishop of Nevers, Michel Vial, organised a competition to build a chapel in her honour and Virilio persuaded Parent to join with him at the beginning of their friendship in 1963 in entering it. The partnership of Parent and Virilio was successful in the competition. The bunker-like church building that Parent and Virilio produced is now officially a historical monument in France (Virilio and Lotringer 2002: 27). Parent and Virilio's oblique church of Saint-Bernadette du Banlay, developed and, eventually, built between 1963 and 1966, was a brutalist, menacing building which has been interpreted as deriving from the architecture inspired by the German bunkers of the North Atlantic wall that Virilio had photographed in their thousands and that he had already seen as embodying an architecture of disequilibrium some years prior to this first joint architectural venture with Claude Parent. The church building symbolised much for this rather odd architectural pairing, one self-confessedly 'not a practising Christian', the other deeply spiritual and already engaged in several religious art projects. For the secular, professional architect Claude Parent, the church expressed what he felt as a righteous angry man about the 'architecture and society of the time' (Virilio 1996b: 19).

The three years' work on the church of Sainte-Bernadette and the completion of its construction preceded the sustained development of the experimental theories around the idea of oblique function. In some ways, though, the Sainte-Bernadette project was seen as a bunker church, and expressing a military vocabulary, more in retrospect than it was as the work went along. Parent has recalled that the 'decision to apply this language' of the German bunkers 'to the form of the church came at a late stage in the project's development' so 'the formal references to bunkers should therefore be seen as a secondary element' (Virilio 1996b: 19). Parent, perhaps over generously, too, has said that Paul Virilio, despite not being an architect and effectively hanging out in his friend's office each day, was the one in the partnership who had the radical ideas. According to the self-effacing later testimony of Claude Parent, Paul Virilio (Virilio 1996b: 51):

> had an admirable, and legitimate, ambition to make architecture and he contributed to the project in a very real way. It was Virilio who said that we should put a slope on the floor planes of the church . . . The challenge of working together on a real, concrete project inspired a fundamental break-through – the first application of the function of the oblique. The military vocabulary of the bunkers dominated our early projects – the church as well as the cultural centre in Charleville. Virilio saw the bunker as the apotheosis of twentieth-century architecture.

Certainly the radicalism of retheorising the horizontal by Virilio in the early 1960s gave energy to the idea of living on inclined planes and having furniture coming out of the floor, which became a serious utopian project for Parent and Virilio as the 1960s wore on. But in reality Claude Parent and Paul Virilio came to the partnership as independent thinkers with interesting backgrounds in architecture and art, as well as in Virilio's case Gestalt psychology and phenomenological philosophy. They worked jointly in these years and, as Parent notes, each came with 'a set of design ideas that we wanted to develop to the full' (Virilio 1996b: 19).

Claude Parent and Paul Virilio conspired to launch Architecture Principe in the milieu of 1960s French architecture and by extension the new aesthetic movement of art, sculpture and painting that had originated in the utopian decade of the 1950s. But it was Virilio, rather than Parent, who was to go on from this early tentative postion and achieve international fame as a 'dromologist' with a growing host of global fans promoting the idea of the 'dromocratic condition' as a possible replacement for the postmodern era. Where Virilio today has an increasing global critical literature about him (Der Derian 1998; Armitage 2000, 2001; James 2007a and b; Virilio 2009b), Claude Parent has few texts written about the man and his work and he is little known or acknowledged outside France, though his own professional colleagues and citizens did award him the accolade of Laureate of the Grand Prix National de l'Architecture in 1979. Eventually developing architecture formally as his academic profession through his post as professor of architecture, Parent's protégé Paul Virilio became part of the furniture at the Ecole Speciale d'Architecture in Paris for thirty years, beginning in the late 1960s when he was elected by the students after the events of May 1968, as his productive association with Claude Parent was coming to an end. Professional architectural recognition was eventually forthcoming from his peers and Virilio was awarded the Laureate of the Grand Prix National de la Critique Architecturale in France in 1987. As the director of the Ecole Speciale d'Architecture in Paris, a post which essentially stemmed from 1972 when he was made co-director, he held a chair of architecture for three decades and was latterly president of the Ecole for several years. Virilio retired from the Ecole only at the close of the 1990s, with an emeritus professorship, when he was in his late sixties. As Claude Parent has emphasised, however, Paul Virilio never actually formally qualified as an architect at any time. Virilio's role at the Ecole, where he produced tracts on everything from international relations and terrorism through art history and media to the complexities of military technology, was as an architecture theorist and teacher, a trainer of architects, as he himself has noted mundanely, for 'the real world'. But to all intents and purposes Virilio left architecture behind in 1968 when he and Parent went their separate ways. It was left to Claude Parent to continue the architectural side of the function of the oblique partnership.

In the mid-1960s Parent and Virilio needed an organisation. The year they met, 1963, Claude Parent formed the Architecture Principe group with Paul Virilio and their mutual friend, Michel Carrade, the painter. A fourth member was also recruited, Morice Lipsi, a sculptor. The aim of Architecture Principe was to investigate and promote a new kind of architectural and urban order. Sylvere Lotringer (Virilio and Lotringer 2002: 12) has stressed the root meaning of the Parent and Virilio Architecture Principe group's moniker as 'urging architecture to begin again'. The Architecture Principe group lasted formally until 1969 when Claude Parent and Paul Virilio split over Virilio's participation in the momentous events of May 1968. In 1966 the group produced a magazine entitled *Architecture principe* which ran to nine issues and a tenth, retrospective special issue thirty years later, in 1996. All the manifestos of *Architecture principe*, in original French with English translations, together with separate specially written introductions to the whole volume by Paul Virilio and Claude Parent and several contributions from celebrity international architects such as Daniel Libeskind, were published collectively (Parent and Virilio 1997). A German edition was also published in the same year. Only Claude Parent and Paul Virilio put their signatures to the short articles in the publications, which, as they claimed, constituted the group's permanent manifesto. It seems, in retrospect, that Lipsi and Carrade did relatively little in *Architecture principe*. From the fragile beginnings of the group in 1963 there were eventually nine numbered issues of *Architecture principe* published between February and December 1966. The final number, ten, was published as an anniversary issue in September 1996 with contributions from associates such as Bernard Tschumi, Jean Nouvel and Daniel Libeskind, who had by then become celebrity architectural theorists in their own right, as well as critical, reflective essays from Paul Virilio and Claude Parent themselves. Each of the original Architecture Principe manifestos was emblazoned with a specific title. These were, in order of publication: *The Oblique Function*, *The Third Urban Order*, *Potentialism*, *The Nevers Worksite*, *Habitable Circulation*, *The Mediate City*, *Bunker Archaeology*, *Power and Imagination* and *Blueprint for Charleville*. These themes made up the first nine issues, all published in the mid-1960s. *Disorientation or Dislocation* was the rather tantalising title of the tenth and last issue in 1996. By today's publishing standards the magazine's issues were very short on word length but high on rhetoric and conceptual innovation. For instance, the *Bunker Archaeology* issue 7 of *Architecture principe* was published in September/October 1966. It comprised the short essay by Paul Virilio entitled 'Bunker Archaeology' which actually dated from 1958 when he was actively and obsessively photographing the German bunkers (Redhead 2009; Virilio 2009a). This was followed by another short essay from Virilio written in September 1965 entitled 'Cryptic

Architecture' which contained enigmatic statements such as (in English translation from the original French of the manifesto): 'cities are episodic and cerebral, they are a permanent and genetic crypt'; 'cryptic architecture is thus an infra-architecture'; and 'cryptic energy, itself indissociable from the survival of all living species'. 'Architecture cryptique' was the label Paul Virilio used in the early 1960s for the theoretical ideas spawned by his 'bunker archaeology'. Claude Parent's contribution to issue 7 was only slightly more than three short paragraphs. He proclaimed prophetically, several years before Virilio actually gained an academic post, that 'Paul Virilio is a reader of reality. He holds the university chair of the real; he is not in the analytical domain, but is a creator. In the present he is hunting for future portents. He sifts, chooses, gathers.' Parent went on in this brief, rather bizarre, but strangely accurate eulogy to describe the highly religious Paul Virilio as a 'man of faith' and 'in a state of permanent disequilibrium' who 'in order to triumph over original sin' has 'us discover today the masterpieces of an ancient world of terror'. With phrases like these, and permanent manifestos in their back pockets, the utopian post-architecture purveyors of the oblique function of the mid-1960s were making their mark.

Claude Parent in the 1960s was integrally associated with the idea of what was regarded then as the 'new society' especially by the most 'militant modernists' (Hatherley 2008). Parent, besides being the older partner in the architectural partnership with Paul Virilio was by the mid-1960s more cautious than his friend and also less utopian than he himself had been in the 1950s. It was Parent who was becoming more the world weary professional architect and Virilio who could say of his eventual election by the students as a professor at the Ecole Speciale d'Architecture in the late 1960s, 'I was happy I ended up teaching. It kept me from selling floors. As for Parent he ended up building nuclear reactors which I would never have agreed to do' (Virilio and Lotringer and 2002: 50). But the urban theorist and planner in Virilio was also beginning to take shape in the theoretical and practical collaboration with Parent, who had an established office and architectural practice in Paris where he had worked on a daily basis for over a decade. The partnership may have started as an artistic enterprise but it was also always, already connected to the city, to the idea of a future society, and the future of modernist urban planning. However, the first building venture illustrating the function of the oblique, though it more or less unfolded from its original conceptual structure, did not immediately open the floodgates of the Parent and Virilio architectural partnership. Virilio had prepared some stained glass windows for churches and through this 'sacred art' link managed to secure the Sainte-

Bernadette construction commission for himself and Claude Parent after some religious cultural entrepreneurship. Unfortunately, clients for the products of the function of the oblique were not exactly queueing up to pay for new projects. Further projects with Parent for a cultural centre in Charleville and a house in Saint-Germain-en-Laye, though they followed the lines of the original project, were never actually built. The December 1966 issue 9 of *Architecture principe* was entitled *A Blueprint for Charleville* because that is exactly what it remained: a blueprint. However, eventually another Parent and Virilio collaboration, namely the Thomson-Houston Aerospace Centre in Velizy-Villacoublay, was seen to fruition. In the meantime the Parent architecture practice built blocks of flats at Neuilly-sur-Seine and a series of supermarkets. Eventually, with Virilio out of the picture in the 1970s, apartments and shopping centres and the much praised French Pavilion at the 1970 Venice Biennale came out of the Parent practice. There followed, too, much to Paul Virilio's disgust, the design and construction of atomic plants in the late 1970s. In some of the building projects Claude Parent undertook in the 1960s and early 1970s the traditionally horizontal surfaces were replaced by planes sloping by as much as 28 per cent. What is clear is that they were all influenced by the function of the oblique theory that he had forged with Paul Virilio at the height of the mid-1960s utopian vision of what they both hoped would be a 'new society' (Virilio and Lotringer 2002: 13).

Theoretically the partnership of utopian architectural ideas blossomed for Parent. There is clear evidence that Parent and Virilio aimed the theory of the oblique function at social movements which conceived themselves as part of the design for the invention of a new, post-industrial society. Parent and Virilio debated these issues far and wide – at conferences and in their new magazine *Architecture principe*. In 1965 and 1966 Claude Parent and Paul Virilio presented papers to various conferences and seminars. Those given at Lyons, Locarno, Bologna and Lurs were collected together as the November 1966 issue 8 of the magazine. The pair closely collaborated personally, politically and theoretically in this period, despite being regarded as 'mad' and 'jokers' by some critics. The collaborations were not restricted to the jointly authored magazine manifestos. For example, in June 1966 at Folkestone across the channel in England, the French duo joined a panel on experimental architecture at a symposium organised by the International Dialogue of Experimental Architecture (IDEA) which included representatives of British utopian architectural groups like Archigram. For Owen Hatherley (Hatherley 2008: 130) the 'new brutalism' in British modernism in architecture and art of the 1950s and 1960s is symbolised by 'the futuristic fantasies of Archigram (some of whose members worked on the South Bank Centre's ferroconcrete walk-ways by day)'. The Archigram project was part of 'serious British modern-ism', an outgrowth of 'Brutalism not the International Style' (Hatherley 2008: 130). The intervention by Parent and Virilio, a presentation on 'oblique cities' delivered by the two Frenchmen dressed all in black, bizarrely led to audience uproar still remembered decades later by those present. The presentation was provocative in form and content. If their intention was to provoke trouble in England the idea succeeded and they were duly booed off the stage and even received a Nazi salute from those they were addressing. Audience memory suggests that their choice of all black clothes (this was after all the year of the emergence in New York of the Andy Warhol influenced rock group the Velvet Underground led by Lou Reed and John Cale) rather than the pyschedelic garb worn by other symposium participants probably alienated the other architects present as much as what they said. But the fact is that Parent and Virilio were not just disrupting the conference by the way they looked. They were after all talking about the futuristic possibility of 'oblique cities' right across the globe. The extent of the radicalism of Architecture Principe in the context of the architecture theory, and indeed practice, of the period should not be forgotten. It is clear with the benefit of many decades of hindsight that the Folkestone incident symbolised the break they had already made with previous ideas, including the utopists of the 1950s. The 'horizontality' of the pre-industrial era and the 'verticality' of the modernist, industrial epoch was in the mid-1960s, for Parent and Virilio, to be transformed by the 'oblique' of the post-industrial. Looking back, the fact that the 'post-architects' were seen as outsiders in England in the year 1966, and treated with suspicion and hostility, is hardly surprising.

In the context of May 1968, especially as seen by French theorists like Alain Badiou who were there the first time around (Badiou 2010), architecturally and theoretically, things would eventually come to a close, however, for the group work of Parent and Virilio. The Thomson-Houston Aerospace project, assisted by Virilio's good relationship with the engineer, turned out to be the duo's final completed collaboration. External rather than internal factors were responsible. The powerful utopian association more or less came to an end by 1968 because a new and bold joint project to construct a full-scale experimental model of the function of the oblique was overtaken by rapidly developing global politi-cal events. The grandly named project, 'The Pendular Destabiliser No. 1' (there was also a No. 2, at least in the drawing stage) which Parent and Virilio intended to inhabit for some weeks to test the equilibrium and habitability of buildings on an incline, and to determine the best choice of angles for the different living spaces, was in the process of being built at the university of Nanterre in the first few months of 1968. It was an experimental structure which was raised twelve metres from the ground to isolate it from the outside world. 'No telephone, no post, no means of communication – except for a little hole in the wall that we could talk to each other through' was how Claude Parent recalled 'The Pendular Destabiliser No. 1' as it was envisaged in its design (Virilio 1996b: 55). It is clear that the senior architectural partner, Claude Parent, was worried about the strangeness of the project and the possibility that he and Virilio would reap the ridicule (Virilio and Lotringer 2002: 43) if it was publicised. Parent certainly felt relief when the experiment was eventually dropped. The bold psycho-physiological experiment with the two of them 'trapped like rats in a laboratory' was curtailed not because of the impracticability of experimental living on inclined slopes (though that may well have been the end result of the behavioural tests, measured by electrodes, which were envisaged by Parent and Virilio under strict medical supervision) but because of wider political and cultural happenings in France, and in Western society generally. This just happened to be the era of May 1968, and, in France, Nanterre's campus was where the spark was lit for the spectacular May 1968 events in Europe, an upheaval which politically separated the previously close two architectural colleagues.

May 1968, with its student and worker uprisings, and the notorious riot police action, saw the beginning of the end for the architectural partnership that had flourished for five years around the theory and practice of the function of the oblique. Situationism, especially in the figure of Guy Debord (Merrifield 2005; Hussey 2001), and its effect on left politics in France and especially on the theories and practices of cities (McDonough 2009), was obliquely at the centre of the disagreement between Paul Virilio and Claude Parent that ended their work together, though neither of them was, or is, a Situationist, despite what has often been written about their endeavours. It was undoubtedly a traumatic time for those who had seen themselves as part of radical cultural politics in France during the 1950s and early 1960s. Claude Parent has remembered that he was 'upset that the political climate had so corrupted a friend of six years' (Virilio 1996b: 57). Moreover other conflicts in the partnership were surfacing. For instance, both Virilio and Parent were anti-militarist but their critique of militarism was different. Claude Parent has argued that Virilio 'did have a certain respect for the power of a collective organisation to achieve extraordinary, almost magical results that are beyond the power of the individual' (Virilio 1996b: 51). However, D-Day in 1944 and the might of the US military-industrial complex to achieve its goal in the Second

World War as a whole apparently held a fascination for Virilio that Parent could not share. Furthermore, Parent was not a Christian whereas Virilio was, and is, deeply influenced by his religious faith and has been a practising Catholic since the age of eighteen. Perhaps most damningly, in 1968 of all years, Parent did not believe the function of the oblique theory itself to have a 'political agenda' (Virilio 1996b: 55). Parent, as if to underline the argument, wrote in an architectural essay two years after May 1968 that the function of the oblique was never envisaged as a political movement. Virilio seemingly never forgave him.

According to his later testimony, looking back on the whole affair of the break up of his partnership with Virilio in the 1960s, the more restrained Parent plainly thought that the politics of May 1968 (Hussey 2001; Badiou 2010: 43–67) were simply 'idiotic'. He has said that he 'didn't even know what Situationist meant' at the time, whereas Virilio evidently threw himself into the 'spontaneous' situation with gusto becoming one of the 300 who 'took' the Odeon on 15 May 1968, an act that appalled, but also amused, his older architectural colleague (Virilio and Lotringer 2002: 231–40). Virilio has further recalled his part in the event of the occupation of the Theatre de l'Odeon in Paris (Virilio and Lotringer 2002: 46–9) where he stressed the influence of Living Theatre on his actions that day. Claude Parent (Virilio 1996b: 55) has reminisced that:

> Virilio's experience of the time was very different. He was close to the hub of things. He wrote an article . . . and he joined the group occupying the Odeon. When I went to see him, I was told that he was now calling himself 'Comrade Paul'. Those people all took themselves very seriously, forming 'revolutionary committees' and 'sub-committees'. I have no stomach for that kind of thing . . . I don't like that mob mentality . . . he was very much involved in the movement as a whole. He said it was something he'd been dreaming of all his life – 1789 revisited. All the same, he was no fool. The day the police stormed the Odeon and drove everyone out with their batons, he wasn't there. He'd gone home to take a bath.

Parent was right in remembering that as far as May 1968 is concerned, Paul Virilio 'was very much involved in the movement as a whole' though he was not in fact aligned with any group in particular, despite Claude Parent's suspicion that Virilio was probably 'at the time much influenced by the Situationists' (Virilio 1996b: 55). For his own part Paul Virilio (Virilio and Lotringer 2008: 82) has rather romantically looked back on May 1968:

> I remember the speeches in the Richelieu Amphitheatre of the Sorbonne, before the taking of the Odeon Theatre at the very beginning of May '68. I

went in: the place was packed. I heard a guy, probably a communist, say 'I read on the walls of the Sorbonne: "Imagination comes to power!" That's not true, it's the working class!' I answered: 'So, comrade, you deny the working class imagination.' It was pretty clear, one referring to a horde able to take power like a mass of soldiers, and the other (me) referring to the active imagination.

Claude Parent, a radical utopian in the 1950s and early 1960s, was simply not prepared to go along with any of this ultra-leftism and wanted to maintain his position as modernist social critic through his architectural practice. Virilio has said that May 1968 marked a 'political' rift with Virilio going to the 'left' and Parent to the 'right' after May 1968 (Virilio and Lotringer 2002: 48) but it may have been a dispute that was terminologi-cal, and even generational, as much as anything. Parent maintained that the questioning of society and the challenging of architectural processes (Virilio 1996b: 55–7) had nothing whatsoever to do with the 'politics' of May 1968 (Badiou 2008, 2010: 43–67). Virilio, too, was younger and possibly more impetuous, around the same age as Situationist leader Guy Debord (Hussey 2001), whilst Parent looked on askance at what he regarded as the youthful and vengeful anarchism of the mob. To someone like Paul Virilio who has continued to see himself until today as an 'Anarchist Christian', the problem was not so much one of order. For Parent order was central and indeed he was disappointed that May 1968 did not produce a 'new order', or 'realistic alternative', displaying only acts which seemed designed to tear 'everything apart' (Virilio 1996b: 55). Whatever the precise cause of the split between Parent and Virilio the bust -up meant that they could no longer work together. May 1968, and its aftermath, proved effectively to be the end of the joint journey for the previously patient Parent.

Although May 1968 symbolically put an end to the partnership, theoretical and practical, of Claude Parent with his 'artist' colleague Paul Virilio, the outriders of the movement of 'architecture beginning again' did continue for a while, independently of each other, with some further development of the ideas surrounding the theory of the function of the oblique. Even before the break up with Virilio, Parent had designed radical oblique dwellings (with Ionel Schein, his first utopian partner) for an extravagant business client, Mr Woog, a young Swiss millionaire, who wanted to live on the banks of Lake Geneva. Once the split with Virilio was irrevocable, Claude Parent further continued to explore the function of the oblique in a whole series of practical architectural projects, design-ing an oblique house in 1969, the oblique French Pavilion in 1970 and several other urban projects in the 1970s and 1980s. He also published single authored texts in French specifically about the oblique function in 1970 and 1981 (Parent 1970, 1981; Virilio 2009b). As for Paul Virilio, he has emphasised in retrospect (Virilio 1996b: 13) that his work on the function of the oblique was not only conducted with Claude Parent:

> After I became co-director of the Ecole Speciale d'Architecture in Paris in 1972, my teaching concentrated on the development of technical research into the organisation and the precise morphology of oblique volumes. Several student theses were devoted to this theme, but after a few years the overwhelming difficulties of building an oblique habitat led us to abandon this work which seemed to offer no practical benefit to young architects starting out in the working world.

Effectively by this time the utopian architectural game was up. The pair of arch radicals whom the French architectural press of the 1960s had mischievously labelled 'post-Corbusians' had finally given in to the more prosaic demands of the 1970s and ultimately the neo-liberal world of the 1980s, 1990s and 2000s. Paul Virilio, to the extent that formal architecture figured much in his life after 1968, taught generations of students to become 'technical architects' in the Ecole Speciale d'Architecture on Boulevard Raspail in Paris. As Virilio has said, he was training them for the real world. Essentially he was 'not building much of anything' but 'doing theory' (Virilio and Lotringer 2002: 49). For Claude Parent the subsequent forty years were business as usual. After the Virilio partnership broke apart, another young hopeful came to hang out in the Parent architectural practice. This turned out to be Jean Nouvel, today one of the best known contemporary French architects and theorists. Parent, as architectural entrepreneur and writer, has for many years continued to champion his famous protégé's cause and to promote Jean Nouvel as a theorist as well as an architect. Parent has also continued to practise as an architect professionally since 1968. He has designed Paris buildings well into his seventies including a theatre in 1990 and offices in 1998, as well as a controversial trade centre, the Myslbek Centre, in a central business district of Prague, just off Wenceslas Square, in 1997. Yet, after more than fifty years of practice as an architect in his home city, Claude Parent has felt that 'his big mouth' has prevented him from being offered work in larger scale urban projects and really getting a 'chance to show what he can do with a piece of the city' (Virilio 1996b: 57).

In the context of the Architecture Principe group in the 1960s, Parent and Virilio's work was seen by critics to 'subvert Modernism's quest for stable foundations' and the two of them in harness did radically put into practice Virilio's idea of a negative, critical aesthetic on the 'negative horizon' (Virilio 2005b) where the 'vocabulary of the bunker was intended to create a repellent architecture that would overrun established perceptions and provoke a response from the user, in the same spirit as the Situationists' (Virilio 1996b: 62). The partnership of Parent and Virilio, though it did not endure, was a formative period in both men's life and work and repays the close 'archaeological' study I have conducted here. For Parent it had been an exercise in critical architecture, in critical modernity, which he has continued to pursue. He has achieved, late in the day, a place in the pantheon of French architecture of the last one hundred years which without allocating him leadership of a school or genre has lauded his persistent questioning of modernist architectural orthodoxy. However, although the excavation of the intellectual and cultural history of Claude Parent undertaken in this essay is significant in its own right, it is also a possible signpost to new directions within a field of contemporary social and cultural theory that is moving away from theories of postmodernity and towards rethinking of new modernity, and indeed new modernities. Parent's work within what he called critical modernity is one possible resource for this rethinking of modernity. Uncannily, even though it is Paul Virilio, and particularly his work from the 1970s onwards, who in contemporary debates receives the attention of social and cultural theorists seeking to replace the outmoded idea of the postmodern condition with the 'Virilian' notion of the 'dromocratic condition', it is more productive, as argued here, to plunge further back into Virilio's oeuvre, especially into his work with Parent in the 1960s.

As seen here Claude Parent's architectural and theoretical work, alone and together with others, is important primarily because of the concept of critical modernity that he has applied to it. Parent was to experience a more localised response to his work than Virilio over the subsequent four decades but it does not diminish its significance or mean that it cannot be seen as useful outside of narrow limits of modern architectural practice. To Claude Parent's mind, the 'body in motion' aspect of the oblique function was present from the very beginning of the work in the 1950s, when he was influenced by the innovative sculpture of Nicolas Schoffer and other artists. Virilio's work on perceptions of motion, unlike Parent's which had been highly influenced by the very different art and architecture aesthetic of the 1950s, had been formed by the ideas of Gestalt psychology and phenomenology of perception that he learned at the university of the Sorbonne in Paris in the early 1960s, from teachers such as Maurice Merleau-Ponty, Vladimir Jankelevitch and Jean Wahl. He confided to interviewer Philippe Petit 'I was a follower of Gestaltheorie . . . I am a man of the percept as well as the concept' (Virilio with Petit 1999:

22). The 'motion', or mobility, of the bunkers was a convenient jumping off point when he met Virilio. Virilio and Parent's work in the 1950s and 1960s on motion and mobility was prescient and far sighted in all kinds of ways and has implications for today's trends in social and cultural theory; for example, the work of John Urry (Urry 2000, 2003, 2007) and others at the Centre for Mobilities Research (CeMoRe) at the University of Lancaster in the UK has to some extent already radically refashioned social theory of the age around the idea of 'mobilities'. As Parent himself has argued, 'some bunkers also have a sense of movement, (i)f you look at them for long enough, they seem to be advancing towards you – like tanks' (Virilio 1996b: 51). The work that he and Paul Virilio did together in the 1960s certainly did envisage a new post-architectural and urban future that would force the body to adapt to disequilibrium and promote fluid, continuous movement. It was bred in the context of utopian times in the 1950s and 1960s as a reaction to the stultifying orthodoxy and results of the earlier aspects of the 'modern movement' in art and architecture. Rejecting the traditional axes of the horizontal and the vertical they have influenced what new globally recognised architects like Daniel Libeskind have done in contemporary architecture, attempting to combine incompatible structuring principles within the same building such as the horizontal/vertical and oblique cubes (Žižek 2010: 245). Parent and Virilio used oblique planes to build architecture in motion, the architecture of disequilibrium, in an attempt to anticipate, or to create, a dynamic era of the body in movement. But just as Claude Parent carried on with the idea of the oblique function after his time with Virilio, as an individual theorist and professional architect, he was actually working on an embryonic architecture of disequilibrium well before he met Virilio. As early as 1957, when he built his own house in Paris, he was already developing the spatial syntax of a critical architecture, of the architecture of disequilibrium, in the example of a dwelling house which 'seemed to rise up, fracture and then tumble back down to the ground' (Virilio 1996b: 60). Parent has remarked about other dwelling house buildings he designed in this period before he met Virilio that he 'simply wanted to make a house that appeared to be toppling over'. Parent was, in these formative years, constantly working with the idea of buildings having a sense of movement, planning an architecture no longer 'rooted in the ground' but apparently 'erupting out of it' (Virilio 1996b: 49). This embryonic critical architecture of Parent was to come to fruition with the function of the oblique worked out with Paul Virilio in the Architecture Principe group where the idea of the oblique was to induce a constant awareness of gravity, bringing the body into a tactile relationship with the environment. The critical architecture of Parent continued thereafter, going beyond the oblique and regularly shocking and provoking with his many different buildings, drawings and designs even if the reaction, critical and public, did not quite reach the heights, and venom, it achieved in the 1960s. The drawings and models of Parent, in fact, have always had the potential for media notoriety, constituting almost a punk, or post-punk, architecture and a new, associated aesthetics. For example one of his most startling was not connected to the idea of the oblique at all but an experimental architectural project to create a monumental 'bellybutton' at the geographical centre of France. Conceived for the village of Bruere-Allichamps near Bourges with collaborator Ben Jakober, a sculptor, Parent based the idea on plaster models he made of a woman's navel.

Late in his life Parent started to receive some of the recognition he has so richly deserved for the last half a century. In 2005 he joined the Academy des Beaux- Arts in France. The 15 March 2007 edition of the magazine *Wallpaper* featured Claude Parent as its 'icon'. In 2010, between January and May, Claude Parent was given a full and fitting retrospective of his life and work at the La Cite de l'Architecture exhibition in Paris. Jean Nouvel, appropriately, designed the exhibition for Parent and a comprehensive catalogue of Parent's work was edited for publication by Frederic Migayou and Francis Rambert (Migayou and Rambert 2010), a document comprising 400 pages and 700 illustrations. Parent himself, looking sprightly at eighty-six years old, attended the opening night. The overall assessment that can be made of Claude Parent from the narration told, and retold, in this chapter is of an architect who has made significant contributions to the development of French and international modernist architecture for over half a century and has almost single-handedly opened an interesting and cutting edge chapter in post-space, post-architectural studies. The lesson we can take from his oeuvre is that constant, watchful critical practice from within modernist architecture, and modernism in general, is always necessary and that a 'militant modernism' is still possible and desireable (Hatherley 2008). Those critical modernist contributions have been seen here to have influence beyond the boundaries of architectural practice within a particular nation state, even if international recognition has been rather late in the day. However, architectural theory, like that of Jean Baudrillard (Proto 2006; Redhead 2008) has also lately had an impact on theory within the social and human sciences. If the 'spatial turn' has any lasting importance as a label it is a reference point for a period when architects and architectural thinkers, such as Daniel Libeskind, Rem Koolhaas, Zaha Hadid, Renzo Piano, Santiago Calatrava, Bruce Mau and Jean Nouvel among many others, came to be symbolic for, and of, trends in cultural politics and social theory. It is noteworthy that in the past decade 'star' architects, or those who have been referred to cryptically as 'starchitects' (Callaghan 2010), like Libeskind, Koolhaas, Hadid, as well as other well established practitioners such as Frank Gehry and Norman Foster 'crossed over' as celebrity social theorists who would attract large academic and intellectual crowds. Owen Hatherley (Hatherley 2008: 53) has described them much more critically as 'erstwhile avant-gardists' and contributors to 'the aesthetics of Capital'. Their fame is global; in 2000 the ICA (the Institute of Contemporary Arts) in London hosted a cultural theory conference at which Rem Koolhaas and Daniel Libeskind eclipsed those whose profession it was to theorise social and cultural phenomena. Similarly, the visit of Bruce Mau to Perth in Western Australia in 2002 drew widespread academic esteem as well as devotion from architectural and design practitioners. Once the digital revolution of the 1990s took hold, and the the modelling software used in aircraft and car design was perceived as applicable to buildings, the kind of post-architecture that Parent epitomised became a real, lasting possibility for the 'starchitects' (Callaghan 2010) of 'post-space'. As Owen Hatherley has pointed out (Hatherley 2008: 12) in the 'first decade of the twenty first century' nobody 'actually designs postmodernist buildings' whilst 'urban architecture is dominated by the "signature" architecture of the supermodernist star designers, ranging from the the expressionism of Zaha Hadid to the glassy, glossy International Style redux of Norman Foster'.

That such celebrity architectural thinkers and practitioners have been taken up by global movements in the social and human sciences seemingly exhausted by two decades of focus on postmodernism, postmodernity and the postmodern is in many ways down to the pioneering efforts of Claude Parent and Paul Virilio. Virilio's celebrity intellectual status has spanned both eras, the 1959s and 1960s and today. Parent's new topicality is partly as a result of this 'spatial turn' in the late 1990s. Much as his theorisation of critical modernity is useful for a critical architectural practice, it has wider import too. As Owen Hatherley says (Hatherley 2008: 32) the 'new urbanism' that emerged in British modernism with all its brutalist instincts was also 'Pop – an architectural equivalent' to colleagues like 'Richard Hamilton and the Independent Group'. As can be seen from the next chapter there are important links between Claude Parent, Paul Virilio and the politics of post-Pop.

Modernity, or to play with Lyotard's notion mischievously, the modern condition, is often viewed as a 'single condition' but there are in fact many ways to be modern (Gray 2003, 2009a). Claude Parent has said that 'we still confuse modernities' (Parent and Virilio 1997: 15) but 'modernities' remains a useful concept in an era when theories of modernity and postmodernity are undergoing significant change and challenge as they are in theoretical work in the human and social sciences today. Part of the problem in such theorisation in the humanities and social sciences, stimulating and innovative as it is, remains the binaries created that are in need of deconstruction: modernity/postmodernity, modernity/late modernity, solid/liquid modernity, first/second modernity and so on (Gane 2004; Giddens and Pierson 1998; Beck and Willms 2004; Bauman 2000, 2007a). The alternative idea of theorising contemporary modernities, overlapping and competing, is an appealing one and can avoid the debilitating problem of periodisation of the binary divides. Those problems of periodisation, such as when does modernity become late modernity, or modernity become postmodernity (in the sense of after modernity), or first modernity become second modernity, or solid modernity become liquid modernity, or original modernity become reflexive modernity, are persistently troubling and unresolved questions of contemporary theorisation of modernity. Although Parent has never styled himself as a social theorist, the idea of critical modernity that he has promoted and worked with for more than fifty years, in the sense of a constant questioning of modernity, and indeed modernism, from within, can be of use to theorists of modernity employing the idea of modernities. A new or critical modernity can be promulgated without seeking anything after modernity or any radical transition within modernity. For those theorists interested in the retheorisation of modernity without postmodernity Parent's work in critical modernity may yet come to be a more useful general concept and approach than it has been seen to be so far. I began this whole enterprise in this chapter by parodying the French theorist Bruno Latour's notion of 'we have never been modern' (Latour 1993) and have emblazoned the parody in the title of this book. The counter claim that we have never been postmodern is nevertheless no homage to the idea that there is no modernity, or that there is as I write a process taking place which could be called the 'end of modernity' (Sim 2010). Utilising the work of Claude Parent on critical modernity, this chapter marks out a position in the rethinking of modernity within contemporary social and cultural theory that strongly asserts that there is only modernity, nothing after it. Critical modernity is an idea that Claude Parent has made contemporary and urgent.

CHAPTER 4

Post-Pop

In this chapter I want to take a look at some contemporary issues from the cultural politics of Pop. Everything is Art nowadays, as the author Gordon Burn demonstrated so well in his writings on Damien Hirst, Tracey Emin and many others (Burn 2009). But Pop, too, is everywhere. And Pop is into Art, 'Brit' and other myriad versions (Burn and Hirst 2001; Burn 2009). Contemporary art is part of Pop culture but Pop is also part of the accelerated culture of non-postmoden contemporary art. For Paul Virilio, 'critic of the art of technology' and theorist of speed, the accident and technology in modernity, the notion of duration has been destroyed as contemporary art production is now sucked in by the news market for twenty-four hours (or twenty-four seconds). The acceleration of technologies of presentation and reproduction, according to Virilio, by reducing the time and space between subject and object to zero, has eliminated duration. In this accelerated life of popular culture it is possible to glimpse what Andy McCluskey of pioneering synth pop band OMD (Orchestral Manoeuvres in the Dark) has seen as the 'history of modern', which is also the title of their 2010 album with two separate tracks called 'history of modern', respectively parts 1 and 2. McCluskey has convincingly argued that 'the last modernist movement' was indeed 'English electronic pop music at the end of the twentieth century' (Lynskey 2010), a scene embracing OMD themselves, Human League, Heaven 17, New Order, Pet Shop Boys and recent inheritors like Delphic, all pervasively influenced by German pioneers Kraftwerk.

I want to introduce this foray into the cultural politics of Pop in accelerated culture by briefly considering contemporary pop artefacts that demonstrate the move of Pop into Art: the Pet Shop Boys' *Catalogue* (Hoare and Heath 2006), Peter Saville's *Estate* (Saville 2007) and Kevin Cummins' *Juvenes* (Cummins 2008) are three evocative examples. Then I will consider in this context the life and career of an iconic figure in the cultural politics of Pop: the writer Hanif Kureishi.

Pet Shop Boys released *PopArt* in 2003. One CD comprised dozens of previously issued singles plus a couple of new tracks. Another contained forty-one videos plus a three-hour band commentary. A 2006 TV documentary on Pet Shop Boys, subsequently released on DVD, hailed them as having lived 'A Life in Pop'. In the same year the CD of their live collaboration with the BBC Concert Orchestra came out, entitled *Concrete*. Pet Shop Boys' world tour in 2007 was labelled 'Cubism'. Pet Shop Boys have always been one of the best examples of what Simon Frith and Howard Horne, writing about the impact of the British art school movement on popular music culture, once succinctly called 'Art into Pop' (Frith and Horne 1987) but we have, today, the reverse of this process, the culmination of the effects of fifty years of Pop culture, particularly British, as opposed to American, Pop (Heath 1993). Pet Shop Boys, biographically, did not completely fit the art school into pop culture mode (Heath 1991) but were acutely aware of the legacy of the link in their work. Neil Tennant, from the same Newcastle milieu as Bryan Ferry and Roxy Music (Bracewell 2007) went to North London Polytechnic to read history in the early 1970s. Chris Lowe, a Blackpudlian, studied architecture at the University of Liverpool between 1978 and 1981. As the cultural commentator and novelist Michael Bracewell (Bracewell 2002a: 24) has pointed out, for Pop artist Andy Warhol, as an aesthetic and a style, 'Pop was the totality of popular culture, of which popular music was simply a strand.' The relationship, as Neil Tennant once insisted to Bracewell (Bracewell 2002a: 30), 'goes back to the start of Pop Art in the 1950s when artists in Britain began to respond to pop music'. Pet Shop Boys' *Catalogue*, edited by Philip Hoare and Chris Heath (Hoare and Heath 2006), released in 2006, comprised 1,955 illustrations (1,727 in colour). Organised chronologically, it illustrated the first two decades of Pet Shop Boys (1986 was the year of the first album release but they had first recorded with Bobby O in the USA a couple of years before). Each principal format was reproduced as a large image and other formats were illustrated where the design differs. All Pet Shop Boys videos were highlighted in double-page spreads of stills. All concert tours were represented, too; even Christmas cards. *Catalogue* assumes that Pet Shop Boys' 'influence has been as much visual as musical'. Their visual aesthetic project had drawn on architects, designers and artists and the 'catalogue' provided pictures from the twenty-year exhibition; truly Pop into Art, or what Jacques Ranciere has called 'the future of the image' (Ranciere 2009). In the opening pages of *Catalogue*, entitled 'Practice', it was argued that 'the art of the Pet Shop Boys' had 'its roots in the early 1980s'. It was clearly, then, a 'post-punk aesthetic'. Pet

Shop Boys, as Michael Bracewell (Bracewell 2002a) has astutely noted, are manifestly a 'post-punk' group. Post-punk aesthetics are being revisted again in the early decades of the twenty-first century. For writers like Simon Reynolds (Reynolds 2005, 2009) and Owen Hatherley (Hatherley 2008) 'post-punk' is linked to the 'art forms' of a 'militant' British modernism of earlier times, of George Orwell and working-class culture. Hatherley (Hatherley 2008: 124) has written of the experience of watching New Order in its early days after the death of Ian Curtis and Joy Division:

> I watched a DVD of New Order playing in Brussels in 1981. These three men and one woman, all from working class backgrounds in post-industrial, council estate Manchester – the grandchildren of those sturdy Wigan men reading the racing pages – were playing music which would have astonished and mortified Orwell, what with its blocks of overwhelming electronic sound, unnatural bass rumbles and technocratic shimmers . . . But if ordinary people are so hostile to new forms, new noises and new shapes, then how did the last forty years of all kinds of jarring, avant-garde street music manage to happen? Were the teds, the mods (modernists, as they were originally known), glam rockers, punks, junglists, even the kids in provincial towns getting wrecked on Saturday nights to the ludicrously simple and artificial hard house or happy hardcore, all somehow class traitors?

There has in truth been a Pop aesthetic in British popular culture for decades. And punk and post-punk in the years between 1977 and the early 1980s speeded up the process. Items of Pop are a pleasure to behold: think of a mid-period Factory record cover design by Peter Saville, a 'cool modernist' as I would label him after Marshall McLuhan (McLuhan 2003: 38–50) via Jean Baudrillard, heralded by London's Design Museum in the 'Peter Saville Show' exhibition of his work (soundtrack by New Order) and the Frieze edition *Designed by Peter Saville* (Saville 2003) copiously illustrated coffee table book. Saville spent the early part of his career designing record sleeves for Factory Records (Robertson 2006), the Manchester based label which went bankrupt in 1992 in which he had a 6 per cent stake (Nice 2010). In 2010 he was asked to design the new shirts for the England football team by the Football Association, reprising the 'World in Motion' collaboration by Factory's New Order in 1990 for England's role in the soccer World Cup in Italy. Sleeves for the likes of Joy Division, then New Order, became legendary as 'low art' riding on a wave of 'high aesthetic minimalism' and Saville's recollections on the battles to produce (and reproduce) them are as fascinating now as they have ever been (Nice 2010). His work has nevertheless been in much more than the popular music field including forays into fashion, advertising and contemporary art. Peter Saville is still perhaps the most influential graphic designer of his generation, alongside other 'cool modernists' like Neville Brody who designed *The Face* and *New Socialist* in the 1980s. Best known for classic 1970s and 1980s Joy Division and New Order record covers, including more recently in 2003 New Order's *Retro* and in 2005 New Order's *Waiting for the Siren's Call*, Saville has also art directed catalogues and advertisements for fashion brands such as Yohji Yamamoto and Christian Dior and created corporate identities for Givenchy, Mandarina Duck and London's Whitechapel Gallery. He has designed other music covers such as CDs for Pulp and Suede and art directed the print campaign for Stella McCartney, Paul McCartney's daughter. For over thirty years Saville has been advertised as one of the most revered individuals working in the creative industries and one of the best graphic designers working today. The intensity and timelessness of his work has ensured a cult status. *Creative Review* magazine readers in 2002 voted Peter Saville the most admired figure in the design world. In 2004 Manchester City Council appointed him as their 'creative director' in what they referred to as 'the original modern' city, a label widely used in the promotion of the regeneration campaign. His career trajectory though has been almost a refusal of commercial success. Saved from insolvency in the early 1990s by working for the design group Pentagram, Saville has argued that he does not conduct his life in a businesslike, professional way. He has always mused about retiring, even after more than three decades doing what he does. In 2003, as well as featuring in his own retrospective at the Design Museum, he was one of the case studies for a British Council international exhibition entitled *The Twenty First Century Dandy* examining the wardrobes and look of British men. Punk, and post-punk, was Saville's inspiration from Joy Division onwards. Peter Saville's 'elegaic' modernism is of an organic, esoteric kind. A catalogue retrospective from a 2007 exhibition Peter Saville *Estate* (Saville 2007), containing 127 items from a 2005 exhibition in Zurich, underlined what arch chronicler of 'Pop life' Michael Bracewell (Bracewell, Watson and Edwards 1988; Bracewell 1988, 1992, 1995, 1997, 2001, 2002b, 2007, 2009) has seen as the 'monolithic metaphor for both the passing of modernism and the replacement of modernist ideals with postmodern re-arrangements of context and quotation' (Saville 2007). Michael Bracewell's essay in the catalogue 'Estate 1978–2007' has comprehensively encapsulated Saville's post-punk aesthetic:

> Since its earliest public expression in the closing years of the 1970s, in the form of design work for the packaging and promotional materials of Factory Records, there has been a certainty of purpose in Peter Saville's

meticulous placement of his aesthetic sensibility. At once declamatory and
covert, its mission as elegy masked as modern elegance, Saville's entrap-
ment of 'beauty' has made eloquent the sense of an ending . . . Enshrined
as an arbiter of contemporary taste and trend, Peter Saville has concerned
himself, rather, with the ways in which the language of design might speak
the truths most often ascribed to fine art. This is a project which began in
Manchester, in the North West of England, during the closing years of the
1970s.

Another artefact from life in a northern town, Joy Division in the
Manchester of the late 1970s, was the early inspiration for the photographs
of Kevin Cummins. His pictures from all kinds of 'low culture' adorn the
National Portrait Gallery and the Victoria and Albert museum in London,
beautifully aestheticised in art gallery permanent collections. Kevin
Cummins has also drawn on a version of Pop for his aesthetic outlook
but contemporary art for its production and marketing. Cummins, pop
music photographer professionally since the late 1970s, released collections of photographs from the 1980s and early 1990s called *The Smiths
and Beyond* in 2002 (Cummins 2002), a volume which he personally felt
was 'not quite up to scratch in production terms'; a comprehensive collection on Manchester music in 2009 (Cummins 2009) and a complete
black and white retrospective on Joy Division in 2010 (Cummins 2010).
By 2008 he had already released a special limited edition collection of his
photographs of Joy Division/New Order called *Juvenes* which cost £200
a copy. *Juvenes* was produced in an edition of 226: 200 at £200, signed
and numbered; twenty-six at £500 with the inclusion of signed photo.
Fuel were the designers for Cummins' project and it was handmade and
boxed in Belgium. In Kevin Cummins' own view 'it was a lovely col-
lectable'. Previously, despite years of denial that his work would include
his obsession with a lifelong football fandom of Manchester City FC, he
also set in motion in 2002 a collaboration with Mark Farrow, of Farrow
Design, a fellow Manchester City fan and record sleeve designer for
Factory Records, Pet Shop Boys and M People amongst others, whose
aesthetic, like Cummins', was 'born out of punk'. The collaboration would
result in the 413 colour photographs in the book *We're Not Really Here:
Manchester City's Final Season at Maine Road* in 2003 (Cummins 2003),
a photo diary of Manchester City's last year before moving to the City of
Manchester Stadium, built originally to host the 2002 Commonwealth
Games, after being at Maine Road in Moss Side, Manchester for eighty
years. Cummins, viewing himself as akin to an anthropologist, was given
'access all areas' for a year by Manchester City. He has since said that 'it
was a joy to do 'and that 'everyone at the club was so supportive – even the

players'. Five different themed limited editions of the book, case bound and boxed, apart from the standard edition, showcased football fandom, 'post-fandom' in my jokey, ironic term (Redhead 1997b), as an art form.

Into this already painted picture accelerated culture of post-Pop, I want to situate a provocative, emblematic writer, Hanif Kureishi, seeing his life in the context of post-war Pop art and culture; what I have termed the general accelerated culture of the late twentieth and early twenty-first centuries (Redhead 2004b). I want to assess critically Hanif Kureishi's thirty-year career in theatre, film and popular modernist writing in the context of this accelerated popular culture. In doing so I draw on the documentary *Hanif Kureishi: South Bank Show* made by Melvyn Bragg for Carlton TV in 2003 but also many personal and intimate conversations with Kureishi himself when he gave time freely for my earlier, related project on the 'realism' and 'post-realism' of 'the repetitive beat generation' (Redhead 2000) writers clustered around Nicholas Blincoe, John King, Irvine Welsh, Emer Martin, Sarah Champion, Mike McCormack and Alan Warner. Approached about becoming an interviewee in that book, Kureishi was at once interested in what was touted in the 1990s as the emergence of a new breed of contemporary 'cult' fiction authors already challenging the dominance of his own Pop oriented 'boomer' generation of writers (Redhead 2000). In 2005 Hanif Kureishi wrote the screenplay for the film *Venus* (Kureishi 2007) starring Peter O'Toole as an old man infatuated with a young girl and directed by Kureishi's long-time film collaborator Roger Michell. *Venus*, drawing on Kureishi's reading of Japanese modernist fiction, was released to critical (in both senses) acclaim in autumn 2006. In 2007 his award winning short story 'Weddings and Beheadings', where Kureishi 'dared to inhabit the consciousness of an unnoticed character, the cameraman filming a terrorist execution' (Kureishi 2006a), was banned (from being read on air) by the BBC, but by this time had been granted a CBE by the British New Labour establishment for 'services to literature'. Hanif Kureishi's 'psychoanalyis' novel *Something To Tell You* (Kureishi 2008) was published in March 2008 and once again greeted by media uproar as his own sister complained of Kureishi's fictional misrepresentation and dishonour.

In his late fifties Hanif Kureishi remains one of the leading critical writers of his generation with a substantial back catalogue of fiction, plays, screenplays, films and non-fiction to his name. The film *My Beautiful Laundrette* (Kureishi 1986), starring Daniel Day Lewis as a gay (former) skinhead, and the debut novel *The Buddha of Suburbia* (Kureishi 1990), later made into a popular TV series of the same name, have become established classics of international post-millennial popular culture intimately capturing the 'feel' of the times, which have often been misleadingly seen as the postmodern era. The 'cool modernism' of Pop, or 'history of modern' as OMD/McCluskey have conceptualised it, is exemplified best in a volume with Pop music writer Jon Savage called *The Faber Book of Pop* (Kureishi and Savage 1995). This weighty 862–page text was the most comprehensive collection of writings on and from the history of Pop as a cultural style. It has remained a much neglected statement of Pop as an aesthetic, whether in music, fiction, fashion, film, architecture and design, or as a cultural politics in general. Kureishi's style of writing is now, after more than three decades, finely honed into an art form in itself, self-conscious of its own construction but beautiful in its detached modernist, minimalist simplicity. As Kureishi's co-editor Jon Savage for the iconic volume on Pop, himself another emblematic writer of Pop in popular music culture, quoting liberally from 1960s popular music 'modernists' Pete Townshend (Wilkerson 2008) and The Who (Neill and Kent 2007), has noted: 'the simple things you see are all complicated'. 'The Simple Things You See Are All Complicated' is indeed the title of Jon Savage's own separate introduction to *The Faber Book of Pop* book, and boasts a cryptic lyric borrowed from The Who's best song 'Substitute'. Though Kureishi contributed his own pithy editorial introduction, 'That's How Good It Was', where he celebrated the American Pop modernist legacy of writers like Tom Wolfe and Philip Roth, in fact it was Jon Savage who did most of the work on the compilation of the pieces for the massive volume, drawing on a life spent in TV research and pop interviewing and reviewing. Savage's own books on the history and context of pop music and popular youth culture are themselves important and outstanding examples of Pop as a cultural aesthetic. A first retrospective of his essays from 1977 to 1996 (Savage 1996) brilliantly exposed the cycles of pop, and their speeding up from the late 1970s onwards. A later, palimpsest history of the origins of youth culture from the nineteenth century up to 1945 by Savage (Savage 2007) was, for Pet Shop Boys' Neil Tennant 'a remark-able exploration of what it meant and how it felt to be young in the early modern era'. Savage's illustrated biography of the The Kinks, sharpest of all the 'mod' (modernist) bands in 1960s Britain (Savage 1984), was an exemplary Pop artefact as was his award winning books on 1970s punk and The Sex Pistols, entitled, liberally plundering a punk anthem, *England's Dreaming* (Savage 2004, 2009).

With the 9/11 and 7/7 events in New York, Washington and London, Kureishi's writing on religious fundamentalism and racism, pervasive in his career, can now be seen as prescient and prophetic. What I call here the 'cold modernity' of the present period is starkly illuminated by a new critical vision in Kureishi's late work. Post-Pop, accelerated as a new cultural politics, is urgent and influential again, as it once was in an earlier era which produced the Pop art of Richard Hamilton and the Pop music of bands like Roxy Music (Bracewell 2007). Hanif Kureishi is still one of the most prolific critical writers of his generation with a large collected stories back catalogue (Kureishi 2010) and a substantial critical literature (Kaleta 1998; Moore-Gilbert 2001; Yousaf 2002; Ranasinha 2002; Thomas 2005; Buchanan 2007) about his life and work. He now, eventually, has a substantial legacy – fiction, plays, films, screenplays and non-fiction stretching originally back into the 1970s. His cultural production has been in and out of style, globally, since the beginning of the neo-liberal era of the 1970s and 1980s. Once patronised as only 'the British Asian' writer and film-maker, Kureishi has raised the bar on critical writing. In the so-called 'postmodern condition' of the 1980s and 1990s what I see as Kureishi's 'low modernism', or what Marshall Berman labelled 'modernism in the streets' (Berman 2010), saw him touted as an 'enfant terrible', with provocative film projects involving sex, drugs and race such as *Sammy and Rosie Get Laid* (Kureishi 1988) and *Intimacy* (Kureishi 1998) causing widespread moral panic largely because of their explicit, explosive sexual content. The era of hyper neo-liberalism, however, especially in the later 1990s and early twenty-first century, saw him languishing in middle age, and inevitably new outsider writers (for instance Irvine Welsh, the author of *Trainspotting*, in the mid-1990s) emerged to take his place at the centre of global public outrage. With the onset of the 9/11 and 7/7 events in New York, Washington and London, Kureishi's writings on multiculturalism, religious fundamentalism, the West and Islam, war, violence and racism have been once again seen as offering a warning about the dangers of the onslaught on Western liberalism. In reviewing his life and work in an accelerated time for popular culture, it is possible to see how the self-conscious cool modernism of Kureishi's writing can illuminate the current condition – the cold modernity of today, dominated as it is by decade long neo-conservative adventures in Afghanistan, Iraq and Pakistan and their political and cultural fall-out (Ali 2005) in the West. I want to situate Hanif Kureishi in the context of post-war Pop as a cultural aesthetic and as a cultural politics and assess his potential contribution to the urgent task of capturing accelerated culture. In a time where postmodernism and postmodernity are out of fashion, and where, according to the arguments in this book (Redhead 2008: 1–13 and 217–24), we can confidently proclaim that 'we have never been postmodern', Kureishi's cool modernist approach is worth taking seriously, especially in an era when 'cool capitalism' (McGuigan 2009) is perceived to be on the rise.

Hanif Kureishi was born in English suburban Kent in Bromley on 5 December 1954. His father Rafiushan Kureishi was originally from an upper middle-class military family in India and worked as a civil servant in Britain though he had trained as a journalist. His mother is English and comes from south- east England. He used to ask his father 'Why are we here?' after hearing tales of his father's life in India (Kureishi 2004). The colonial legacy, though, meant that as Kureishi says they 'were Pakis', and, curiously, thought of as 'Indian and Paki at the same time'. In his view they 'were stuck in history, the history that is colonialism'. Kureishi has a younger sister and has three children of his own – twin boys, Carlo and Sachin and a younger son, Kier. Kureishi went to primary school in Bromley until the age of eleven where he remembers 'screaming at the gate' as he was separated from his mother, just as his own children later did when separated from him. He recalls swimming in Bromley's open air pool as a child. He was then educated at Bromley Technical High School from 1965 until the early 1970s. He has said he 'was frightened until he 'cycled out of there'. He has remembered being 'scared the whole time' and being 'rather small' and 'the only Asian kid in the school'. Racism was blatant and normalised in Kureishi's childhood in 1950s and 1960s Britain (Gilroy 2004). For instance, he was picked on by a teacher who called him 'Pakistani Pete', a stereotypical racist label repeated by a character in his own coming of age novel *The Buddha of Suburbia*. The racism 'offended' and 'bewildered' Kureishi (Bragg 2003; unreferenced quotes following are all from this documentary). The labelling provoked him into a suspension when the conflict with the teacher led to him being summoned by the headmaster when Kureishi refused to be caned. Instead he 'was suspended from school' and 'used to wander about Bromley high street' on his own because he was too frightened to tell his father about the suspension. Being called a 'Paki' at school was the result of 'a lot of the kids' being 'skinhead'. Kureishi has recalled the 1960s youth cultural styles with some trepidation: for Kureishi 'some of the kids were greasers or rockers' and the 'more middle class kids became hippies'. Hanif Kureishi, in time, became 'a hippie'.

David Bowie (David Jones, as he was in ordinary life) had been to the same Bromley Technical High School as Kureishi slightly earlier in the 1960s. Souxsie and the Banshees and Generation X were also to emerge from the same suburban milieu in the punk era of the 1970s and the 'Bromley Contingent' became a well known label in the history of British Pop culture. A seventeen-year-old Bowie had even been interviewed on national television in the mid-1960s for having founded the Society for Cruelty to Long Haired Men. In the early 2000s, Kureishi gleefully took an interview commission from a British Sunday newspaper which involved him 'hanging out' with the by then global rock star David Bowie for a weekend at Glastonbury pop music festival in Somerset along with hundreds of thousands of fans, before submitting his copy. As Kureishi has reminisced about his childhood's dreams of Bowie at his school 'for hippies among us he became a symbol' of what it was to be 'creative'. For Kureishi, even into middle age, 'you could be an oddity in Pop'. Indeed a 'certain sort of creativity' always appealed to him 'in Pop'.

Sport, too, has also always interested Kureishi. But it is sport as popular culture that catches his eye. He is a casual Manchester United soccer fan. He was named by his father after the great Pakistani cricketer Hanif Mohammed, stimulating a life long interest in the glories of international cricket, and he has interviewed the emerging British Asian boxer Amir Khan (Kureishi 2006b) amongst other celebrities in popular culture in recent years. Pop, though, in all its modernist facets, has always taken precedence. Pop is the pervasive, often hidden, influence in all his work from young man to middle-aged writer. Kureishi in the 1950s and 1960s when he grew up, although a staunch fan of all the British Pop music of the time, 'was too isolated to be in a band' and like Stephen Patrick Morrissey of The Smiths sometime later 'became a bedroom boy', something he admits to still being today as a full-time, professional writer. Kureishi 'found it much harder to be with people' and constantly felt plagued by the question 'how do you get out of this room?'

Between 1971 and 1973 Hanif Kureishi studied for his A levels at Ravensbourne College of Arts in Kent in south-east England. This art school educational background was a basis for the development of a dis-tinctive aesthetic in popular culture (especially popular music) in Britain from the 1950s onwards, a process of 'art into pop' brilliantly encapsulated by Simon Frith and Howard Horne in their pioneering book *Art into Pop* (Frith and Horne 1987) from their research into art schools in the period from the 1950s to the 1980s, first published as an International Association for the Study of Pop Music (IASPM) pamphlet in the 1980s, and a classic popular cultural studies text today. Michael Bracewell (Bracewell 2002b: 24) has noted, for the likes of Andy Warhol, as an aesthetic and a style, that 'Pop was the totality of popular culture, of which popular music was simply a strand'; and the relationship between pop music and art for Bracewell 'goes back to the start of Pop Art in the 1950s when artists in Britain began to respond to pop music'. 'It is no accident' that John Lennon of The Beatles and Pete Townshend of The Who went to art college because 'in Britain the relationship was particularly strengthened by the existence of foundation courses at art schools' as Neil Tennant of

Pet Shop Boys has emphasised (Bracewell 2002b: 30). Hanif Kureishi himself has cited Pete Townshend, a former student at Ealing Art College in London, who heard the auto-destructive artist Gustav Metzger speak there in the early 1960s, as a model of inspiration. Kureishi says, 'When you saw Pete Townshend smashing up his guitar, you thought that is what it is to be a teenager.' Hanif Kureishi left art college in 1973 to study philosophy at Lancaster University, but was expelled after one year. He instead re-enrolled at Kings College, London from 1974, where he was awarded a degree in philosophy in 1977. He studied in the day whilst working at the Royal Court theatre (Devine 2006) in London in the evening. He thought that he had 'a double education, which was in Philosophy and Culture' a job at night 'after college in the day'. Kureishi has said, looking back on these years, that he can 'see now how many major decisions of your life are made before twenty-five'. Subsequently, in 1982 after becoming an award winner with a number of plays (Kureishi 1992) to his name, he was made writer in residence at the Royal Court theatre, where he first met lifelong friends and collaborators such as Roger Michel. It was a culture shock for Kureishi to be at the Royal Court in the 1970s and early 1980s. 'Everyone was upper class, everyone had been to Oxbridge' whilst Kureishi knew acutely that he 'came from the suburbs . . . the ultimate Thatcher place' and 'hadn't met any really posh people before'. However he realised, once at the Royal Court, that 'things I was interested in – books, Pop – other people were interested in too'. Shortly afterwards, with the experimental early Channel 4 television station having just started in Britain, he was dubbed 'the Asian writer' alongside the likes of iconic outsider white male artists such as Derek Jarman and Ken Loach. This rather patronising labelling did however lead to Kureishi making films for Channel 4; first *My Beautiful Laundrette* then *Sammy and Rosie Get Laid*, both with screenplays by Kureishi and filmed by director Stephen Frears. They represented a significant cultural breakthrough in the 1980s for a non-Oxbridge young British Asian writer. As Kureishi has stated, 'At that moment, that's when the door opened. A few years later he directed a film himself for the first and only time, entitled *London Kills Me* (Kureishi 1991; book) with a superb contemporary pop, reggae and rock music soundtrack selected by the DJ and writer Charlie Gillett. The critics weighed into him and the first phase of his career was over. 'Enfant terrible' no more: as far as the media were concerned, just terrible!

Kureishi, when pushed for reflection, has labelled himself as an 'artist' and his 'art' as a respectable profession, writing being something he does today, as always, 'because it is an obsession' and, moreover, to help him 'have a purpose'. Much self-reflection is beneath the surface of Kureishi's

carefully constructed modernist art form and inevitably for a 1970s philosophy student and a self-confessed countercultural liberated 1960s child of
the twin theorists Karl Marx and Sigmund Freud, psychoanalytic theory
is prominent. An interest in fashionable leftist theorists of psychoanalysis, such as the Slovenian Marxist Lacanian theorist Slavoj Žižek (Myers
2003; Žižek and Daly 2004; Butler 2005; Bowman and Stamp 2007; Žižek
2010) and the practice of psychoanalysis itself, which he has personally
undergone for some time, led Kureishi to write his late middle-age novel
Something To Tell You which is based on a character who is a psychoana-
lyst. Kureishi believes that for the writer 'as it is in psychoanalysis', it is
the 'censorship, the resistance you work for', wherein you 'look for the
interruptions, the silences'. But it is, in truth, Slavoj Žižek 's often outra-
geous public performances and readings (like Pete Townshend's earlier
auto-destructive modernist guitar smashing), which Kureishi himself has
witnessed as something of a fan, that remain influential on Kureishi as a
writer, rather than any lingering post-Marxist, post-Lacanian theoretical
edifice. His youthful experiments with ultra leftist politics are long gone.

It is the contention here that it is post-war Pop that provides the key
to what I call Hanif Kureishi's cool modernism, and to his usefulness for
contemporary cultural politics and theory. The cool modernism of Pop
is no accident in Kureishi's work. There has always been a low modernist, Pop aesthetic to Kureishi's oeuvre. Even the sleeves to his books,
put out by the London based Faber and Faber publishing house, are a
pleasure to hold, like a mid-period Factory record cover design by Peter
Saville, another 'elegiac' modernist beginning his work in the late 1970s
and still culturally producing today. Beholding Saville's own *Designed by
Peter Saville* (Saville 2003), the book of the travelling exhibition, entitled
the 'Peter Saville Show', originating at London's Design Museum in
2003, together with the Michael Bracewell catalogue piece 'Peter Saville:
Estate 1978–2007' in Peter Saville *Estate* (Saville 2007) and Matthew
Robertson's *Factory Records: The Complete Graphic Album* (Robertson
2006), elegiac modernism is almost perfectly defined. Saville worked for
Pentagram, the designers of Hanif Kureishi's Faber and Faber books,
between 1990 and 1993. Another enigmatic Pop artist, Peter Blake, who
designed The Beatles' *Sergeant Pepper's Lonely Hearts Club Band* album
cover in 1967, itself a revered artefact for Kureishi, a devoted Beatles fan,
was commissioned by Faber and Faber to design the book jacket for *The
Buddha of Suburbia* debut Kureishi novel in 1990. The cover had distinct
echoes of The Beatles' gatefold sleeve in its images. The subsequent
regular use by Kureishi of the same company, the designers Pentagram,
for his cover designs unified them as modernist 'cultural product'.

Furthermore, Kureishi and Savage's volume *The Faber Book of Pop* once again boasted a Pop art cover designed by Pentagram. Kureishi's style of writing, too, especially since the mid-1990s, has become hewed into an art form in itself, self-conscious of its own construction but beautiful in its detached minimalist simplicity, too. Roger Michel, Kureishi's collaborator as director of *The Buddha of Suburbia* TV series and *Venus* movie, and friend from Royal Court days, saw one controversial film they worked on together in 2003, called *The Mother* (Kureishi 2003), morally lambasted for its portrayal of an older woman enjoying a sexual relationship with a much younger man (played by soon-to-be James Bond, Daniel Craig), as 'creative' in its pure, 'simple' modernism.

The view of the astute contemporary cultural critic and novelist Michael Bracewell is that Pop is as important as ever it was in the politics of culture. In a sea of realist, magic-realist or even post-realist, contemporary British fiction Hanif Kureishi's 'mod' or low modernist approach stood out in the 1990s and early 2000s. It still does. This much misunderstood cool modernist approach has certainly brought Kureishi public notoriety in the press and broadcast media, and literary attacks on him have been frequent in recent years. John King, one of the younger generation of British contemporary working-class new wave 'realist' fiction writers I have elsewhere dubbed the 'repetitive beat generation' (Redhead 2000) saw Hanif Kureishi and his ilk as the 'enemy', as much in class terms as anything else. Hanif Kureishi is often pilloried for apparently raiding his own life for the content of his fiction. Kureishi's late 1990s novel *Intimacy* caused a furore partly because the subject matter was so close to autobiography – a man who leaves his partner and two young children. In ordinary life Kureishi's ex-partner (a Faber and Faber editor) and their twin children lived close by the West London home he shared with his partner Monique and their own child. The novel *Intimacy* perceived simply as autobiography brought allegations of sexism against Kureishi and considerable end-of-century bile from all sides. Kureishi has said about writing in general that in his view 'there is only autobiography actually'. He also has argued that *Intimacy* was the product of wanting to 'write a book about my generation' where 'most have got divorced'. He emphatically, he has remembered, really 'wanted to write a hate book' and not a book about love. Many of Kureishi's autobiographical social and political concerns, which do clearly pervade his writing, surround parenting and forty- and fifty-something men's problems in coming to terms with breakdown in relationships and, in his own words, seemingly 'making the same mistakes each time' – a state widespread enough to be described in some quarters as an especially modern masculine cultural condition, and which has forced Kureishi into occasionally dubious dalliances with groups seeking 'justice for fathers'. Kureishi's assured and thought provoking collection of short stories around these issues, entitled *Midnight All Day* (Kureishi 1999), was, in his personal life, followed by a brief, intense involvement in a workshop on precisely this kind of modern masculine malaise, which he and others promoted at the Royal Court theatre, the very venue where he had been a young writer in residence twenty-five years earlier.

Kureishi's cool modernism can sometimes be capable of being (mis) read as detachment and disengagement, or, worse, as reactionary politics. One of a number of books published about Kureishi's life and work, by American academic Kenneth Kaleta (1998), called him a 'post-colonial storyteller'. This is an interesting characterisation but I would rather label him 'post-love' in this accelerated Pop context. 'Post-love', as a notion, more accurately describes Kureishi's generation, particularly the men, influenced massively by feminism and gay and lesbian politics in a host of contradictory ways, who were borne on a wave of love, sex, drugs and rock'n'roll before punk, post-punk, dance culture and neo-liberalism eclipsed 1960s and 1970s hedonism, leaving behind what I have called elsewhere a 'hedonism in hard times' (Redhead 1997a: ix–xi). Kureishi still listens, he has stressed, to the 'Beatles, Rolling Stones, Bob Dylan, Davis Bowie, Led Zeppelin' musical nexus which spawned his first published writings and underlie the Pop novel *Gabriel's Gift* (Kureishi 2001) which happens to feature a Bowie-type 1970s rock star central character called Lester Jones. Kureishi certainly listens to the sounds of other musical eras, too, and is eclectic in his taste: he loves jazz, and the Bristol sound of what he sees as a 'great band' like Massive Attack. Rather, it is just that for him 1980s through to 2010s pop music no longer has the same effect on him that even a group like Uriah Heap did 'in the rain in Bromley in Kent' when he was growing up in the 1960s and early 1970s. Pop music is certainly less of an influence on his fiction these days: divorce and break-ups and bombings were the soundtracks for much of his twenty-first century output until the novel *Something To Tell You* which he views as 'featuring popular music again'. But Pop as aesthetic and cultural politics are less easy to shake off. The comic novel *Gabriel's Gift* with which Kureishi greeted the new millennium is essentially a story of father and son – a relationship which Kureishi often explores in his various writings but done with much more panache than multi-million dollar writers like Nick Hornby or Tony Parson can manage, despite their book chart sales figures. A short story Kureishi wrote as the twenty-first century dawned, published in *The Body* (Kureishi 2002a), a collection of seven original short stories plus a novella, drew on his own current life experiences as a father of a young son, but with typical Kureishi twists and turns envisaged the parents making a video for the small child so that he can show his friends in decades to come what his parents were like when the son grows up and reaches his mid-forties.

Able regularly to draw on an impressive back catalogue with many collected works of non-fiction and screenplays (Kureishi 2002b, 2002c) Hanif Kureishi has moved from the deviant enfant terrible of contemporary British fiction to a 'grown up' writer struggling with the onset of middle age. Controversy, though, usually involving age and sexuality, for Kureishi is always just around the corner. *Intimacy*, the film, directed by celebrated French auteur director Patrice Chereau, and based largely in fact on a short story 'Nightlight' from an earlier collection of stories by Kureishi called *Love in a Blue Time* (Kureishi 1997a) as well as the novel *Intimacy* itself, was released in 2001 to much grinding of potential censors' teeth, especially because it purported to show lingering 'real' oral sex on the screen for the first time in British mainstream cinema. Kureishi himself described it as a 'dark' film and fully expected it to cause a stir, particularly in his 'home' country. In the case of the book, Kureishi thought that 'the form in which it was written, a confession, would convey their suffering' and he confessed himself that he had 'put in a whole melange of stuff': some that had really happened in his life; and some that had not. In terms of the portrayal of the central narrative event, a man leaving his wife and two children, he 'wanted it to be seen as awful as it would be'. The media critics certainly sharpened their word processors for the film version of *Intimacy* as they did for the subsequent film *The Mother* featuring disturbing performances by Anne Reid and Daniel Craig. Criticism of *The Mother* prompted Kureishi to retort that 'you might write a film about your mother but at least she gets laid'.

It is, however, the insecurity, confusion and sheer placelessness of cold modern globalisation, post-9/11, that Kureishi has managed to evoke in his post-millennial writings better than anyone else. The idea of 'home' country is a concept Kureishi says he 'couldn't care less about anymore after years of worrying about being called a Paki and wondering where he was from', as he put it once in a public lecture. He was, however, always perturbed as a youngster when his answer 'from Bromley' to the question 'where are you from?' drew blank stares in the streets of south London. His mid-1990s work on religious fundamentalism and the problems of multiculturalism and young British Muslims in the form of the novel *The Black Album* (Kureishi 1995), and the short story made into a film by Udayan Prasad *My Son the Fanatic* (Kureishi 1997b) remain uncannily relevant for a re-energised cultural politics post 9/11 and 7/7 and were predicated on long periods of ethnographic research in the mosques of London in the early 1990s. He was initially allowed free access to many London mosques to observe the young Muslims at prayer but was eventually thrown out. As Kureishi points out in the introduction to his screenplay for *My Son the Fanatic*, 'Muslim fundamentalism has always seemed to me to be profoundly wrong, unnecessarily restrictive and frequently cruel.' Nevertheless, he has acknowledged that 'there are reasons for its revival that are comprehensible'. Visiting Pakistan in the mid-1980s made Kureishi aware of the oncoming crisis of Western culture for its Islamic immigrant populations. He has said on recalling such travels that he met his family but what he 'didn't like in Pakistan was political Islam'. He has remembered that he 'got a real sense of what a theocratic society was like' where 'the country was actually being run by the Koran'. In the 1980s, when these trips to Pakistan took place, religious fundamentalism was sweeping the Middle East and the Iranian fatwa against his friend, the writer Salman Rushdie (for the novel *The Satanic Verses*), provoked Kureishi into getting 'very involved' in fighting what seemed to him at the time 'a version of political Islam' which was 'very close to fascism'. Kureishi began to see a 'hostility to the West' which was 'sort of shocking' to him, a 'radical theocratic' move which cloaked 'a really sophisticated political agenda, based on Puritanism'. For the fanatical fundamentalists, as he has pointed out many times, 'there is only one book'. For Hanif Kureishi, on the other hand, there are many books. According to Kureishi we were seeing then, in the 1980s and 1990s, an emergence of a new version of Britain, a country changing very rapidly, yet in his opinion 'still managing to cope very well with large amounts of immigration since the 1950s' (Kureishi 1997: xii).

In the wake of the 7/7 event in London, and even the subsequent 21/7 attack, on the London underground and road transport system, Hanif Kureishi's views on the state of fundamentalism amongst young British Muslims and the state of multiculturalism in Britain today and in the past two decades were widely sought. Kureishi wrote short acidic essays for *The Guardian* newspaper on precisely these issues – modernist prose pieces that harnessed his Pop minimalism to great effect, stimulated by a strongly committed belief that the Iraq war was 'the most politically stupid act' and bolstered by his own 1990s ethnographic research for the cutting edge fiction that eventually emerged as *The Black Album* and *My Son the Fanatic*. His 'The Carnival of Culture' in *The Guardian*, 4 August 2005 and 'The Arduous Conversation Will Continue' in *The Guardian*, 19 July 2005, initially like bombshells fragmenting into contemporary culture and politics, were both quickly featured in a book published in 2005. Faber and Faber in London, Kureishi's sole book publisher in his long career, collected together the two *Guardian* articles, a chapter from *The Black Album*, the short story *My Son the Fanatic* and several other essays he had written on Islam and the West over the last two decades under the umbrella title *The Word and the Bomb*. A stunning polemic on liberalism essay 'The Word and The Bomb' prefaced the 'simple modernist' packaged collection of these previously published writings. A few months later, Kureishi published another comment on the same lines, a newspaper essay on these themes entitled 'Reaping the Harvest of our Self-Disgust' (Kureishi 2006d). They constituted powerfully effective prose pieces in harness to a modernist cultural politics and were widely recognised as such. An article on a website in July 2005 by June Thomas, Slate's foreign editor, at intpapers@slate.com nominated the film of *My Son the Fanatic* as the 'first 7/7 movie', a cultural text that helped to answer the question ringing out after the first of the devastating London events in 2005: 'How could apparently assimilated British-born Muslims end up stuffing bombs into their backpacks and murdering dozens of their compatriots in the Tube and on a London double-decker bus?' In the view of the writer on the website, the film, stemming originally from a 1990s *New Yorker* short story by Kureishi, showed 'how the British-born son of a Pakistani immigrant morphs from a clothes-obsessed, cricket-playing, music-loving accountancy student into a devout muslim who rails against the corruption and emptiness of Western society, much to the uncomprehending consternation of his father'. After what Kureishi has called the 'virtual wars' in Afghanistan, Iraq and even Pakistan, and especially after the London attacks, this sociological and cultural transition was a key feature of the post-millennial politics, much of it reduced to slogans such as 'Londonistan' and 'Islamaphobia'. The website argued that 'My Son the Fanatic is too subtle a creation to fall into a simplistic religious-belief-bad/Western-assimilation-good dichotomy'. Hanif Kureishi took up this issue in all its complexity with gusto in the initial *Guardian* essay, published under the title 'The Arduous Conversation Will Continue' though originally called more bluntly 'The Consequences of War'. Kureishi (Kureishi 2005: 91) wrote:

> We no longer know what it is to be religious, and haven't for a while. During the past 200 years sensible people in the West have contested our religions until they lack significant content and force . . . The truly religious, following the logic of submission to political and moral ideals, and to the arbitrary will of God, are terrifying to us and almost incomprehensible. To us 'belief' is dangerous and we don't like to think we have much of it. Confronted by this, it takes a while for our 'liberalism' to organise itself into opposition and

for us to consider the price we might have to pay for it. We also have little idea of what it is to burn with a sense of injustice and oppression, and what it is to give our lives for a cause, to be so desperate or earnest. We think of these acts as mad, random and criminal, rather than as part of a recognisable exchange of violences.

For many years Hanif Kureishi has been well aware of how 'consumerism' (which to him emerged in the 1960s at the same time as Pop offered a kind of cultural politics) has already 'traded its moral ideals for other satisfactions' and that has emphasised that 'consumerism' is precisely what the West wishes to export, 'masquerading as "freedom and democracy"' though the West keeps 'silent about its consequences'. For instance, take the invasions of Afghanistan and Iraq in the early 2000s; Kureishi saw these events as producing the 'smooth idea of "virtual" war that we have adopted to conquer the consideration of death'. Again, Kureishi noted with sharp observation on the equivalence of what he called 'the exchange of violences' in provocative, insightful writing perhaps only matched by the equally extreme essays on symbolic exchange by Jean Baudrillard on George Bush's 'war on terror' and American military excess. Jean Baudrillard scandalised mainstream media in the West by seeing the attack on the twin towers in New York in September 2001 in terms of symbolic exchange, and he went still further when commenting on the images of Abu Ghraib and other atrocities of contemporary warfare (Baudrillard 2004b, 2005a, 2005b, 2010a, 2010b; Redhead 2008). Kureishi and Baudrillard come to very different conclusions on the question of 'critical intelligence' (Baudrillard 2005a: 14), and on their perspectives about the 'real' (Redhead 2008; Žižek 2002a, 2005). Furthermore, Kureishi is a low modernist figure while Baudrillard, if anything, was anti-modernist as well as anti-postmodernist. Nevertheless, the writings of Baudrillard and Kureishi are, in my view, indispensable texts for our quest to understand the complexities of our time. For his part Kureishi (Kureishi 2005: 91–2) has argued that:

'Virtual' wars are conflicts in which one can kill others without witnessing their deaths or having to take moral responsibility for them. The Iraq war, we were told, would be quick and few people would die. It is as though we believed that by pressing a button and eliminating others far away we would not experience any guilt or suffering – on our side. By bullying and cajoling the media, governments can conceal this part of the war, but only for a while. If we think of children being corrupted by video games, imitation violence making them immune to actual violence, this is something that has happened to our politicians. Modern Western politicians believe we can murder real others in faraway places without the same thing happening to us, and without any physical or moral suffering on our part.

The only way out of the spiral of 'violence, repression and despair' according to Kureishi was not only to replace the 'exchange of violences' with a 'moral honesty about what we have brought about', but also with a thorough going exchange of ideas rather than a simplistic multiculturalism of festivals and food. 'Culture', in Kureishi's own Pop definition of it as 'literature, the theatre, newspapers', is as important and relevant as ever it was and creates a Cultural Politics of Pop which has been investigated in this chapter as a whole. For Kureishi culture 'continues the arduous conversation' which urgently must take place. In the second of his *Guardian* essays in the wake of the 7/7 and 21/7 London attacks, entitled 'The Carnival of Culture', Kureishi reflected on the research he did in the 1990s for *The Black Album* and *My Son the Fanatic*, when he visited Whitechapel and Shepherd's Bush mosques to observe, to his shock and horror, but also fascination as a writer seeking material for his stories, young, idealistic men listening intently to the regular 'diatribes against the West, Jews and . . . homosexuals'. For Kureishi it was not only 'sexuality that was being excluded here, but the whole carnival of culture that comes from human desire'. In Kureishi's eyes, the 'body hatred and terror of sexuality that characterises most religions can lead people not only to cover their bodies in shame but to think of themselves as human bombs'. Indeed for Kureishi 'culture', or 'our stories, dreams, poems, drawings', enables us to experience ourselves 'as strange to ourselves' and shows us 'how we think we should live' (Kureishi 2005: 97–100).

Hanif Kureishi has truly lived 'a life in accelerated popular culture', since his birth in the post-war Britain of the 1950s. I have demonstrated how Kureishi, especially in his work on Islam, neo-liberalism and Western liberalism, but moreover throughout his career, has maintained a critical intelligence through his writing. As he said pointedly in *The Word and the Bomb* 'live culture is an exploration', 'the Word is dangerous' and 'independent and critical thought is more important than ever' (Kureishi 2005: 10). In what Tariq Ali (Ali 2005) has called, also in indispensable writing about 9/11 and 7/7, these 'scoundrel times' Hanif Kureishi's contribution to our critical culture is a cultural politics of Pop; a post-Pop cool modernism in a cold modernity.

CHAPTER 5

Pastmodernism

'Good evening ladies and gentlemen. Would you please welcome Columbia recording artist, Bob Dylan.' Night after night, year after year, dating from the late 1980s, the dulcet tones of his resident announcer introduced Bob Dylan, ageing song and dance man, troubled troubadour, pulped pop star, to his devout live audience; or what was left of it. Never ending tour. Never bloody ending. Same words, same voice, every night. In the middle of the noughties Dylan, then sixty-five years old, could say (Lethem 2006), 'I see that I could stop touring at any time, but then, I don't really feel like it right now. I think I'm in my middle years right now. I've got no retirement plans.' But in Bob Dylan's art there is detectable what might be called a 'late style' as Edward Said (Said 2006), via Theodor Adorno, who himself wrote copiously about 'modern music' (Adorno 1994), has coined it in writing about the subject of death and its effect on an artist's life and work. Bob Dylan's own late style emerged in the early 1990s (Sounes 2001), as I show here, and it is likely to persist until his own death, whenever that may be. In earlier parts of his career, the record was 'an art form' for Dylan which 'maybe (he) was never part of'. Instead, he has pursued for years the 'something that's coming through . . . today . . . to make it just as real. To show you how it's real' (Lethem 2006). Rereading his many interviews, it is clear that the fate of art in posterity, the 'politics of his art' (Marqusee 2003) in other words, has always been a Dylan concern from the very beginning (Cott 2006; Sounes 2001). As this late style developed over the years though, scholarly critics (as well as fellow musicians like Joni Mitchell) lined up to seriously and persistently question Bob Dylan's 'originality' and charged him with 'postmodern plagiarism', in truth 'copying' others, on a mammoth scale for most of the last fifty years. Michael Gray (Gray 2000) in *Song And Dance Man III*, his 900-page third edition of 'the art of Bob Dylan' first published in the early 1970s, has shown in page after page the huge range of other 'authors' in Dylan's words and music. Clinton Heylin (Heylin 2010) has detailed the many different influences, direct and indirect, in 309 Dylan songs from 1974 to the present day, as well as many instances of 'borrowing' in lyric and tune in his earlier work (Heylin 2009). Most notable of all, Sean Wilentz (Wilentz 2010: 263–86) has pointed out just how much Dylan was indebted to others for the later 'work', essentially since the early 1990s. He has also noted Dylan's own jokey, ironic quotation marks around the album title for 2001's *'Love and Theft'* itself the title of cultural historian Eric Lott's book about the origins of American blackface minstrelsy. Wilentz has emhasised though that

> at the most basic legal level, the charges of plagiarism were groundless . . . many of the words as well as the melodies that Dylan appropriated had long ago passed into the public domain and were free for appropriation by anyone . . . The exceptions . . . involved isolated lines – images and turns of phrase – that hardly represented passing off another person's memoir as his own. According to American copyright law, as affirmed by the Supreme Court, transforming the meaning of a copyrighted work can constitute fair use. (Wilentz 2010: 309–10)

It is possible to trace the emergence of Dylan's late style to the New York Supper Club shows in the early 1990s. Dylan's own voice as he hit the first notes of the opening 'Ragged and Dirty' song on both nights in November 1993 at the exclusive Manhattan Supper Club in New York, captured for posterity on a four CD bootleg available in the late 1990s, in a cool blue box if you were lucky, was in sharp contrast to the announcer's sweetness. The entirety of the stunning four shows over two nights was captured on audience tape on the bootleg CD. In July 2002 another bootleg CD became available comprising the late show on 16 November 1993 straight from the soundboard, complete and professionally mixed. Eventually, in 2008, one track, 'Ring Them Bells' was officially released on *Tell Tale Signs*, volume 8 of the official Bootleg Series.

The 'voice is gone, man', Dylan once groaned hoarsely, in 1965, to the studio engineer in an aborted early solo waltz piano take of 'Like a Rolling Stone' (Marcus 2005: 1), at the high point of his powers, in the mid-1960s. By the early 1990s it was, sadly, true. Whether through chain smoking in his early decades until the late 1960s, or just singing on stage virtually every night for thirty years from the mid-1970s onwards, his once sweet, distinctive and engaging voice was shot to pieces, veritably 'ragged and dirty'. But the upside was that it made him sound uncannily like his old heroes, the blues, folk, gospel, cowboy and country singers he listened to on faraway American radio stations in his Minnesota youth, and, who

Michael Gray has evidenced at length, gave unwittingly so many of the musical notes and vocal lines Dylan has sung to us ever since. Dylan's vocal range, once wide, was narrowing by the performance but like the multi-skilled musician he remains today, the sound of his live work at the Supper Club was an object lesson in finding, eventually, like a blind man in the dark, a place, a subject position even, from which to sing well into his own old age. He was, in 1993, the age he sounded on his records in 1963 and 1964. But he sounds much older than that now.

In the early 1990s, too, Bob Dylan was – at last – shaking off the debilitating curse of his Born Again Christian period, which dated back to the late 1970s. Professionally at least, if not personally, the effects of his conversion in 1978, just as America swung viciously to the right under the fundamentalist Christian banner, took a decade to wear off. In many ways, the muse that had abandoned him probably was fundamentally lost in the mid-1960s (depending on the listener's take on the mid 1970s *Blood on the Tracks* Dylan, before Born Again, it might be argued that this loss came a little later). In 2005, forty years after the release of 'Like a Rolling Stone', Dylan's pre-1966 period was celebrated in various extremely public ways, as if his whole life was, in the words of one of his own songs, 'not dark yet' but 'getting there', not least in the publication of Greil Marcus' majestic book of the origins of the production and recording of his best known song 'Like a Rolling Stone' (Marcus 2005). Other memorabilia followed at pace in this particular cycle of pop which has lasted until the present: for instance, a fan obsessive driven *The Bob Dylan Scrapbook: 1956–1966* (Santelli 2005) was put out and quickly remaindered in the bookshops; film-maker Martin Scorcese's four-hour TV documentary *No Direction Home*, echoing a lyric from 'Like a Rolling Stone', was widely distributed featuring seemingly refreshingly candid, 'honest' and revealing extracts from a lengthy, filmed Dylan interview given originally to his manager in 2001; writer Mike Marqusee's political look back at Bob Dylan and the 1960s was given a new updated paperback edition (Marqusee 2005); a paperback edition of the best selling autobiography *Chronicles: Volume 1* (Dylan 2005a), Dylan's acclaimed, utterly riveting, beat poet reminiscences of various parts of his life, in particular the early 1960s, also hit the stores; the much reviled, and exasperatingly reviewed, Dylan novel *Tarantula*, first written in 1966, again saw the light of day in a reprinted version with a 'cool modernist' black cover (2005b); black and white photos of 'early' Dylan from 1964 were published in book form with an accompanying text by eminent rock writer Dave Marsh (Gilbert 2005) and enjoyed a successful London exhibition; lastly, Benjamin Hedin's *Bob Dylan Reader* (Hedin 2006) was republished in a mass market paperback edition, as if a textbook for global courses in 'Dylan studies'. Forty years on, the mid-1960s were back in vogue and Dylan was their ultimate popular cultural symbol. Plans were even made (and then abandoned), for a fortieth anniversary celebration of the Free Trade Hall concert, given in Manchester in May 1966 when Dylan was loudly branded a 'Judas' for his 'electric turn' (Sounes 2001; Heylin 2000: 246–60). In the subsequent years there has been no let up in Dylan's burgeoning 'cultural product' in the pop marketplace. In 2006, for example, D.A. Pennebaker's black and white film of the 1965 acoustic Dylan tour of England *Dont Look Back* was reissued on DVD along with a book and second full length DVD of outtakes from the 'original' film. In 2010 Dylan's record company released a box set of his first eight albums in mono, marketed as the 'authentic' modern way to listen to these legendary recordings from the 1960s in the accelerated twenty-first century. He even signed a six-book deal with a publisher; not bad for someone approaching seventy years of age.

There is, it seems, a lost moment in this history of modernity in popular music culture: the early 1990s. This was a period, against the backdrop of Grunge and Nirvana, especially in the USA, where Bob Dylan finally emerged from the relative slumbers of more than two decades and pre-pared to haul himself back to the American, and global, marketplace for the fine late trilogy of middle-age albums, namely *Time out of Mind* (1997), *'Love and Theft'* (2001) and *Modern Times* (2006). By the time of the Supper Club concerts in New York in 1993 two superb acoustic albums *Good As I Been To You* (1992) and *World Gone Wrong* (1993) had already been recorded, simply and cheaply, in Dylan's own West Coast home garage. Excellent outtakes, 'Mary and the Soldier' and a cover of Robert Johnson's '32–20 Blues' were later released on the official bootleg series' *Tell Tale Signs* and proved to be as good as most of the content of the original albums. On these early 1990s albums, Dylan went back to his roots with brilliant covers of wilfully obscure folk and blues tunes like 'Jim Jones' and 'Jack A Roe', as well as another outtake, the haunting version of Jo Stafford's 1952 hit song 'You Belong To Me', recorded at the time but only released on the soundtrack of Oliver Stone's film *Natural Born Killers*. Nevertheless, the live performances with his band on the Never Ending Tour were in this period as maddeningly inconsistent as ever, especially when it came to literally strangling his best known 1960s material.

The rare exception to this standard interpretation of an icon in decline is the two nights Dylan and his band played at the intimate Manhattan Supper Club in November 1993, two shows each night of the 16th and

17th of that month. Dylan biographer Clinton Heylin has noted that these shows were a rare, but important example of Dylan sustaining the 'performing side of his craft' into his fifties (Heylin 2000: xvii). Dylan was contemplating making the event his contribution to the MTV Unplugged series and recording of the Supper Club rehearsals and concerts was duly organised at his own expense. Two performances from the shows, 'One Too Many Mornings' and 'Queen Jane Approximately', have long been available for viewing on the *Highway 61 Revisited* interactive CD Rom offi-cially released in the mid-1990s. With the advent of 'new media' they have subsequently been available across the internet for a number of years for anyone who wished to access them. Dylan paid from his own pocket for the film crew and multitrack digital console, and then quietly buried the project. In fact, the officially released MTV *Bob Dylan Unplugged* (1994) concert was recorded somewhere else altogether in 1994 and featured mainly Dylan's 1960s hits material, albeit played by the same band who performed at the Supper Club, with one addition of producer Brendan O'Brien who played organ, thereby rendering it manifestly electric not acoustic, plugged not unplugged. A very limited edition bootleg CD of the unplugged/acoustic Supper Club revealed new renditions of various obscure forgotten Dylan songs like 'Queen Jane Approximately', 'Tight Connection to My Heart' and 'My Back Pages' together with several American music gems such as 'Delia', 'Blood in My Eyes' and Blind Boy Fuller's 'Weeping Willow'. The CD captured Dylan and the group of musicians he hauled from town to town most nights at the joyful apex of their collective glory, barely recognisable from the run of the mill, often shambolic 'metal' journeymen on tour the rest of the year if the myriad bootlegs available from this period are anything to go by. Bob Dylan has commented (Lethem 2006) in contrast that the band who recorded *Modern Times* with him in 2006, his then touring band (Gray 2006), comprising Tony Garnier (bass), George C. Recile (drums), Stu Kimball (guitar), Denny Freeman (guitar) and Donnie Herron (steel guitar, violin, mandolin), was 'the best band I've ever been in, I've ever had, man for man' (Lethem 2006).

Here, below, just for the historical record, are the little known precise details of 'the last supper club' shows:

The Supper Club Tapes: Bob Dylan and his band
Manhattan Supper Club, New York, USA, 4 sets, 16 and 17 November
1993
(Bootleg CD, The Complete Supper Club, 4 volumes)

THE BAND
Bob Dylan, guitar, vocals
Tony Garnier, stand up bass
Winston Watson, drums
Bucky Baxter, dobro, banjo, steel guitar, mandolin
John Jackson, guitar

THE PLAYLIST
16 November
Volume 1
Absolutely Sweet Marie
Lay, Lady, Lay
Blood in My Eyes
Queen Jane Approximately
Tight Connection to My Heart (Has Anybody Seen My Love?)
Disease of Conceit
I Want You
Ring Them Bells
My Back Pages
Forever Young

Volume 2
Ragged and Dirty
Lay, Lady, Lay
I'll Be Your Baby Tonight
Queen Jane Approximately
Jack a Roe
One Too Many Mornings
I Want You
Ring Them Bells
My Back Pages
Forever Young

17 November
Volume 3
Ragged and Dirty
Lay, Lady, Lay
Tight Connection to My Heart (Has Anybody Seen My Love?)
Weeping Willow
Delia
Jim Jones

Queen Jane Approximately
Ring Them Bells
Jack A Roe
Forever Young
I Shall Be Released

Volume 4
Ragged and Dirty
One More Cup of Coffee
Blood in My Eyes
Queen Jane Approximately
I'll Be Your Baby Tonight
Disease of Conceit
I Want You
Ring Them Bells
My Back Pages
Forever Young

As Clinton Heylin has pointed out, the shows at the Manhattan Supper Club were indeed 'exceptional', culminating with the final night, or the 'last supper', which Heylin has assessed as 'his finest performance of the nineties' (Heylin 2000: 679). This truly was the 'last supper club' as the dearth of creativity following the Christian conversion was finally laid to rest. It was also, in contrast to the legend of 1960s pop history, Dylan going 'acoustic'. On the Supper Club tapes the listener finds Dylan playing, lovingly, the 'old, weird' (Marcus 1997) 'Americana' he always so revered and which can be heard best in all its glory on the original five CD bootleg Basement Tapes of over 100 songs (Griffin 2007; Wilentz 2010) recorded in 1967 in Woodstock and the surrounding area. *The Old, Weird America* was the later, USA-targeted title for the Greil Marcus book originally published as *Invisible Republic* (Marcus 1997, 2001, 2010). 'The Old, Weird America' was also the title of Marcus' essay in the package for the CD reissue of Harry Smith's *American Folk Music* anthology. Dylan's stint as radio DJ in 2006 for his own satellite radio programme could have carried this label, too; in the event it was called, more prosaically, 'Theme Time Radio Hour'. Greil Marcus in 2010 published a huge retrospective of most of his Dylan writings from 1968 onwards, much of it stressing Dylan's eventual absorption into the 'old, weird America' from the early 1990s onwards. This Bob Dylan 'epiphany', what might be called the 'acoustic turn', in the early 1990s took place nearly three decades after the Manchester Free Trade Hall audience 'Judas' taunt at the electric half of the World Tour, with what later became The Band, in 1965 and 1966, now etched in fading colour in Scorcese's *No Direction Home* showcasing Dylan angrily turning his back on the crowd as he implored tour drummer Mickey Jones, formerly mainstay of Trini Lopez' band, to 'play fucking loud!' The main musicians who played on the Supper Club shows, Tony Garnier, Bucky Baxter, Winston Watson and John Jackson, regulars in Dylan's touring band of the time, may not match Robbie Robertson, Rick Danko, Richard Manuel, Garth Hudson and Levon Helm in Dylan's all time support band competition but they gave subtle and sympathetic interpretations of all the songs Dylan played in the intimate surroundings of the Manhattan Supper Club at 240 West 247th Street, New York, jammed full with 200 lucky holders of the free tickets distributed for the shows. Jon Pareles (Pareles 1993) reported for the *New York Times* at the time of the shows that Dylan 'performed with a fire, tenderness, playfulness and ornery charm that have surfaced only fitfully in recent years'. Pareles noted that Dylan 'not only sang with careful attention to every phrase, spontaneously transforming every line, but also played plenty of acoustic lead guitar'. The observant writer called Dylan 'an American syncretist' pulling 'together blues and country and gospel styles to sound both deeply rooted and utterly individual', singing songs of 'love, death, war, poverty, desolation and faith' a view underlined in Sean Wilentz's look at *Bob Dylan in America* (Wilentz 2010) and captured neatly in Greil Marcus' evocative phrase, coined specifically about Bob Dylan, 'American vernacular music' (Marcus 2010: xvi).

The Supper Club 'moment' is the exact point of the emergence of Bob Dylan's late style of American syncretism. Late style was, actually, originally the idea of Theodor Adorno. Edward Said (Said 2006; Ali 2006) held a seminar on writers' and artists' 'late style' in the mid-1990s in an American university where he taught literary studies and launched Adorno's concept anew. Jean Genet, Benjamin Britten and Richard Strauss were among his subjects, but Bob Dylan's post-Supper Club life and work can be accorded a 'late style' nomenclature, too. As the writer, and long time Bob Dylan fan, Hanif Kureishi (Kureishi 2006c: 52) has put it succinctly, Edward Said's work on late style provokes the questions, 'Does the apprehension of decay and death bring more meaning to an artist's work, or less?' and 'Does the "ultimate knowledge" mean wisdom and serenity, or fury and despair?' Said's 'musings on endings and death', as Kureishi has labelled them, recall Dylan's own revived attempt to arrest decline and desire. *Modern Times* indeed. Or, songs for the New Dark Ages. As music critic Andy Gill has cleverly put it 'Dylan plays on our associations of modernity with speed, wealth, technology, all the benefits of progress. But this is an old man's view of modern times . . . and Dylan's observations are tempered with hard won experience, if not a little cynicism' (Gill 2006). Dylan is not so much a 'postmodern' thief in the night, as so many critics have presented his supposed widespread and longstanding 'plagiarism' (Gray 2000; Heylin 2009, 2010; Wilentz 2010). He is more than this. He is a seeker of the art of the 'old, weird America'. In the podcasted self-reflexive words of an old friend of Dylan's, Beat poet Lawrence Ferlinghetti as he looks back from his nineties, Bob Dylan is 'a pastmodernist, not postmodernist'. Or, in a nod to Orchestral Manoeuvres in the Dark: he is an arch purveyor of the 'history of modern' (Lynskey 2010).

CHAPTER 6

Post-Sports

In this chapter I want to investigate some aspects of the speeding-up of sport and sports media in contemporary accelerated culture alongside a generalised rethinking of the sociology of modernity. In a 1990s book of essays entitled *Sport and Postmodern Times* Brian Pronger (Pronger 1998) coined the term 'post-sport' when reviewing the transgression of the body in sport within queer theory. But the term 'post-sport', or 'post-sports', also connotes a more apocalyptic place for sport and sport media: the world, for instance, of ubiquitous illegal betting dominated scandals in international cricket and the corrupt practices of financial incentives for sport media event bids like the World Cup within FIFA, the governing body of world soccer, from the 1990s onwards, and the 'live' global sport media coverage of such events. For columnist Simon Jenkins (Jenkins 2010):

> the truth is that international sport has become so bloated by national pride and celebrity as to lose all sense of proportion. The Geneva centre of housing rights and evictions reckons sport to be one of the biggest displacers of humanity, perhaps second only to war. In two decades some two million people have had to make way for Olympic stadiums and villages.

Paul Virilio (Virilio and Depardon 2008a: 184) has warned that, officially, it is being estimated that 'the future environmental migrant' numbers will be 'one billion'; moreover that 'six hundred and forty five million people will be displaced from their homes over the next forty years' and that 'two hundred and fifty million will be displaced by phenomena related to climate change', all part of a demographic resettlement' of the globe on a massive scale as exodus from cities (and also, even, the planet) gathers pace in the next fifty years (Virilio 2010a). Sport mega events, in various cities around the world will, far from regenerating the urban environment as has been the orthodoxy in the past, be a cause of part of this resettlement.

It could be argued that sport has always gone hand in hand with imperialism and colonialism, but in post-sports it is possible to glimpse a long media revolution. Tara Brabazon (Brabazon 2006: 194) has argued that the 'key for sports theorists is not to celebrate the spectacles of imperial sport, but to demonstrate how cultural figures like David Beckham . . . feed English identity after the loss of empire', and to help citizens to adapt national sporting culture to what Paul Virilio has called a new age of globalisation. Sporting labour markets (Lanfranchi and Taylor 2001) and sport media rights, and their scholarship, are subject to these processes too. As the sociologist of sports media culture Raymond Boyle (Boyle 2010: 1307) has argued:

> Until we stand back and take a longer view of what Raymond Williams famously called the 'long revolution' of communications, culture and democracy it is hard to accurately make sense of some of the underlying changes that are evident in the sports media relationship of the last few decades. In doing so however we find something quite profound and less commented upon appears to have happened. Sports have lost their veneer of innocence, with regard to the impact that the world of business and capital has on their practices and culture. For media and sports scholars, of course, have long argued that the discourse of sporting innocence has been largely mythological in its nature.

Sport in the media 'in the digital age' (Boyle 2010), too, especially sport in tems of sexuality, gender, ethnicity and the body, is increasingly used to symbolise the 'politics of postmodernism' (Ross 1989) where 'postmodern man or woman' is a cultural production – what Terry Eagleton refers to as 'cool, provisional, laid-back and decentred' (Eagleton 2010: 15). Think, again, of David Beckham, single-handedly raising the global profile of US soccer, who Ellis Casmore has portrayed in this light (Cashmore 2006: 229–46), held up as the ultimate 'metrosexual' in the modern era where new forms of subjectivity (Lash and Friedman 1992) are created, especially for masculinity and 'the lads' (Blackshaw 2003).

I want in the context of post-sports to review some of the ideas of Paul Virilio, veteran French theorist of 'dromology' and 'dromocracy' and suggest that this controversial work may at least give us an outline of what this book labels in its subtitle, 'theory at the speed of light', or 'post-theory'. Theory at the speed of light in my usage is part of a conceptual discourse of claustropolitan sociology which can illuminate the impact of new information and communications technologies in a world collapsing time and distance as never before. Virilio's notion of 'city of the instant' in the 'futurism of the moment' is where billions of people come together (through live broadcasting, streaming on the internet and so on) at the same time all over the world. Although many contemporary cultural and social theorists are drawn upon regularly to give a critical edge to sociological studies of sport, culture and the media, Paul Virilio is usually conspicuous by his absence in these debates. I seek here to begin to rectify this state of affairs, looking anew at modernity, media and sport. I suggest, for example, that spectators attending an English Premier League football match in the twenty-first century watch from an inert, sedentary position an accelerated, and accelerating, spectacle flash by in a blur like the swerving lightweight, highly technologised ball, itself acting like an unmanned military drone, a method of 'pure war' analysed so succinctly in Virilio's myriad little books. This sport media event is beamed around the globe 'live' to 'other' watching millions by virtue of the global communications revolution. Moreover, the mode in which the spectator watching at the stadium actually sees the speeding spectacle is conditioned by decades of absorbing such matches live on television, sofa-surfing in the comfort of his or her armchair, a state of 'polar inertia' or 'pathological fixedness'; again to quote Virilio, 'those absent from the stadium are always right'. 'Those absent from the stadium are always right' as has been asserted by Paul Virilio, in conversation with long time interlocutor, Semiotext(e)'s Sylvere Lotringer, in the early 1980s (Virilio and Lotringer 2008: 99–100). Virilio, as the pre-eminent theorist of speed in our age, is worth taking seriously when he provides us with such pithy slogans. Today speed, like power, is everywhere in the era of new, mobile modernities and mobile city cultures. This is especially evident in sporting culture and more specifically in mediatised sporting events. Test match cricket and even 50–over limited overs matches are being eclipsed by high speed, accelerated Twenty20 games where batsmen run to the wicket. The Twenty20 World Cups and the Indian Premier League (IPL) games are huge global media events only a few years after their origin. In football the hyper thin 'modern ball', exemplified by the Jubilani ball in the World Cup in South Africa in 2010, has become something of a 'lethal weapon' (Moore 2005: 70) giving new meaning to film-maker Wim Wenders' phrase the 'goalkeeper's fear of the penalty' as players grapple with the 'art of the impossible' (Moore 2005: 70) in a split second. The key question is: how can contemporary social and cultural theory make sense of these changes in the 'art of technology'?

As I have pointed out Paul Virilio's work comes with something of a health warning (Der Derian 1998; Armitage 2000, 2001; James 2007a and b) but it is still possible that a rigorous reading of his work will, in some part, pay dividends (Kinsella et al. 2002; Patrick 2003) in the study of post-sports. His own concentration on the accident through photographic, film and video images of disasters and catastrophes such as Chernobyl in 1987 and 9/11 in 2001, as well as common or garden earthquakes and building collapses, excludes, tellingly, sporting event speed 'accidents' such as the Heysel disaster of 1985 at a European Cup Final between Liverpool and Juventus in Belgium or the Hillsborough debacle (Brennan 2008; Scraton 2009) at Sheffield Wednesday's ground at a FA Cup semi-final between Liverpool and Nottingham Forest in 1989 in England.

The legacy of Virilio is clearly controversial. This is partly because, unfortunately for some writers who wish to use him in this way, he cannot be seen as a conventional social theorist or indeed, any kind of 'postmodernist'. His work *may* be a necessary condition for the necessary rethinking of the sociology of modernity but it is certainly not sufficient. He is, as he has told interrogators many times in interviews, a 'critic of the art of technology' rather than a theorist to be pigeonholed in any conventional academic discipline. As if to re-emphasise his current importance in global intellectual circles, Virilio was recruited as a member of the editorial board of *Cultural Politics*, an international cultural studies journal published by Berg from 2005, but his presence is an alien one. As the social and cultural theorist Scott Lash (Lash 1995) has correctly pointed out, Paul Virilio, like his friend and contemporary Jean Baudrillard, has been taken up by the art world as much as by academia, although not without hostility and, ultimately, rejection (Baudrillard 2005c; Redhead 2008). In the decade since Lash made the point, Paul Virilio has been feted by art critics and his art history taken seriously by academics (Virilio 2003b, 2007a; Virilio and Lotringer 2005).

In the context of rethinking social theory, post-sports and modernity, Virilio might seem to be an odd choice as prominent theorist, given the haphazard progress towards the academy through the 1950s and 1960s and the problematic Christian humanism that his work often expresses and that endorses the concept of the possessed individual which Arthur Kroker has rigorously critiqued (Kroker 1992). Virilio's biography was unusual to say the least. It included a period where he spent his time photographing the wartime German bunkers (Redhead 2009) as well as the spell where he trained as a stained glass painter. However his ultimate claim to international relevance in the contemporary search for more adequate theorising of modernity is that he has over many years developed a theory of speed, technology and culture which, whatever its flaws, is worth taking seriously, even if it is ultimately jettisoned by its once enthusiastic disciples. This theorising of speed and modernity alone marks him out as a major contemporary thinker. As the speeding up of modernity, in effect the entire intellectual territory of accelerated culture (Redhead 2004a), continued apace, ever shortening the time between departure and arrival, Paul Virilio could be said to be always on the verge of 'arriving' as a celebrity academic. The late 1990s and early 2000s is seemingly Virilio's time. High priest of speed, he has been dropping his 'logic bombs' for thirty years. Today, 'Virilians', adopting Virilio's own terminology of 'dromology' and 'dromoscopy' and 'dromocratic revolution' (Virilio 2005b), increasingly promote the current period as the 'dromocratic condition'. In Virilio's highly idiosyncratic tales of accelerated culture, or what has elsewhere been labelled by a number of critics as 'accelerated modernity', the speed of mass communications as well as the speed of 'things' is what counts. In this scenario we have all been invited to become historians of Virilio's instant present where immediacy, instantaneity and ubiquity rule.

However, this is not the whole story of either Paul Virilio or accelerated culture. There are conflicting interpretations of Virilio's theorising in the books about his work but essentially Virilio's contention is that the speeding up of technologies in the twentieth and twenty-first centuries, especially communications technologies like the internet, the world wide web, e-mail and mobile phones, have tended to abolish time and distance. Speed, crucially for Virilio, has had a largely military gestation. The way in which mass communication has speeded up at the same time has meant, in his view, that old-fashioned industrial war has given way to what he calls, following Albert Einstein, the information bomb or information war. As military conflict has increasingly become 'war at the speed of light' – as he described the first Gulf War in the early 1990s (Redhead 2004b) – the tyranny of distance in civilian as well as military life has almost disappeared. This does not mean that there is no deceleration, or slowness, though. Inertia, or better still what Virilio termed 'polar inertia' (Virilio 2001), has set in for even the supersonic airplane traveller or high-speed train devotee. Paul Virilio eventually left his post in academia in France to write a long planned book on the accident (Virilio 2007b), a concept which has over the last decade become more prevalent in his thinking. It is also an idea that encapsulates some of his most specific pronouncements about speed, technology and modernity. 'The accident', though, is a very specific term in Virilio's work and suffers in the translation from the French. There is a philosophical dimension to the concept, derived from Virilio's phenomenological background in academia at the university of the Sorbonne in the early 1960s where he studied under Maurice Merleau-Ponty amongst others. The accustomed use of the word in English is not really what Virilio has in mind. Each technology, for Virilio, contains within it the capacity to self-destruct. Planes crash. Skyscrapers collapse.

The field of critical sociology of sport and sport media is rapidly expanding. Examples would be the numerous books in the Routledge series Critical Studies in Sport (edited by Ian McDonald and Jennifer Hargreaves) and the collection of essays edited jointly by John Sugden and Alan Tomlinson (Sugden and Tomlinson 2002) and subsequently, alone, by Tomlinson (Tomlinson 2006). The label is wide in its inclusiveness, incorporating diverse work from many scholars (Hargreaves 1994; Miller et al. 2001; Boyle and Haynes 2004, 2009; Bairner, Magee and Tomlinson 2005; Whannel 2002; Giulianotti 2005; Rowe 2004). In this burgeoning area, as in many other academic fields, though, Paul Virilio is often conspicuous by his absence. Perhaps just as Virilio's late countryman Jean Baudrillard's 'time' was the USA (and further afield) in the 1980s and 1990s, the 2010s (Baudrillard 1997, 2006b), the time of the concept of war conducted by unmanned predator drones, will be, in retrospect, Paul Virilio's. In the mid-1990s publishers, and their coterie of referees, could say 'why Virilio?' to suggestions that he be featured in academic series about well known thinkers. Today, that is unlikely to be the response in general social theory book series. Furthermore, publishers commissioning a text book profiling contemporary social theorists in the mid-2000s are now just as likely to ensure that it features a section on Virilio as they are on seasoned key theorists, such as Michel Foucault or Pierre Bourdieu. Such a book was published at the turn of the millennium (Elliott and Turner 2001). Paul Virilio's celebrity, though deserved, however, will probably never be of the same order as Jean Baudrillard or Slavoj Žižek, who have online academic journals devoted solely to their oeuvre (*International Journal of Baudrillard Studies* and *International Journal of Žižek Studies*) and books updating developments in such studies (Bishop 2009).

I want to concentrate here on how these thinkers might impinge on the sub-discipline of the sociology of sport and sport media and more specifically what has been labelled as a 'critical sociology of sport' where class, gender and ethnicity are high on the research agenda. Some critique of critical sociology of sport and sport media has already taken place (Blackshaw and Crabbe 2004) and my contribution is meant to build on such critique. In this field it is my contention that reading both Paul Virilio and Jean Baudrillard rigorously could conceivably illuminate the contemporary accelerated culture of sport and sport media (Redhead 2004a) with 'theory at the speed of light' but that much more also has to be done to accomplish anything like a satisfactory result in this task. That figures like Virilio, and to some extent Baudrillard, have not thus far figured prominently in this sub-discipline is down to two factors: where they have been acknowledged in social theory, either their work is misleadingly contextualised as neo-Marxist social theory (Poster 2001), or else as 'postmodernism' (Kellner 1994) or 'hypermodernism' (Armitage 2000, 2001), frequently triggering denigration of their utility for 'critical' thinking.

Critical sociology of sport and media studies relies heavily on contemporary cultural and social theorists. Indeed challenging books have been produced, centring on sport and modern social theorists (Giulianotti 2004). Paul Virilio is nearly always absent in these enterprises despite his frequently uncanny contemporary relevance especially in his work on what he calls the 'city of panic' (Virilio 2005c) and the spaces of the 'city of disaster' (Armitage 2005; Virilio 2005c, 2005d; Thrift 2005; Conley 2005). Norbert Elias, Pierre Bourdieu, Michel Foucault and even Jean Baudrillard feature prominently in these discussions but not Paul Virilio. Critical sociology of sport and the media texts which have made significant contributions to the field in different ways have not lodged a reference to any of Virilio's work (Miller 2001; Miller et al. 2001; Sugden and Tomlinson 2002; Boyle and Haynes 2009, 2004; Crawford 2004; Rowe 2004). There is, nonetheless, a growing recognition that 'accelerated culture' (Redhead 2004a) is a term to be taken seriously in a critical sociology of sport and media cultures (Bairner, Magee and Tomlinson 2005) and in one or two cases an explicit consideration of at least some of Virilio's writing has been undertaken. Earlier attempts to cite Virilio in the context of sport fandom, and more specifically post-fandom (Redhead 1997b), have provoked some response from other scholars in critical sociology of sport and media cultures. This lack of critical engagement with Virilio in these fields has begun to change, as it has in other disciplines such as criminology (Wilson 2009b). For example, Garry Whannel (2002) in his work on masculinities, moralities and sport media mentions some of Virilio's early work on the way to developing his own useful notion of 'vortextuality'. Further, Tony Blackshaw and Tim Crabbe (Blackshaw and Crabbe 2004) in their pioneering exploration of sport and deviance have skilfully used a text by Virilio (Virilio 1997) in part three of their book, a section entitled 'Watching the Game'. Their concentration on the Premiership, the English Premier League soccer competition underwritten by Rupert Murdoch's part owned media company BSkyB, for this theoretical enterprise is intriguing and provocative and their development of the idea of 'cruising' as a mode of spectatorship is enhanced by Virilio's logistics of perception, especially his notion of 'eye lust' (Blackshaw and Crabbe 2004: 138, 144–5). The compatibility of the work of Paul Virilio, though, with cosmopolitan sociological theory used by Blackshaw and Crabbe, such as the idea of an era of 'liquid modernity' (Bauman 2000)

which Blackshaw and Crabbe borrow from Zygmunt Bauman, is question-
able. Virilio is an observer of the claustropolis rather than the cosmopolis.
Virilio, as critic of the art of technology, has no background in sociology
whatsoever – he has often placed himself explicitly 'against sociology'.
Other contemporary critical sociologists of sport have begun to utilise
Virilio. Richard Giulianotti, in his wide-ranging critical sociology of sport
text book (Giulianotti 2005) has briefly discussed Virilio's general contribution to the enterprise of critiquing the sociology of sport as it presently
exists, and to expanding and developing the field. Giulianotti has usefully
pointed to Virilio's 'intriguing elaboration of the time-space compres-
sion thesis' (Giulianotti 2005: 177). However in what has been a body of
general theoretical work on speed, technology and modernity produced
over a long period Virilio does not explicitly reference sport very often,
and few clues are signposted. Based much more on the military origins
of speeded-up technological change, it is not easy to 'apply' Virilio, or
be a Virilian. He is, like Baudrillard, a singular thinker of post-theory.
Giulianotti (Giulianotti 2005: 177) has, nevertheless, seen Virilio's ideas
and the development of contemporary sport media rights as linked:

> Compared to warfare, sport inhabits a secondary, albeit symbolic and
> strategic position in Virilio's framework. Non-white or developing-world
> athletes may dominate many sporting disciplines via the old velocity
> in physical movement. However, the instantaneous digital mediation of
> sports symbolises the high-tech potency of the white-dominated West's
> military-industrial complexes. Commodification of televised sport advances
> the material-speed divisions between the haves (who buy instant televised
> rights) and the have-nots (who receive old, inferior highlights packages).
> Strategically, the surveillance and social control of sports spectators using
> advanced gadgetry, allow the military industrial complex to test its latest
> techniques in cases of more overt political resistance. Thus Virilio promotes
> our general understanding of how time-space compression connects to tech-
> nological exercises of power.

However problematic the outcome, Giulianotti, Whannel and Blackshaw
and Crabbe are to be commended for their pioneering use of Virilio in the
sociology of sport domain.

How might we read Virilio to better effect in the study of post-sports? In
Virilio's world, speed enables us to see and foresee. It changes our 'logistics
of perception' to echo Virilio's words, our ways of seeing. Let us take a
prosaic example, culled from popular sporting culture. The high modernist Virilio rarely takes notice of 'low' culture such as sport at all. But Virilio
might be useful in considering the notion of the speeding up of sport,

and especially sport media, in modernity. The spectator at a Premiership professional soccer match in England at the beginning of the twenty-first century is witnessing a spectacle that is highly accelerated in all sorts of ways compared even to a game at the beginning of the Premiership itself twenty years ago. In the 1992–3 season when the Premier League began such matches in England were played at a very high pace in the first half, gave everyone a breather at half time, and then proceeded to speed up until around three quarters of the game had been played. This in itself was in great contrast to the way Football League First Division games had been 'sensually' played for over a hundred years (Winner 2005) prior to the early 1990s. In 'modern' soccer culture, essentially since the 1960s, techno-logical changes in the sort of footwear worn, the ball used, the shorts and shirts chosen, grass (or other surface) played on, floodlighting employed, not to mention training regimes for players, have had the overall effect of speeding up the process of the game to the extent that there is now literally no stopping for ninety minutes, plus any extra time for injuries and time wasting. Tactics in professional sport like soccer now include how many balls a club's ball boys carry, which can also affect how fast or slow a game can be. For instance, when Stuart Pearce took over from Kevin Keegan as manager of Manchester City in the English Premier League in 2005, for his first game in charge against Liverpool at the City of Manchester Stadium he instructed the ball boys each to carry a ball and to make sure whenever the match ball went out of play another ball was thrown in quickly to ensure a high, non-stop, tempo for his team. Pearce pointed out in a press confer-ence that the previous manager Kevin Keegan had 'only played with one ball'. Positivistic sport science analyses of such speeding up of technological change, and their impact on the outcome of soccer matches, have become popularised in recent years (Bray 2006). A spectator at a Premiership match or game in Spain in La Liga today consequently watches, from an inert, sedentary position in a seat an accelerated, and accelerating, spectacle flash by in a blur like the lightweight, highly technologised ball, itself operating like one of Virilio's favourite unmanned 'drones'. The 'old ball didn't move unless you were playing in thin air like Mexico' ex Scotland and Arsenal goalkeeper Bob Wilson has noted, but the new ball 'moves like a beach ball, it's so thin . . . you have a split second to decide' (Moore 2005: 70). As the former England and Chelsea, Spurs and AC Milan player, and TV pundit, Jimmy Greaves (Greaves 2005: 84–5) has put it, one of the reasons:

> for the standard of goalkeeping not being as high as it once was is down to
> the type of ball used today. In my day as a player, and in subsequent years,
> the type of football commonly used was the Mitre Matchplay. When that

ball was hit at goal it travelled more or less true; there was little deviation through the air. Should a goalkeeper's positioning and angles be correct, he would be able to judge the flight of the ball and execute a save. From the fifties through to the eighties, the standard weight for a ball was set at exactly sixteen ounces – the equivalent of 0.45kg. Over the years the weight of a football has gradually decreased. The ball used in the Premiership in recent years, the Nike Total 90 Aerow, is far lighter than the footballs used years ago.

This accelerated sporting spectacle is beamed around the globe 'live' to watching millions, be they in a Canadian airport terminal or a suburban house in India, by virtue of the global communications revolution also ushered in since the increasing ubiquity of television in the 1960s and the satellite and cable revolution of the 1990s and the further internet accelerated changes of the 2000s. Moreover the way the spectator at the game watching 'live' at the stadium actually sees the speeding spectacle is conditioned by decades of watching such matches 'live' on television, sofa surfing in the sedentary comfort of his or her armchair, an example of Virilio's 'pathological fixedness' or 'polar inertia'. In many grounds, too, the spectator can watch 'live' (with slight delay) replays of the action on giant screens at one end of the ground just in case 'nodding off', or what Virilio refers to as 'picnolepsy', has occurred. The case example I have cited of Premier League soccer would so far fit the notion of an accelerated culture found in very different language and different instances in the work of Paul Virilio. There is, though, no inexorability about the process I have described. For instance top league professional soccer in other countries – say Argentina, Japan, Italy or Spain – is not necessarily as fast as the Premiership in England. Soccer style, culture, tradition and tactics in these other countries determines a slower pace of the spectacle even though the same technological changes mentioned persist. Moreover, the 'live' televising of Premiership soccer matches from England around the globe is often subject to delay, not only the slight 'digital delay' which means a fractional time of delay in arrival of a signal or message, but the organisational delay of broadcasters in other countries showing 'live' matches delayed by a few minutes, hours or even days to fit in with domestic television schedules ('as live', as they are referred to in the global sports media industry). This example serves as a warning that all might not be as it seems in this supposed accelerated culture of the instant present.

Virilio has been labelled as a postmodernist, partly because of the mediatising of the events he discusses in the 'city of the instant' in the 'futurism of the moment'. Equally, he has been bracketed with Jean Baudrillard, another so-called 'postmodernist'. The life and work of Paul Virilio and

Jean Baudrillard often overlaps but there are significant and irresolvable (Gane 2003; Hegarty 2004) differences between them. Further, it is a misnomer to bracket them as 'postmodernists' (Hegarty 2004; Redhead 2004a, 2004b) at all. John Bale and Patricia Vertinsky in their stimulating and otherwise interesting collection of essays about sport, space and place and the 'sites of sport' (Bale and Vertinsky 2004: 1) explicitly refer to them as the 'postmodernists Paul Virilio and Jean Baudrillard'. It is unusual to cite Virilio at all in critical work on sport and media cultures so their inclusion in an important text in critical sports geography is welcome and necessary, but the description (which is a standard one in other fields, it should be said) of both Virilio and Baudrillard as 'postmodernists' is most misleading. Richard Giulianotti, too, sees both figures as 'postmodernist'. The discussion of Paul Virilio in Giulianotti's critical review of the sociology of sport (Giulianotti 2005) is explicitly included in a chapter on 'the postmodern' and this is where the idea of the 'era of postmodernity' is developed. Further, for Giulianotti (Giulianotti 2005: 226) 'one does not need to reinvent the basic definition of the postmodern to include Virilio. Indicatively Virilio and Baudrillard attract similar communities of scholars'. It is certainly true that Virilio and Baudrillard 'attract similar communities of scholars', but both theorists are better understood outside of discussions of postmodernism (and for that matter post-structuralism).

Virilio's enigmatic phrase, 'those absent from the stadium are always right' was, in some ways, a typically quirky Virilio pass back to inter-locutor Sylvere Lotringer, originally spoken in conversation as long ago as 1982 (Virilio and Lotringer 2008). It is pertinent today given the power of media companies and media moguls like Rupert Murdoch in the battle over sport media rights and the trend for spectators to turn away from attending grounds because of cost. In contrast to the early years of the Premiership in England in the 1990s, many top flight professional soccer clubs in recent seasons (Blackburn Rovers, Middlesbrough, Wigan Athletic, Bolton Wanderers amongst them) have witnessed regular mass absences of their paying spectators. The context of Virilio's pithy phrase, though, was actually very specific. It was a conversation in the wake of the 1980 Olympics in Moscow when the USA was 'absent from the stadium' and also the 1978 football World Cup in Argentina, run at the time by a military junta when the 'disappeared' were absent from the stadium. Virilio's phrase does have a more eternal ring to it, too, connoting the media and business moguls whose buying and selling of television rights has given a supposedly new consumer power to passive couch potatoes all over the world. One aspect of the notion of non–postmodernity that has been identified here is the way in which in mediatised sporting events in accelerated modernity the stadium is effectively transformed into a television set and, as Paul Virilio has noted, the situation where 'those absent from the stadium are always right' is placed on the agenda. Sean Smith's blog SportsBabel, subtitled 'Disconnect in the Sportocracy', 'explores the impact of digital media and other technologies' on what he tantalisingly calls 'the sportocracy' – in a blog located at http://www.sports-webconsulting.ca/sportsbabel. Smith's phrase neatly encapsulates the sport and media cultures in accelerated culture. Some might even argue that the twenty-first century is an era of 'sportocratic condition', but that would be to compound the essentialism associated with those who would endorse the idea of a 'dromocratic condition' or a 'postmodern condition'. Nonetheless, the notion of 'sportocracy' may prove fruitful as sport and media cultures invade the 'city of the instant'. SportsBabel frequently invokes the writings of Paul Virilio and has explicitly analysed Virilio's phrase 'Those absent from the stadium are always right'. Under the title of 'The Privilege of Absence' Smith has suggested that:

> Virilio is certainly correct here to an extent, in that the stadium becomes a sort of television set, with each game filmed before a live studio audience . . . what I think he misses, however, is how this inversion has doubled back on itself, to the point where the absentees are watching a broadcast of the participants watching a broadcast in a weird twist on reality TV. When at the track, we spend the majority of a horse race watching the steeds on the big screen television in the centre of the infield, only to turn to the charge down the home stretch. At a baseball game, only a small portion of the crowd need actually watch the game at any particular moment to alert the rest as to when the live action should begin – the rest of the time we will socialise with our friends and catch replays on the Jumbotron between the commercials.

The sort of scenario sketched here by Sean Smith, and further in his mercurial contribution to the post-aesthetics of sport, or what I call here post-sports, a subsequent collection by and on Virilio entitled *Grey Ecology* (Virilio 2009b), is compounded daily at professional soccer matches as the 'absent' spectators watching on live television (or via the internet) are treated to the spectacle of spectators within the grounds watching not only the replays of incidents on giant screens but who are watching the game 'live' on screens on their mobile phones. Moreover, spectators use those mobile phones to take pictures of incidents within the ground, on or off the field, and send those photos instantly to friends who are absent from the stadium anywhere in the world, or upload them to social networking sites, or, increasingly, submit them to news media companies who request fans' pictures of events at games as part of user generated content news gathering in the global 'land' of Web 2.0 (Leadbeater 2008).

I have looked here at aspects of the speeding up of sport and sport media in contemporary accelerated culture; in other words, at post-sports. I have suggested that the controversial work of Paul Virilio, most recently arrowing in on the 'city of panic' in the 'futurism of the instant' (Virilio 2005a, 2010a), constitutes theory at the speed of light which is necessary to illuminate the impact of rapidly changing new information and communication technologies in a world collapsing time and distance as never before. Looking anew at modernity, media culture and sporting events in what Virilio labels the 'city of the instant' there is some lasting legacy for a claustropolitan sociology project. To conclude, let us leave the last word to Virilio as he told Sylvere Lotringer (Virilio and Lotringer 2008), and by extension all of us who would listen and learn, about the lessons of the Maracana stadium in Rio de Janeiro in Brazil (currently being rebuilt for the 2014 World Cup) and the Moscow 1980 Olympics:

> [T]he serious problem is that those present, those who participate, those for example who attend an auto race are disqualified by the absentees. The billion people who watch the Olympic Games in Moscow, or the soccer championship in Argentina, impose their power at the expense of those present, who are already superfluous. The latter are practically no more than bodies filling the stadium so that it won't look empty. But their physical presence is completely alienated by the absence of the television viewer, and that's what interests me in this situation. Once, the stadiums were full. It was a magnificent popular explosion. There were 200,000 people in the grandstands, singing and shouting. It was a vision from an ancient society, from the agora, from paganism. Now when you watch the Olympics or the soccer championship on television, you notice there aren't that many people. And even they, in a certain way, aren't the ones who make the World Cup. The ones who make the World Cup are the radios and televisions that buy and – by favouring a billion and a half television viewers – 'produce' the championship. Those absent from the stadium are always right, economically and massively. They have the power. The participants are always wrong.

CHAPTER 7

Post-Politics

In this chapter I want to sound a warning about the possible knee jerk return to past theorists in the detritus of the collapse of faith in the neo-liberal ideas that have ruled the globe since the 1970s. All theory is produced in a political and social context, so it is important to trace the context of the production of previous theories which now may be turned to in the midst of crises, once again, even if they ended up the first time around in some kind of 'post-political' vacuum. In the early 1990s it could be written in a book of essays on postmodernism, politics and culture (Perryman 1994: 1) that 'after postmodernism, post-fordism, post-marxism, we are now being offered the post-political . . . the implication is that we are entering an age where the central focus of new thinking and collective activity is moving away from the political party'.

It was the Italian Autonomists who became most strongly associated with the vexed notion of the 'post-political' (Redhead 1990), or 'post-politics', in the 1970s and 1980s. As Sadie Plant has situated it historically, the Italian Autonomists were part of a late twentieth-century development of situationism in one country in 'a postmodern age' (Plant 1992). But in the land of that particular brand of left libertarianism, it was ultimately the right-wing magnate Silvio Berlusconi, proprietor of Italy's largest media empire (Anderson 2009: 285–92), who inherited the throne and became a long-term prime mover, and prime minister, in the nation's recent history. As Berlusconi's reign entered what seemed like the end game a supposedly 'post-fascist party', the Future and Freedom for Italy movement (FLI), emerged on the 'post-political' stage. The Italian Marxist philosopher, Lucio Colletti, who was born in 1924 and died in 2001, became Berlusconi's ally in his flight from Marxism, but delving back into Colletti's life and work can actually be a useful enterprise for an analysis of the 'crash' of 2008 and the uneven economic, cultural and political global development that has followed. Colletti developed theories of value, aesthetics, law and politics that are still relevant today but have strangely been sidelined, even within contemporary Marxist discourse. In the 1970s he was described as the most important living Italian Marxist philosopher, eclipsing even extremely influential European Marxist figures such as Antonio Gramsci and Galvano Della Volpe. By the 1990s he was in the arms of the right and, in particular, Silvio Berlusconi. Not so much 'From Rousseau to Lenin' (Colletti 1972) as one of Colletti's books was entitled, more From Marx to Berlusconi! I want here to put Colletti's life and work into perspective, suggest reasons for his rightward political trajectory and compare and contrast his work with that of another scientific materialist European Marxist, Louis Althusser. Althusser and Colletti had something of a secret dialogue in their lifetimes as I will seek to show, but the legacy of their joint, if conflicting and separate, struggles for Marxism as scientific materialism in the twentieth century lives on in today's accelerated culture of the twenty-first, where some on the left such as Martin Jacques (Jacques 2009a, 2009c), former editor of *Marxism Today*, see a 'new depression' beckoning.

In the history of cultural and political theory Lucio Colletti has been a relatively obscure, if iconic, figure. But where his work was used creatively its impact has proved to be long lasting. For example Paul Willis, then part of the Centre for Contemporary Cultural Studies at the University of Birmingham (CCCS), used Colletti extensively when he wrote *Learning to Labour* (Willis 1977), a classic account of 'how working class kids get working class jobs', which is justly famous for its first half 'Ethnography'. The book derives much of its overall theoretical strength from the use of the pioneering and sustained work of Lucio Colletti in the second part, entitled 'Analysis'. Especially in his analysis of 'general abstract labour' Willis skillfully uses Colletti's conceptual apparatus, translated by then into English and widely available through New Left Books and *New Left Review*. Willis (Willis 1977: 143) has, however, pointed to problems with Colletti's analysis, too:

> I take Colletti's case absolutely that abstract labour is much more than a mental category in the analyst's head. It is a central factor of real social organization and the real basis of the exchange of commodities (including labour power) and is recapitulated every time in that exchange. Abstract labour as a social force is also indicated in subjective processes such as the separation of the self from labour . . . However, Colletti's equation of abstract labour with alienation forecloses too early the fixed nature of man and denies the possibility of a progressive and contradictory edge to the split between concrete and abstract labour which capitalism enforces. I dissent from Colletti as he follows Lukacs in equating the self-consciousness of the

working class with knowledge of the operative principle of abstract labour as a force for reification, and recognition of its own labour power as the source of value. It is this error which allows him to attribute the simple possibility of a correct political analysis to working class consciousness. This is where both he and Lukacs can be justly accused of empiricism and historicism.

In the specific context of the CCCS it was Louis Althussser as a representative of scientific materialism who was much more influential than Colletti in the Centre's theoretical and ethnographic stance over many years. Colletti's influence in the global academy as a whole waned from about the late 1970s to the early 2000s. But today Lucio Colletti is a growing inspiration to new theorists and scholars, especially in the specific theorisation of the new social and economic forces of neo-liberalism.

Let us look at why Colletti is once again seen to be a model theorist, especially to younger scholars. Lucio Colletti, the former Italian communist and Marxist theorist, was born in Rome on 8 December 1924. He died in Livorno, Italy of a sudden heart attack, at the age of seventy-six, while taking a bath on 4 November 2001. As John Stachel has noted (Stachel 1988) 'at the time of his death he was a Senator in the Italian parliament, representing the Lombard League, one of the most reactionary parties in Italy'. He had, by his death, 'long departed from an adherence to any variant of marxism' as he had himself symbolised in his chosen title of *Le Declin du Marxisme* (Colletti 1984) for a collection of essays in French translation – 'the decline of marxism'. Colletti was survived by his second wife Fauzia and daughters from each of his two marriages. His death provoked events in Italy that were described as almost a state funeral but the dearth of recognition of his work subsequently is the really strange story. Lucio Colletti developed theories of value, the state, aesthetics, law and politics that are still relevant today although his own intellectual legacy is not as great as it might have been. The 2007 to 2008 global credit crunch (Smith 2010) and the onset of what some see as a prolonged new depression which may last decades, however, may well see Colletti's renaissance (Mann 2009) as an important analytical theorist of capital, the state and modernity. In the 1970s he was described as the most important living Italian Marxist philosopher, eclipsing even influential twentieth-century figures in his country of birth such as Antonio Gramsci and Galvano Della Volpe, and had been elevated to the pinnacle of a small band of high theorists including Louis Althusser and Jurgen Habermas, who were said at the time to constitute a 'Western Marxism' (Anderson 1977). For Perry Anderson, then the editor of *New Left Review*, Colletti was a major 'contemporary author' rapidly producing 'new texts as the NLR was sending its numbers to press (Anderson 2000: 7). The 1980s, however, saw a global demise of the theoretical power of Marxism as scientific materialism, and the influence of Marxist theorists in general. Lucio Colletti in particular went from hero to zero. By the 1990s Lucio Colletti was in the arms of Silvio Berlusconi and served as an elected politician in Berlusconi's party in the Italian parliament for a number of years. Yet this remarkable political trajectory was not opportunist; he self-reflexively was always on 'the left', and an avowed anti-fascist, for his entire career.

What was the specificity of this trajectory? Born in the 1920s, in 1950 Colletti became a member of the Italian Communist Party (PCI) following in the footsteps of Italian communism's founding philosopher Antonio Gramsci (Colletti 1971). In Italy, Lucio Colletti was variously remembered in obituaries as an intelligent Marxist, the Galileo of social sciences, a rigorous thinker with a critical spirit, an irreverent, sarcastic but free spirit, and as a formerly dangerous communist. But Colletti was also much criticised by many liberal media commentators for his part in Berlusconi's first elective dictatorship which eventually came to an end in April 2006 before another right-wing term ensued, which has lasted, despite prosecutions, until the present day.

Lucio Colletti was determined to study philosophy from a young age. His youth was dominated by the fascist background of Italy in the 1930s and he had to wait until 1945, and the age of twenty-one, before he could enrol at the university of Rome. Colletti is perhaps best known for his major theoretical treatise on Marx, the book *Marxism and Hegel* (Colletti 1973) entitled *Il Marxismo e Hegel* in the original Italian (Colletti 1969a), though few commentators on Colletti, from whatever political persuasion, seem to have read the whole text. For Colletti the link between Hegelian dialectics and Marxism was much overblown in Marxist philosophy (Smith 1986; Colletti 1975b; Gottfried 1978) and his own book-length work stressed what he regarded as the singular importance of Immanuel Kant as a philosophical ancestor of Marx well before it was fashionable to do so. Colletti (Colletti 1975b: 3) summarised his own arguments on the problem of the difference between Kant's notion of real opposition and Stalinist dialectical contradiction as threefold:

1. The fundamental principle of materialism and of science, as we have seen, is the principle of non-contradiction. Reality cannot contain dialectical contradictions but only real oppositions, conflicts between forces, relations of contrariety . . . 2. On the other hand, capitalist oppositions are, for Marx, dialectical contradictions and not real oppositions . . . For Marx, capitalism is contradictory not because it is a reality and all realities are contradictory, but because it is an upside down, inverted reality (alienation, fetishism) . . .

3. All the same . . . it is nonetheless true that it confirms the existence of two aspects in Marx: that of the scientist and that of philosopher.

For Lucio Colletti's theoretical and political enterprise the goal was to produce a real, scientific basis for Marxism that had no place for Hegelian consciousness and humanism. In this context he developed important sustained critiques of the brands of Marxism espoused by Lukacs and by the Frankfurt School of Adorno and Horkheimer amongst others.

The problematic binary division of scientist and philosopher in Marx (and in Lucio Colletti's work subsequently) was to persist for Colletti long past the crisis of Marxism which he and others identified during the 1970s. In the remainder of the quarter of a century of Lucio Colletti's life it would be the deconstruction of Jacques Derrida that would wrestle with the scientist and philosopher in Marx, and indeed in the play of language between science and philosophy themselves. Such deconstruction, sometimes misleadingly defined as 'postmodernism', ironically culminated in a global celebrity culture of the philosopher as public intellectual, with figures including Jacques Derrida himself, as well as Edward Said, Slavoj Žižek and Jacques Lacan, celebrated either on DVD and 'consumed' all over the globe (Derrida 2002; Said 2005; Žižek 2007; Lacan 2008a), or marketed in a populist way through the production of (slightly) more accessible popular texts (Lacan 2008b; Žižek 2002a; Badiou and Žižek 2009). It was a celebrity that in his global heyday Lucio Colletti had also experienced to some extent. However, Lucio Colletti and Western Marxism did not make much more progress in this direction of deconstruction of Marx as scientist/Marx as philosopher and Colletti's identification of a real and serious theoretical problem in Marx would find no ultimate solution in his lifetime. Colletti's subsequent collection of essays *From Rousseau to Lenin* (Colletti 1972), including *Ideologia e Societa* when it was originally brought out in Italian in 1969 (Colletti 1969b), won the Isaac Deutscher Memorial Prize in 1973 and is probably his most widely read, and cited, work in English. For Colletti, Jean-Jacques Rousseau was the first to develop a fundamental critique of the 'bourgeois representative state' and an analysis of the separation of civil society from the state, and the fact that Marx's own development of theories of the state barely moved beyond Rousseau suggested to Colletti that Marxism lacked a true political theory even in the wake of Lenin's writings. Colletti also memorably contributed a fascinating and sustained introduction to an English edition of Karl Marx's *Early Writings* in the 1970s (Colletti 1975a) and later a preface to an Italian edition of Marx and Engels' most famous statement of intent, *The Communist Manifesto* (Colletti 1985; Marx and Engels 1998).

The papers in *From Rousseau to Lenin* were culled from a decade of writing about themes such as 'Marxism as Sociology', 'Bernstein and the Second International' and 'Lenin's State and Revolution', while he held a professorship in philosophy at the University of Rome in the 1960s. Early on, he taught at the University of Messina and was at the University of Salerno in a faculty which included Italian luminaries such as Gabriel de Rosa and Carl Salinari. In the 1970s he also taught philosophy at the university of Geneva after his intellectual and political activities at the university of Rome became increasingly controversial for the Italian right. Colletti was always what one obituary writer called an extraordinary polemicist but there is surprisingly little written about him in the English language and even less attention given to his fall-out with Marxism from the 1970s onwards (Mann 2009).

One major contemporary influence on Colletti's work was the Italian Marxist philosopher Galvano Della Volpe who died in 1968. Colletti always remembered first discovering Della Volpe's work in 1951. Della Volpe had been a professor at the university of Messina where Colletti had also taught before going to teach at the university of Rome. Della Volpe's *Critique of Taste* published in 1960 (Della Volpe 1978) was a treatise on Marxist aesthetics and his most significant book at a time when he was seen as Italy's leading Marxist philosopher. Colletti took over Della Volpe's mantle as Italy's most important living Marxist philosopher in the mid-1960s, and especially as the 1960s gave way to the 1970s. Indeed apart from the challenge of Antonio Gramsci, and later, still current today, Giorgio Agamben (Agamben 2005), it is possible to cite Lucio Colletti as the twentieth century's leading Italian left philosopher overall and the inheritor of Della Volpe's pioneering efforts. Della Volpe was one of the few professors who remained in the PCI (Communist Party of Italy) after the Hungarian revolt in 1956. Colletti remained, too, and witnessed a period of Della Volpean influence inside the PCI especially in the late 1950s when Della Volpe and Colletti were both on the editorial committee of the party's main cultural journal. Like Galvano Della Volpe, much of Lucio Colletti's life and work was dedicated to an 'absolutely serious' relationship to the work of Marx, based on direct knowledge and real, sustained study of his original texts (Anderson 1974: 3–28). Furthermore, Colletti insisted on the political importance of these texts, emphasising that in the end all Marx's work is essentially an analysis of modern capitalist society and that all the rest of his writing, though important, is secondary to the *Grundrisse* and to *Capital* in all three volumes. In the mid-1970s Colletti gave a fascinating, wide ranging interview to Perry Anderson, at that time the influential editor of the new left journal *New Left Review*, published originally in the July/Autumn issue in 1974 (Anderson 1974: 3–28). This interview, still uncannily resonant today, explored Colletti's creeping disillusionment with Marxist philosophy and politics in the context of his life and work up to that date and was prescient in its rational and incisive break from Marxist theoreticist discourse, citing the pamphleteering tradition of socialism as a lost Marxist politics of the past. Although Colletti acknowledged that both he and Della Volpe had a commitment to study Marxism rigorously, where it is actually to be found in Marx's writings themselves, he felt strongly that the only way in which Marxism could be revived was if no more books like his own *Marxism and Hegel* were published. To Anderson, in the long penetrating interview he conducted with Colletti, Lucio Colletti expressed a profound dissatisfaction with what he had done in his academic career as a professor and confessed that he felt immensely distant from the things that he had written, emphasising strongly that he was in the process of radically rethinking his previous thought. Anderson's interview was published in Italian in the same year as the original Italian version of Colletti's article 'Marxism and the Dialectic' (Colletti 1974) which was translated and published in English a year later (Colletti 1975b). The Anderson conversation with Colletti covered in great detail his own intellectual and political formation and revealed much about the subtleties of his life and work but only hinted at the massive and shocking political move he was to make eventually in the 1990s. However, with hindsight it does lay the theoretical basis for elements of such a move, as can be seen from the detail of doubt in the interview.

Much of Colletti's background is conflated as Gramscian in the existing literature but this is a serious misunderstanding of the milieu of Lucio Colletti. Born in 1924 Colletti grew up in an Italy where the prison writings of Antonio Gramsci (Colletti 1971) were utilised to present Marxism as the fulfilment and conclusion of the tradition of Italian Hegelian idealism, in particular that of Croce (Anderson 2009). Colletti's bachelor degree thesis entitled *La Logica di Benedetto Croce* was written in 1949 on neo-idealistic philosophical logic and Benedetto Croce, and was eventually published as a book in Italian (Colletti 1992). But it was Lenin's materialism that was soon a much more formative influence. Colletti regarded his own intellectual origins as similar to nearly all of the Italian intellectuals of his generation, reacting strongly to Italian fascism but (perhaps) less critical of Stalinism. Colletti always cited Lenin's writings as the main reason for his decision to join the PCI in 1950, and later, in 1958, wrote an introduction to an Italian edition of Lenin's *Philosophical Notebooks* as well as, in the 1960s, a sustained critical essay on Lenin's seminal *State and Revolution* pamphlet. Colletti had been a PCI dissenter after the

Soviet invasion of Hungary in 1956, and consistently held an aversion to
Stalinism in general (Colletti 1970) to such an extent that he was regarded
as a Trotskyist in Italy, hence, partly, his celebration in Trotskyist influenced journals such as *New Left Review* in Britain. 'Hang Colletti' was the
student graffito in the 1970s when anti-Trotskyism was at its height on
Italian university campuses. In the 1950s he was one of the 101 signatories
to a notorious letter from dissident communist intellectuals deriding the
party line on Eastern Europe and lambasting Soviet repression. He told
Perry Anderson of *New Left Review* how he experienced Stalin's death
in 1953 as an emancipation and Khrushchev's denunciation of Stalin at
the Communist Party of the Soviet Union Twentieth Congress in 1956 as
an authentic liberation (Anderson 1974: 3–28). For Colletti the extreme
period of Stalinism comprised ceaseless trials, suspicion, and purges
inside the Soviet Party and all other communist parties (Colletti 1971).
Colletti thought Stalin himself was a cold and despotic man (Colletti
1970). In contrast he praised Leon Trotsky's sober caution and dissection
of Stalinism. However Colletti did not immediately leave the Communist
Party in 1956, waiting in fact until 1964 to exit the Italian party and end
any love affair he might have once had with the Soviet system. He had
joined the Communist Party in his youth as a militant and philosopher and
had no regrets as he told Perry Anderson (Anderson 1974: 5):

> My membership of the party was an extremely important and positive expe-
> rience for me. I can say that if I were to relive my life again, I would repeat
> the experience of both my entry and my exit. I regret neither the decision to
> join nor the decision to leave the party. Both were critical for my develop-
> ment. The first importance of militancy in the PCI lay essentially in this:
> the party was the site in which a man like myself, of completely intellectual
> background, made real contact for the first time with people from other
> social groups, whom I could otherwise never have encountered except in
> trams or buses. Second, political activity in the party allowed me to over-
> come some forms of intellectualism and thereby to understand somewhat
> better the problems of the relationship between theory and practice in a
> political movement. My own role was that of a simple rank and file militant.
> From 1955 onwards, however, I became involved in the internal struggles
> over cultural policy in the PCI.

Colletti was, almost inevitably, firmly against the May '68 movement
in Europe, a reaction as much generational as political. By 1974, when he
was interviewed by Perry Anderson, Lucio Colletti had started to turn his
back on Marxism. He had staunchly regarded dialectical materialism as
an evening-class philosophical pastiche but more seriously for Colletti, at

least in the West, by the mid-1970s it seemed that for too long Marxism
had lived on merely as an academic current in the universities, producing works of purely theoretical scope or cultural reflection. He predicted
to Perry Anderson in the 1970s that Marxism would survive merely
as the 'foible of a few university professors' (Anderson 1974: 28) and
stressed that he did not want any part of it if indeed that was the future
of Marxism, separated from the people it was meant to politically engage.
When Anderson (Anderson 1974: 25) asked him about his initial intellectual origins and entry into political life, Colletti explained how influential
Lenin on the one hand and the international political context on the other
had been:

> It was my reading of certain of Lenin's texts that was determinant for my
> adhesion to the PCI: in particular and despite all the reservations which
> it may inspire and which I share towards it today, his Materialism and
> Empirio-Criticism. At the same time, my entry into the Communist Party
> was precipitated by the outbreak of the Korean War, although this was
> accompanied by the firm conviction that it was North Korea which had
> launched an attack against the South. I say this, not in order to furbish
> myself with an a posteriori political virginity, but because it is the truth.
> My attitudes even then were of profound aversion towards Stalinism: but
> at that moment the world was rent into two, and it was necessary to choose
> one side or the other. So, although it meant doing violence to myself, I opted
> for membership of the PCI – with all the deep resistances of formation and
> culture that a petty-bourgeois intellectual of that epoch in Italy could feel
> towards Stalinism.

Colletti had no sympathy with the Eurocommunist turn in the 1970s
and saw instead the Italian Socialist Party (PSI) as the vehicle for a market
socialist solution, initially under the leadership of Bettino Craxi, to the
problems of Italian capitalism in the 1980s. After the late 1980s collapse
of Eastern European socialism, Colletti eventually settled for backing
Berlusconi, whose Forza Italia party began in December 1993. Colletti
won a safe seat for Forza Italia in the 1996 elections which Berlusconi lost.
In 2001, when Colletti died, Silvio Berlusconi in tribute praised him in an
embarrassing obituary saying he had had courage in rejecting communism
and had been a critical spirit of Forza Italia.

Lucio Colletti's distinctive contribution to Marxist theory in the 1960s
was to claim a modern scientific basis for Marxism as well as to develop
a theorised, anti-Stalinist culture within a Western Communist Party. In
France in the 1960s and 1970s another Communist Party intellectual, this
time in the Communist Party of France (PCF), namely Louis Althusser,

held sway. Ultimately, for Althusser, the condition or state we are in is one condemned to anxiety in the lonely hour of the last instance (which never seems to arrive). It is now twenty years after his death, and international capitalism is (once again, always already) in crisis, a cultural state ripe for a return of the work of Louis Althusser to the international stage, it might have been thought. A living Althusser in the present era would have been a tantalising prospect but, to an extent, his ideas lived on after his death in a more sustained fashion than Lucio Colletti's. As others, including his former students, have argued at various junctures over the last twenty years (Badiou 2009: 54–89; Balibar 2009; Althusser 2001: vii–xiv; Kaplan and Sprinker 1993), it could very well now be an appropriate time to look again at Louis Althusser's specific legacy – his contribution to the project of an anti-humanist, scientific Marxism alongside other partially discredited left public intellectuals of the twentieth century, like his one-time protagonist and colleague on the left, Lucio Colletti (Althusser 2003, 2006).

Louis Pierre Althusser was born in Birmandreis near Algiers on 16 October 1918 and died in Paris from a heart attack, aged seventy-two, on 22 October 1990. The initial twenty-seven years of his life, up until the end of the Second World War, have been recorded in the first volume of a biography in French by his friend Yann Moulier Boutang (Boutang 1992). He was the eldest son of a schoolteacher, Lucienne Berger, and a bank manager, Charles Althusser. He was brought up a Roman Catholic, a faith which pervaded and underscored many of his writings. His Masters thesis, supervised by Gaston Bachelard, was awarded at the Paris Ecole Normale Superieure in 1948. He joined the French Communist Party in 1948 and never left the PCF, although at times it might have seemed that it left him. In late 1945 he met the woman who was to be his lifelong companion and eventually, in 1976, his wife, namely Helene Legotien (nee Rytman). Althusser taught as a university academic for the subsequent forty years at the Ecole in Paris, rising to international celebrity as a Marxist theorist and left philosopher and global intellectual extraordinaire. Many contemporary theorists can claim, like Alain Badiou (Feltham 2008: 1–31) to have had 'Althusserian years', such was his influence internationally.

To the accelerated culture of twenty-first century celebrity, Althusser has become a forgotten icon of an earlier era and is regarded in posterity as a fatally flawed individual, meriting only two references in a long contemporary appreciation of France and its intellectual culture (Anderson 2009: 137–213). He strangled his wife in 1980 (Althusser 1994: 15–17) and suffered from mental illness (what today would be, professionally, referred to as bipolar disorder) for many years, following his incarceration as a prisoner of war in the Second World War. Luke Ferretter (Ferretter 2006: 2) has noted that Althusser in 1939:

> passed the entrance examination to the prestigious Ecole normale super-ieure in Paris in which university teachers are trained, but he was called up before he could begin his studies. He became a prisoner of war in June 1940. Transported to a prison camp in northern Germany, he was initially assigned to hard labour, but after falling ill, worked as a nurse in the camp infirmary. This gave him time to read widely in philosophy and literature.

Five long years in the camp in Schleswig Holstein took their toll. As renowned Althusser scholar Gregory Elliott recalled (Kaplan and Sprinkler 1993: 234) these were 'years attended by a loss of faith and the onset of a long history of depressive illness', a condition which was to last for the rest of his life, another forty-five years.

Louis Althusser, like Colletti an opponent of Eurocommunism, came to the fore in the 1960s, theorising a scientific basis for Marxism in the contemporary capitalist world, as well as creating an anti-Stalinist theo-retical cluster within the PCF. In ground-breaking books like *For Marx* (Althusser 1969) and, with Etienne Balibar, *Reading Capital* (Althusser and Balibar 1970), which have been reprinted endlessly, Louis Althusser was to propose a different, but related, scientific basis for Marxist theory from that offered by Lucio Colletti. *Pour Marx* was Althusser's French language title for his most challenging book, first published in 1965, a year when at the height of his powers he also co-wrote *Reading Capital* (Althusser and Balibar 1970). For the English translation of *Pour Marx*, Althusser spe-cifically addressed a message to his 'English Readers', written in October 1967 (Althusser 1969: 9–15). In the event it was Althusser who became far more influential in Western Marxist circles. There was no Collettiism to rival Althusserianism. Colletti was largely forgotten for decades, and remains in Althusser's trail even today. On Google Scholar internet hits Althusser wins hands down, with Colletti registering only a couple of hundred. However, by 1980 when Colletti published his last major book *Tramonto Dell'Ideologia* (Colletti 1980), Althusser, who died in 1990, was himself becoming a forgotten man, thrown onto the theoretical pyre of Marxist history as his own personal life slid into tragedy, mental illness and confinement (Althusser 1994, 2006). Della Volpe's Italian school predated Althusser and his pupils in its Marxist anti-Hegelianism and Colletti's view of Althusser was coloured by this precession. Lucio Colletti told Perry Anderson (Anderson 1974: 23) in interview conversation of a fascinating, previously unknown, history of dialogue between the two men:

I knew Althusser personally and for some years corresponded with him. Then I would fail to reply to him, or he to me, and gradually the letters between us ceased. When we first met in Italy, Althusser showed me some of the articles he later collected in *For Marx*. My initial impression on reading them was that there was a considerable convergence of positions between ourselves and Althusser. My main reservation about this convergence was that Althusser did not appear to have mastered the canons of philosophical tradition adequately. Della Volpe's discourse on Hegel was always based on a very close knowledge and analytical examination of his texts, not to speak of those of Kant, Aristotle or Plato. This dimension was much less visible in Althusser. On the contrary, it was substituted by the intromission of simplifications of a political type. For example, in these essays there would be a series of references to Mao, which appeared to be an intrusion of another sort of political discourse into the philosophical text itself. Politically, it should be added, none of the Della Volpeans had any weakness towards Maoism. At any rate, with these reservations, the articles which later made up *For Marx* seemed to show a pronounced convergence with the classical theses of the Della Volpean current in Italian marxism. Then Althusser sent me *Reading Capital*. I started to read it, and found – I say this without any irony – that I could not understand the presuppositions and purpose of the work . . . I did not find it particularly interesting as such, and did not pursue it any further.

For Louis Althusser's part, at the time he wrote *For Marx* in 1965, the works of Lucio Colletti and Galvano Della Volpe were of the 'greatest importance, because in our time they are the only scholars who have made an irreconcilable theoretical distinction between Marx and Hegel and a definition of the specificity of marxist philosophy the conscious centre of their investigations' (Althusser 1969: 37–8). A few years later when writing 'The Object of Capital' section of *Reading Capital* Althusser discussed Colletti and Della Volpe at various points but made the clear mistake of conflating Gramsci and Colletti. Essentially, Colletti's own attention to alienation and fetishism in Marx's writings, and his contention that the themes of alienation and fetishism were present in the whole of the later Marx (Anderson 1974: 3–28) in contrast to Althusser's idea of an epistemological break between the early and late (or young and old) Marx, radically separated the two scientistic Western Marxists, even if they both agreed on the pivotal importance of *Capital* and the *Grundrisse*. Lucio Colletti's insistence on his insight that the problems of alienated labour and commodity fetishism are central to the whole architecture of Marx's later work underlies the whole of his own theoretical edifice, and make his work on Marx's theory of value still pertinent in the economic meltdown of global capitalism today. Colletti, at a time when Althusser's star was still on the rise and well before Althusser's tragic decline in mental health at the end of the 1970s, viewed the celebrated French theorist as certainly a highly intelligent person but displaying an organic sympathy with Stalinism – Colletti clearly regarded Althusser's thought as having become increasingly impoverished and arid with the passage of time (Anderson 1974: 3–28).

During the 1990s in the last decade of his own life Lucio Colletti achieved political notoriety of a quite different kind, walking into the arms of the Italian right as his own, earlier contributions to forging a scientific basis (Bongiorno and Ricci 2004) for Marxist philosophy were systematically overlooked by newer theorists and their followers. One Italian language work on Lucio Colletti appeared in 2004 (Bongiorno and Ricci 2004) which has yet to be translated into English but rather surprisingly there has been no biography of Colletti's life and work as such. Such dearth of work on Colletti's biography and legacy leaves major questions about his own personal great moving right show in the 1980s and 1990s. I have suggested here that Colletti was more prescient than his fellow scholars in his rational exit from 1970s theoreticist Marxism even as he was being feted as one of the leaders of Western Marxism. But why did Colletti, a principled leftist, swing right politically as he got older? One clue to this emphatic rightward shift is his fierce anti-Catholicism which he shared with many other European Marxists of his generation (Gottfried 2005) although significantly perhaps not Louis Althusser whose own Catholic background is interwoven with his Marxism and structuralism. The disillusionment with Marxism that Colletti experienced in the 1970s never included a rapprochement with Catholicism in Italian society and his staunch anti-clerical stance persisted to the end. He had chosen Berlusconi over the Christian Democrats because of their mixing of Church and state, and had always fought against the legacy of Mussolini and the fascists in Italy, even though Berlusconi's party was widely seen as containing neo-fascist fellow travellers. There is, for those willing to be sympathetic to Colletti, evidence that before he died there had been considerable falling out with Berlusconi's party.

In the speeded up modernity and accelerated celebrity academic culture (Redhead 2004b) of the early twenty-first century, not too long after the actual death of Lucio Colletti, a Centro Lucio Colletti opened its doors. A fitting tribute to the legacy of Lucio Colletti, collecting together Colletti's books and papers and sponsoring philosophical and political events, Centro Studi Lucio Colletti is housed in a former residence of Lucio Colletti in Rome. The centre is run by Colletti's widow Dotessa Fauzia Gavioli. An exhibition on Colletti's life and work entitled 'Lucio

Colletti: Journey of a Contemporary Philosopher' (in English translation) has travelled to various European cities including Rome, Florence and Oxford. The doubts that had crept into Colletti's work in the mid–1970s as Marxism in the West became, in his own words, a 'purely cultural and academic phenomenon' and the 'foible of a few university professors' (Anderson 1974: 28), still resound amidst the attempt of today's international public intellectuals like Slavoj Žižek (Žižek 2002a, 2002b, 2008a, 2008b, 2009, 2010) to re-energise and re-examine Lenin and his theories of revolutionary violence. However, Lucio Colletti's turn away from Lenin and the choice of his own idiosyncratic personal parliamentary road ensured, unfortunately, that Colletti would not necessarily, initially, be first on the lips of the 'new' New Left in the remainder of the early decades of the twenty-first century. The credit crunch and global crash of 2008 and after, and the 'new depression' confidently predicted by some commentators to be on the global horizon (Jacques 2009a, 2009c) may, ironically, reverse this trend and revive a sustained interest in the life and work of Lucio Colletti.

CHAPTER 8

Post-Catastrophe

Bob Dylan neatly encapsulated the 'structure of feeling' of what I mean by a claustropolitan sociology project in his 'Mississippi', a song given three separate releases on one album in *Tell Tale Signs*, volume 8 of the official bootleg series in 2008: Dylan sang in one version – 'Every step of the way, We walk the line, Your days are numbered, So are mine, Time is pilin' up, We struggle and we scrape, We're all boxed in, Nowhere to escape'. In John Armitage's stimulating article in the West Coast art and politics journal *Left Curve* (Armitage 2006) he proposed a dichotomy between 'cosmopolis or chaosmopolis' when looking at the sociology of the contemporary city. Taking this argument about the breakdown in what I call in this book 'mobile city cultures' further, I want to consider some more possibilities of a claustropolitan, as opposed to cosmopolitan, sociology. I look at how this might help us track 'the trajectories of the catastrophic', an enterprise which heavily involves a further investigation of the stimulating but contradictory work of Paul Virilio amongst other theorists. Claustropolitanism and claustropolitan sociology in my view is not only a potential alternative to the influential thinking of 'cosmopolitan sociology' (of Ulrich Beck, Zygmunt Bauman, John Urry, Anthony Giddens and others). It is, most certainly, a sociology of claustropolis not cosmopolis. But it also points to how social theory might be done now, a social theory from within the claustropolis – a reflection of how it is to live within the accelerated, 'shrunken' world, if even part of Paul Virilio's 'escape velocity' vision is to be fully utilised. A reconstructed theoretical social and human sciences project, which a claustropolitan sociology may comprise, is also part of a more general methodological 'turn' to what I see as a 'bunker anthropology' (Redhead 2009) to reconceptualise and research more adequately, as one recent academic conference call for papers put it, the socio-technologies of connection, resilience, mobility and collapse in contemporary cities. For Tariq Ali these are 'scoundrel' times (Virilio 2005a, 2005b, 2005c, 2005d, 2007b, 2009b, 2010b; Armitage 2005; Thrift 2005; Conley 2005; Kureishi 2005; Ali 2005), coming after the 9/11 events in New York and at the Pentagon (Griffin 2008a and b, 2009, 2010), the London Bombings of and 7/7 and 21/7 (Ahmed 2006; O'Neill and McGrory 2006), the Mumbai and Lahore tragedies and the effects of the long economic 'crash' of 2007–8. Economists have conceived of the 'post-catastophe economy' (Janszen 2010) in 'how to' business oriented books on rebuilding the American economy and 'avoiding the next bubble'. Nine individuals arrested in France in 2008 calling themselves the Invisible Committee (Invisible Committee 2009) proclaimed in a pre-trial pamphlet that 'it's useless to wait – for a breakthrough, for the revolution, the nuclear apocalypse or a social movement. To go on waiting is madness. The catastrophe is not coming, it is here'. Post-catastrophe, post-apocalypse, begins here, but as Eric Hobsbawm (Hobsbawm 2011) has remembered the 'age of catastrophe' from 1914 to 1945 has been with us before. Network failure and system breakdown are increasingly widespread, and increasingly cyclical. Instead of Leon Trotsky's permanent revolution there is the prospect of permanent catastrophe, speeding up in its periods of crisis. Instead of John Reed's 'ten days that shook the world' at the time of the Russian revolution in 1917, by the time the 'world at 2000' (Halliday 2001) was upon us, accelerated culture created a 'September 11, 2001' speed accident that as Fred Halliday has noted produced 'two hours that shook the world' (Halliday 2002).

Paul Virilio is mainly responsible for the contemporary idea of 'claustropolis'. He has characterised this process as part of a 'war on the cities'. Virilio has been theorising war and the city as long as he can remember, but essentially since 1958. He has most recently argued (Virilio and Lotringer 2008) that the nature of deterrence has drastically changed and classical war has failed. For Virilio war is no longer aimed at the military, but at the population. As Sylvere Lotringer has noted in conversation with Virilio, the city has become the new battlefield (Virilio and Lotringer 2008), one example of his theory of the 'accident' – the network failure or collapse or catastrophe or breakdown in accelerated culture. Virilio's theory of the accident is relatively little known and even less discussed. It is becoming, though, more recognised, and even reconceptualised as 'accidentology' whatever Virilio's own frustrations with the speed of its development (Virilio 2007b). He is also a figure whose oeuvre has been generally imported into the English speaking academic world as just another, albeit quirky, complementary element in social and political theory (Armitage 2000, 2001; Der Derian 1998; James 2007a, 2007b) following on from other French theorists such as Jean Baudrillard, Jacques

Derrida, Gilles Deleuze and Michel Foucault. In fact, Virilio's consistent influences over the years have been photography, Maurice Merleau-Ponty's phenomenology, Gestalt psychology, stained glass painting and anarchistic Christianity, a very different intellectual background from the poststructuralists and postmodernists with whom he is often misleadingly bracketed. Paul Virilio is for sure no postmodernist even though he has written of the 'postmodern period' and the 'atheism of postmodernity' as well as the 'profane art of modernity' in one of his books, *Art as Far as the Eye can See* (Virilio 2007a). Alan Sokal and Jean Bricmont (Sokal and Bricmont 2003), in their ill-conceived 'expose' of the supposed scientific inadequacies of 'French postmodernism' and 'poststructuralism', subject Paul Virilio to withering attack (the Virilio chapter is Chapter 10 in the second English edition) alongside Jacques Lacan, Julia Kristeva, Bruno Latour and Felix Guattari amongst many others. Unfortunately for Sokal and Bricmont's project, Paul Virilio has little in common with such figures other than nationality or (formerly) Parisian residence. His theory of the accident (Virilio 2007b) involves what I have elsewhere called an aesthetics of the accident, or in his own words an 'art as far as the eye can see' (Virilio 2007a). Virilio, however, in providing a perspective on the art of the accident in our increasingly accelerated and dangerous modernities (Redhead 2004b), falls short of what is required in the contemporary claustropolitan sociological project. What is required, more generally, is in fact a reinvigorated sociology, not merely an art, of the accident, but, still, Virilio's work remains a part of the routemap. Furthermore, in search in this book for resources for this claustropolitan sociology of the accident I argue for a move firmly towards seeking out the trajectories of the catastrophic, or what Virilio has labelled 'claustropolis', which in his view has replaced cosmopolis. Paul Virilio (Virilio 2007b: 68) poses the question with characteristic aplomb:

> CLAUSTROPOLIS or COSMOPOLIS? A society of enforced seclusion, as once upon a time, or a society of forcible control? Actually, the dilemma itself seems illusory, within the temporal compression of instantaneity and the ubiquity of the age of the information revolution. This interactive society is one in which real time overrules the real space of geostrategy, promoting a 'metrostrategy' in which the city is less the centre of a territory, a 'national space', than the centre of time, of this global and astronomical time that makes every city the resonating chamber of the most incredibly diverse events (breakdowns, major accidents, terrorist outrages etc).

In this scenario we have all to some extent or other become historians of Virilio's instant present where immediacy, instantaneity and ubiquity rule. For Virilio it was with globalisation, through the ubiquitous 'new technologies', that we began to inhabit a world that is 'foreclosed', eerily pertinent in the years of massive foreclosure in the global domestic housing markets, especially in the USA.

For Virilio the globe we inhabit is actually a 'world closed off and closed in'. For him 'the major accident is the Medusa of modernity' (Virilio and Lotringer 2005: 102). He has come to this most recent vision over many years of foraging in the debris of accelerated culture.

Virilio is now in his eighth decade. He was born in France in 1932 of an (illegal immigrant) Italian father and French Catholic mother. He experienced the Second World War first hand. He was sent to his maternal grandparents in Nantes in 1943 when he was ten years old – American and English bombing devastated the city while he was there. He has said that the bombardment was his 'university of disaster' (Virilio and Lotringer 2008: 220). He retired in the late 1990s from his only academic position as Professor of Architecture at the Ecole Speciale d'Architecture in Paris, a post he had held since the late 1960s, after being elected by the students in the wake of the events of 'May 68'. On retirement he was nominated emeritus professor. Armed with his senior citizen card he moved from Paris to La Rochelle on the Atlantic coast of France, a considerable upheaval for someone like Virilio who has long suffered from claustrophobia, has virtually given up driving a car and watching TV and rarely travels outside of his region.

Popular culture music writer Simon Reynolds (Reynolds 2008: 124) has forensically identified 'speed, in the vehicular sense' as 'the central concept in Virilio's thought'. Moreover, Reynolds argues, 'you could just as easily read "speed" in his books like *The Aesthetics of Disappearance* (Virilio 2009c) as referring to both amphetamine and to 'ardkore's ever-escalating tempos'. As Virilio has written, the interest is always in 'speed and stuff' (Virilio and Lotringer 2005). Virilio has described his own role as a 'dromologist', but the idea of the overriding and determining factor of speed for society actually was quite short lived in his work. The notion of a global 'dromocratic condition' comes, from Virilio in a select few, but reasonably well known, writings from the 1970s. The 'society of speed' that this work analysed, was never actually part of a fully formed conceptual apparatus and Virilio soon moved on to other topics and ideas in the maelstrom of the neo-liberal world order of the 1980s and 1990s. The 'accident' was one of them. Initially, he has recalled, theoretical interest in the accident was triggered by an article he wrote (called 'The Original Accident') in 1979 for *Liberation* in France about the Three Mile Island 'accident' in Harrisburg in the USA. The idea of the theory of the accident on the other hand, though full of problems, is a more sustained part of his recent oeuvre and has been in thorough-going genesis since at least the early 1990s as Virilio has continued to accelerate his output of rapid, short books and distinctive, idiosyncratic interviews (Virilio with Petit 1999; Armitage 2001; Virilio and Lotringer 2002, 2008). In this period, for Virilio, 'the world is more and more closed and more and more contracted' (Virilio and Lotringer 2005: 87) and 'claustropolitanism' becomes more and more a spectre on the horizon.

In Virilio's view there have been three distinct eras in the last two centuries characterised by war (in the late nineteenth and early twentieth centuries), revolution (in the twentieth century) and (now) the accident. Virilio asserts that 'the accident has replaced both war and revolution' (Virilio and Lotringer 2005: 82). The eras still overlap of course.

Paul Virilio eventually left his post in academia to write a long planned book (Virilio 2007b) on 'the accident'. The eventual book (published as *L'Accident originel* in 2005 in France) was billed by the English publisher as a 'meditation on technoscientific Progress' and a contemplation of a:

> future overshadowed by the nightmare of an outmoded humanity over-whelmed by a catastrophe of its own making, a kind of catastrophic grand finale that would mirror the original accident, the Big Bang, that some scientists believed created the universe.

Crucially, the same phenomena of speed, accident and war are different today in Virilio's view from what they were when he first started writing about them in any sustained manner in the 1970s and 1980s. He has contemplated this change in a virtual conversation with interviewer Carlos Oliveira in the mid-1990s where he related the issue of the contemporary situation to the general arguments he had been making for a decade or more about the consequences of what he has variously termed 'accelerated temporality' and the 'acceleration of our daily lives' (Virilio 1996a):

> This is because we are witnessing a radical break; it is not my thinking that has become radical, the situation itself has radicalised beyond measure. The end of the bloc-oriented confrontation between East and West, the transition from the industrial to the INFORMATIONAL mode of production, the globalisation that is being achieved through the telecommunication networks and the information (super)highways – all these developments raise grave questions.

For Virilio the 'grave questions' are increasingly explored through the notion of the accident in his writings during the 1990s and 2000s.

The term accident, though, in Virilio's use and specialised terminology, is a complicated and ambiguous notion initially used in the writings of Aristotle. Here, as frequently happens elsewhere in Virilio's original French language writing and speaking, the English translation oversimplifies by connoting merely a catastrophic event rather than the deeper philosophical reference to accident and substance and the phenomenological (James 2007a, 2007b) and existentialist debates Virilio inherited from those he listened to (Maurice Merleau-Ponty, Vladimir Jankelevitch and Jean Wahl) as a student at the university of the Sorbonne in Paris in the early 1960s. Virilio, for his part, has emphasised that (Virilio with Petit 1999: 92–3):

> For the philosopher substance is absolute and necessary, whereas the accident is relative and contingent. So the accident is what happens unexpectedly to the substance, the product or the recently invented technical object. It is for example the original accident of the Challenger space shuttle ten years ago. It is the duty of scientists and technicians to avoid the accident at all costs . . . In fact, if no substance can exist in the absence of an accident, then no technical object can be developed without in turn generating 'its' specific accident: ship=ship wreck, train=train wreck, plane=plane crash, etc. The accident is thus the hidden face of technical progress . . . one thing that must be considered here is the preponderance and role of the speed of the accident, thus the limitation of speed and the penalties for 'exceeding the speed limit'.

The nature of the accident, according to Virilio (Virilio 1996) has changed, and changed speed and everything else in its wake:

> The information revolution which we are currently witnessing ushers in the era of the global accident. The old kind of accidents were localised in space and time: a train derailment took place, say, in Paris or in Berlin; and when a plane crashed, it did so in London or wherever in the world. The catastrophes of earlier time were situated in real space, but now, with the advent of absolute speed of light and electromagnetic waves, the possibility of a global accident has arisen, of an accident that would occur simultaneously to the world as a whole.

Despite the fact that the information revolution has not had a great deal of effect on Virilio himself – he uses the internet only rarely – he has said that he does regard cyberspace as a new form of perspective. Our world is a 'cybermonde' according to Paul Virilio. Especially through cyberspace, for Virilio, history has hit the wall of world-wide time where with live transmission, local time no longer creates history, where, in his view, real

time conquers real space, producing what he calls a time accident, which
he sees as an accident with no equal. According to Virilio (Virilio 1996)
speeding up has meant reaching the limit of speed, that of real time:

> A possible symptom of this globalisation, of the eventuality of such an acci-
> dent, was the stock exchange crash of 1987. We will no longer live in local
> time as we did in the past when we were prisoners of history. We will live
> in world time, in global time. We are experiencing an epoch that spells the
> international, the global accident. This is the way I interpret simultane-
> ity and its imposition upon us, as well as the immediacy and the ubiquity,
> that is, the omnipresence of the information bomb, which at the moment,
> thanks to the information (super)highways and all the technological break-
> throughs and developments in the field of telecommunication, is just about
> to explode.

For Virilio, what took place on 'September 11, 2001' (Chomsky 2001)
was an 'accident and emblematic of the current disorder' (Virilio and
Lotringer 2005: 104).

The 9/11 events, and the critique of the 'official version' put out by
the US government in particular, now has an extensive literature. The
term '9/11' has become code for all kinds of discourse about terrorism,
tradition and modernity (Gray 2003, Ridgeway 2005, Griffin 2005, 2010).
Lawrence Wright writes of 'Al Qaeda's "road to 9/11"' (Wright 2006).
The 9/11 events in New York and Washington have been seen by Virilio
as an explicit example of his theory of the 'accident of accidents', a generalised accident occurring everywhere at the same time, live on global
television and the internet. In Virilio's words 'the live broadcast is the
catastrophe of time' (Virilio and Lotringer 2005: 109). Unlike his long
time friend Jean Baudrillard (Baudrillard 2004b) Virilio makes no reference at all to the myriad suggestions that 9/11 was 'allowed' to happen
by the authorities, or, even, that it was an 'inside job'. He seems in his
writings and interviews to accept the official version of the 9/11 events to
all intents and purposes. He says, for instance, about 9/11 that 'unlike the
first attack against the World Trade Center, there was no missile, no bom-
bardier, no explosions' (Virilio and Lotringer 2005: 104). The cover of the
English edition of his book *The Original Accident* (Virilio 2007b) carried a
photograph of the local effect of the WTC complex collapse. He admitted
to Sylvere Lotringer (Virilio and Lotringer 2002) shortly after the attacks
on New York and Washington that 'the door is open' for what he called
'the great attack' and furthermore that he saw New York as 'what Sarajevo
was' when 'Sarajevo triggered the First World War'. On September 11,
2001, Virilio's earlier prophecy in his work of the 1990s about a generalised

accident or total accident seemingly came tragically true as what he saw as an attack by a small, tightly knit group of men, armed only with Stanley knives, who took over the cockpits of the hijacked planes and flew jet airliners with masses of fuel into the highly populated buildings of the World Trade Center with the loss of nearly 3,000 lives and the destruction of several buildings (including the twin towers of the WTC and WTC 7) in the heart of the financial centre of American (and arguably world) capitalism. These near 3,000 deaths, Virilio has noted, were 'more than Pearl Harbour', the 1941 catastrophe (Virilio and Lotringer 2005: 104). The beginning of this post-Cold War age of imbalance as Virilio has called it, was, as he said at the time of the first 1993 attack on the twin towers (after which, rather bizarrely, he was called on as a consultant) seen in a new form of warfare – the accident of accidents, or the 'Great Accident'. The 1993 attack was precipitous for Virilio (Virilio 2000: 18):

> In the manner of a massive aerial bombardment, this single bomb, made of several hundred kilos of explosives placed at the building's very foundations, could have caused the collapse of a tower four hundred metres high. So it is not a simple remake of the film Towering Inferno, as the age-conscious media like to keep saying, but much more of a strategic event confirming for us all The Change In The Military Order Of This Fin-De-Siecle. As the bombs of Hiroshima and Nagasaki, in their day, signalled a new era for war, the explosive van in New York illustrates the mutation of terrorism.

Virilio noted at the time of the 1993 World Trade Center attack by another small group of terrorists that the perpetrators of such acts 'are determined not merely to settle the argument with guns' but will 'try to devastate the major cities of the world marketplace' (Virilio 2000). Within eight years a slightly larger group had apparently done so (Ruthven 2002; Wright 2006). Many of the features of what Virilio sets out in a contemporaneous essay on the 1993 World Trade Center attack (Virilio 2000) as being on the cards for the future of humanity, were to be put into practice September 11 2001 with exactly the predicted effect of the devastation of a world city. In fact, ironically, 'Towering Inferno' images probably were rife in the minds of many of the watchers of the 9/11 'accident'. In Virilio's own book length musings after September 2001, implicitly about the 9/11 attack, entitled *Ground Zero* (Virilio 2002), he explicitly claimed that as the September 11 twin towers attack was being 'broadcast live many TV viewers believed they were watching one of those disaster movies that proliferate endlessly on our TV screens' and that it was only 'by switching channels and finding the same pictures on all the stations that they finally understood that it was true'. For Virilio, 'overexposure is the live broadcast, it is real time replacing the past, present and future' (Virilio and Lotringer 2005: 109). Aesthetically 9/11 was taken as an 'art of terrorism' in some quarters. Virilio has quoted the avant-garde electronic composer Karlheinz Stockhausen as saying it was 'the greatest work of art there has ever been' (Virilio 2002), though he has also, subsequently, quoted correspondence with the theorist Peter Sloterdijk as evidence for Stockhausen never having said any such thing (Virilio and Dumoucel 2010). Seemingly unknown to Virilio, the Brit-artist Damien Hirst, too, claimed, in the British media, that those responsible for September 11 should indeed be congratulated because they achieved 'something which nobody would ever have thought possible' on an artistic level. The event was in Damien Hirst's view 'kind of like an artwork in its own right . . . wicked, but it was devised in this way for this kind of impact' and 'was devised visually' (quoted in *The Guardian*, 20 September 2001).

The events in Mumbai, India of November 2008 where 173 died and 600 were injured in co-ordinated gun attacks was described globally in the 24/7 news media as 'Mumbai's 9/11'. The crash of 2008 has been dubbed an 'economic 9/11' and '9/11' has become a major global signifier for catastrophe as well as being code for 'untruth' in many of the writings of the 9/11 movements which question the official discourse of governments (Marrs 2006; Griffin 2004, 2007, 2008a, 2008b, 2009, 2010; Griffin and Scott 2007) and point to the emergence since the 1960s of a 'parapolitics' and the 'government of the shadows' (Wilson 2009a, 2009b). The attack on the Sri Lanka cricket team bus in Lahore in March 2009 in which six policemen were killed and six players wounded, confirmed analyses that had described the current condition in the region of Pakistan, Afghanistan and Central Asia as a 'descent into chaos' (Rashid 2008). The attack on the Togo football team bus in Angola at the beginning of the African Cup of Nations tournament in 2010 emphasised for many media outlets the claustropolitan nature of war-torn central African states. The Mumbai attacks were reported to be watched and checked on by the attackers themselves even as they kidnapped, murdered and opened fire. The BlackBerries and mobile phones recovered after their own deaths at the hands of Indian security forces were evidence that the attackers had checked into global 24/7 news channels as the 'live' event was unfolding to monitor how the news media were covering it. Twitter, the real time website with many million members worldwide which elicits rapid response to the question 'what are you doing?' via fewer than 140 characters, was hyperactive during the Mumbai events. It is remarkably fitted for disasters and accidents. Earthquakes, floods or wind storms, or any kind of event happening in real time, induce massive 'twitterfeed'. People use the service to communicate quickly with several contacts at once, or catch breaking news, or network with people they would like to meet, or pass on information or important phone numbers, or simply 'feel' part of a major event. This shared real time communications network aspect is what is crucial. Mobile phone and fixed line phone networks tend to go down when they are most needed. On Twitter people send messages online or via SMS which needs only the weakest of signals to get through. Massive use was made of the service during the Mumbai events.

The National Commission on Terrorist Attacks upon the United States, more widely known as the 9/11 Commission (Henshall 2007; Morgan 2006; Griffin 2007, 2008a and b, 2010), set up by Public Law 07–36 on 27 November 2002, pointed out in its final report that Osama Bin Laden's appeal was partly to people 'disoriented by cyclonic change as they confront modernity and globalisation' (National Commission 2004: 48; Griffin 2007). For John Gray (Gray 2003) the September 11 attacks went as far as to pose the question: what does it mean to be modern? Gray (2003: 1) has posed this precise question explicitly in the title of his sharply drawn short book on Al Qaeda:

> The suicide warriors who attacked Washington and New York on September 11, 2001, did more than kill thousands of civilians and demolish the World Trade Center. They destroyed the West's ruling myth.

Jason Burke has contended that figures like Osama Bin Laden, dead or alive (Griffin 2009) 'aimed not to turn the clock back, which they knew impossible, but to create a contemporary world, a modernity, that was more to their liking and more on their terms' (Burke 2006: 64–5). The activities of groups like Al-Qaeda and the carnage they have spawned, especially in the wake of the events of September 11 did more than just create havoc in dozens of murderous incidents across the globe and huge expansion in 'homeland security' all around the world. They have become part of a new global discourse, a new media, publishing and marketing category of 'modern terror'. Suddenly in the early twenty- first century, bookshops all over the world and carriers like amazon.com started carrying huge numbers of books on previously apparently 'unknown', unresearched areas of the world like Afghanistan (Burke 2006) and Iraq (Cockburn 2006, 2008) and on previously mysterious biographical details of figures such as Osama Bin Laden, Muqtada Al-Sadr and Ramzi Yousef. A mass of books on the rise of Islamic fundamentalism, Al Qaeda and September 11 have now been published. There are a number that are extremely well researched and contribute significantly to the task in hand, of retheorising modernity. They are also amongst the books cited by the National Commission on Terrorist Attacks upon The United States (The 9/11 Commission).

They have in doing so reawakened crucial questions of how we might come to theorise modernity, or better still 'modernities', in the twenty-first century. This new situation has also forced a rethinking of 'war and politics' more generally and the social and legal theory of state formation needed to capture its rapidly changing complexities. 'This is politics not war' proclaimed a T-shirt, produced in Bangkok, depicting Osama Bin Laden, George W. Bush and the World Trade Center in New York. Although aspects of the work surrounding the art of the accident might be instructive, what is needed in my view in future theoretical developments in the social and human sciences is a move towards a claustropolitan sociology of the accident. Virilio thinks this is also an accident of knowledge. For Benjamin Bratton 'there is also an accident contained in theoretical technologies, and in the absorption of Virilio's theory by the institutional positions it seems to criticise so fiercely. "I am studied in military academies" he tells Sylvere Lotringer in Pure War, and indeed he is' (Bratton 2006: 21). For Virilio one of the problems of the highly mediatised modernities we inhabit today is that 'attack' and 'accident' are increasingly indistinguishable. We are unsure whether we are experiencing (terrorist) attack or system or network failure when we regularly consume news of events in the media, especially since the watershed events of 9/11 and the subsequent 'war on terror', itself a kind of mediatised never ending 'live' Fourth World War. The SARS crisis in China, Hong Kong and Canada, BSE scares in North America, train crashes in North Korea, plane crashes in the Middle East and electricity power failures in the USA, UK, Australia and mainland Europe, to take some recent random examples, are cases where an initial denial of terrorist attack shifts the 'blame' to technical failure of systems (in other words a 'real' accident) in such a way that the event is played down. It is only an accident proclaims the news anchor after a few days hype, and therefore everyone can breathe a sigh of relief. What is actually needed is a concentration on the systems and the failure. September 11, for instance, could be seen as as much an instance of systems failure as 'attack', a kind of new Pearl Harbor where the authorities allowed the 'attack' to happen (Griffin 2004, 2007, 2010): failure of intelligence (CIA, FBI), governance (failure to act earlier against Al Qaeda), security (airport, airline), transport (aircraft), military (patrolling of skies) and so on. Accident, along with elements of its philosophical make up as envisaged by Virilio, may be one of the concepts necessary to understand better the modernities and mobile city cultures of the

twenty-first century globe. But the social science in which the sociology of
the accident is urgently necessary is itself a reconstructed urban sociological project; a sociology as John Urry has put it 'beyond societies' (Urry
2000). We need, instead, a new sociology of mobilities, of what we might
call the mobility of modernities around the globe, especially of mobile
city cultures. In a world of mobile city cultures the 'city is already there'
(Virilio 2005a: 5) echoing Virilio's 'mental map' view of his own city,
Paris. As Virilio puts it, 'Paris is portable' (Virilio 2005a: 5). After 9/11,
too, Virilio claims that 'the tower has been motorised' and the 'very high
building has become mobile' (Virilio 2005a: 18) in what he calls 'towerism'
or the 'avant-garde of modernity' (Virilio and Lotringer 2008: 211) while
Lotringer, in conversation with Virilio, asserts that 'towers are bunkers'
(Virilio and Lotringer 2008: 211).

John Urry has rightly argued (Urry 2003) that in contemporary sociology the 'global' has been insufficiently theorised, especially when there
are so many different types of 'capitalisms' (Gray 2009b) in play around
the globe at any one time. Urry, like Zygmunt Bauman, mentions Virilio
occasionally in some of his writing (Urry 2000) but in general cosmopolitan sociology has rarely explored what Virilio has to offer in any sustained
way. One of the contributions Virilio has made more generally to thinking
about modernities is to raise questions about the shrinking of time and
space and the effect of the war induced technologies on the speeding up
of that process; in other words to thinking about the global anew. Virilio's
development of the philosophical idea of the 'accident of accidents' (and
it is the ancient notion that 'time is the accident of accidents' that Virilio
is fond of quoting) is one way of rethinking the global, specifying as he
does that it is the new communications technologies that have created the
possibility of an accident that is no longer local but global; in other words,
that would occur everywhere at the same time. Virilio has stressed that
'time is the accident of accidents' and that 'we have reached the speed
of light with e-mail, interactivity and telework' and that is why 'we are
creating a similar accident' (Virilio with Petit 1999). An event such as 9/
11, eliding accident and attack, was an example of a world wide accident
because it was being screened live as it happened in real time all around the
globe. That said, the theorising of the accident by Virilio, though sugges-
tive and (in his own phrase which he likes to use to describe his personal
intellectual method and enterprise) 'implicit', is often at such a level of
generality that it is not particularly helpful for a rigorous claustropolitan
sociology of the accident. Though Virilio's language sometimes appears
to import what John Urry describes as the 'new physics' (Urry 2003) into
the equation of shrinking time and space, there is relatively little evidence

of Virilio in actuality standing at the cutting edge of these contemporary breakthroughs in science. As other social theorists claim, it is better to view his work, alongside comparable theorists such as Jean Baudrillard, as a 'poetics' (Cubitt 2001) not a form of physics. John Urry argues cogently that the social science enterprise of the twenty-first century which seeks to recruit the thinking of chaos and complexity from 'natural' sciences needs to conceive of systems that are always combining success and failure and are constantly on the edge of chaos. One of the reasons why the 'intellectual impostures' project of the physics pranksters Alan Sokal and Jean Bricmont (Sokal and Bricmont 2003) attacking Virilio and others is so ill judged is that it has not caught up with the 'complexity' of science today, never mind the contemporary complexity of theory in the human and social sciences. These systems that John Urry talks about are systems where Virilio's idea of the accident, a kind of built in component of the constant invention of new technologies, is integral.

What can be said then, of a positive nature, about Virilio's contribution to a theory of the accident, catastrophe, network failure or breakdown in today's mobile city cultures? First, it is important to take Virilio's self-labelling seriously. He is by his own consistent admission a 'phenomenologist', an 'Husserlian' (Virilio and Lotringer 2008) and 'a critic of the art of technology', and an overview of his life and career leave us in no doubt (Redhead 2004a, 2004b, 2009) that he is an 'artist' rather than a social theorist in any conventional sense. He is a high modernist, without connection to the postmodernist and post-structuralist social theorists with whom he is routinely categorised and compared. He is also an avowed Christian who 'does not believe in death' (Virilio and Lotringer 2008: 234). Second, Virilio has had in mind for many years the development of what he calls a 'museum of accidents' to further aesthetically display his theory of the accident. He has argued (Virilio 2007b) for the creation of a Museum of the Accident to fight our habituation to horror and violence, and our daily overexposure to terror. In a sense Virilio is closer to Damien Hirst and Karlheinz Stockhausen when they take the controversial view that an event like 9/11 is an aesthetic question. They are all involved, from different perspectives, in the enterprise of the art of the accident. They are artists rather than social theorists.

The links between 'new media' (computer games, information technology, the internet, the web and so on) and the events of accident/attack that Virilio has analysed (both the 1993 and 2001 World Trade Center catastrophes, for instance) are obviously of interest to students of Virilio given his idiosyncratic focus on the relationships between war, cinema and photography (Redhead 2004b). However the significance of 9/11 in assessing

Virilio's notion of the accident is more complicated than it might appear. For Virilio, unlike other French theorists such as Gilles Deleuze (Deleuze 2006), the cultural forms of cinema and television actually have nothing in common. Paul Virilio actually has a little more to say about 9/11 and its effects on urban culture in later work (Virilio 2005a; Virilio and Lotringer 2002, 2008) but makes no reference to the increasingly available critical literature on the official discourse on 9/11 (Griffin 2004, 2005, 2008a, 2008b, 2009, 2010; Marrs 2006). Paul Virilio has taught us that in the 'crepuscular dawn' of our twenty-first century modernities the attack and the accident are becoming indistinguishable. The 'art of the accident', or what has also elsewhere been termed 'apocalyptic art', is one credible response to this dilemma. However, Virilio asserts that 'this is not the apocalpyse' (Virilio and Lotringer 2005) and such aesthetic practice, a deconstructive play on the distinction between attack and accident, is certainly not sufficient to help us to theorise the new modernities that are catching up with the various new and old capitalisms on offer around the globe. It leaves us, strangely, exhibiting a kind of ghoulish fascination with the effects of the failure of systems; 'rubber necking' at the art gallery and the accident museum or tuning in with compassionless glee to the reports in the media of the latest road crash statistics, a state of mind where (Baudrillard 2004a: 61) 'what people watch above all on TV are the weekend's road accident figures, the catastrophes'. Compare the similar fascination exhibited in the twentieth century by a distinctly unpalatable 'war studies' thinker like Ernst Junger who Paul Virilio has sometimes quoted and cited (Virilio 2005a: 143; Virilio and Lotringer 2008: 112, 218). In Virilio's own words (Virilio and Lotringer 2005: 88):

> When you invent a concept, an art, a sculpture, a film that is truly revolutionary, or when you sail the first ship, fly the first plane or launch the first space capsule, you invent the crash. So it's not simply a footnote on the 'Six O'Clock News' when they show the Concord catastrophe, it's a phenomenon happening every moment.

However, even if this aesthetics of the accident is a necessary condition, it is certainly not sufficient. The claustropolitan sociology of the accident, in my view, needs to take into account thinking around the art of the accident but also fundamentally needs to move beyond it.

CHAPTER 9

Post-Theory

This book as a whole considers the possibilities of an alternative to the direction in social and political theory carved out by cosmopolitan sociology. Cosmopolitan sociology has become a dominant theoretical and methodological discourse in the twenty-first century since the postmodern turn of the 1980s and 1990s but has now run its course. I have looked at some aspects of the always problematic work of the French theorists Paul Virilio and Jean Baudrillard, and suggested some alternative directions for reconceptualisation of modernity and postmodernity, and the features of the accident, collapse and catastrophe today, which go beyond the established discourse of cosmopolitan sociology. I propose here some outline elements of post- theory which would perhaps better capture the stories of our times as a basis for a different agenda from that of cosmopolitan sociology.

The critical question has already been raised: do we need new thinking for social, political and cultural theory *after* the crash? The alternative may be that we simply revive the social and cultural thinkers, and thought, of the past? For some commentators (Rutherford and Chakraborty 2010) the 'era of runaway financial markets is over' and the 'collapse of Lehman Brothers and Royal Bank of Scotland (RBS) marks a progressive moment'. Is this, at last, the denoument for what Perry Anderson (Anderson 2005: 3–28) calls 'the intransigent right' comprising the likes of twentieth-century thinkers such as Michael Oakeshott, Leo Strauss, Carl Schmitt and Friedrich Von Hayek? Will, instead, therefore, Karl Marx, or Louis Althusser, or Nicos Poulantzas (Martin 2008), or Lucio Colletti, armed with their scientific materialist anti-humanism, or the proponents of a sustainable Marxism after post-Marxism (Therborn 2008), suddenly become fashionable again as we hurtle back to the conditions of the 1930s in what has been described by Martin Jacques amongst others as a full blown 'new depression' (Jacques 2009a)? Certainly Marx's idea of the 'double freedom' of the worker in capitalism has never been more relevant – that is, the freedom to sell one's labour power to the highest bidder but *only* to have that labour power to sell. Credit agencies such as Moody's, S and P's and Fitch are now able to decide the fate of formerly sovierign nations, not just economically 'unstable' corporations (Kettle 2010). Hundreds of cities are predicted to 'go bust as the debt crisis that has taken down banks and countries threatens next to spark an urban catastrophe' (Moya 2010). The economic crash can be dated at 9/15, or September 15, 2008, the precise date of the Lehman Brothers investment bank collapse. The 'economic 9/11' is how Nick Clegg the leader of the Liberal Democrats in the UK described the spectacular financial collapse at the culmination of the year long global credit crunch occurring on the world's stock markets between August 2007 and October 2008. There is to be sure a sense of a 'new era' on the horizon, a shift in the fault lines of modernity, which has been around since at least the 1980s and 1990s.

Logistics of catastrophe and trajectories of collapse seem pervasive, and the search for saviours has been accelerating for some time.Vince Cable (Cable 2009) secretary of state for business in the Conservative-Liberal Democrat coalition government in the UK has been described in England as 'the undisputed heavyweight champion of the credit crunch in parliament' in the era of 'the crash'. For some social and economic commentators the times are indeed a sign of a 'new depression', 'entirely new, tumultuous and dangerous' (Jacques 2009b). Now we are, almost overnight, said to be, variously, living in world that is 'post-American', 'post-liberal', 'post-new liberal', 'post-modern' and 'post-free market' – even 'after capitalism' (Mulgan 2009). Belief in 'Markets' has been described as a faith in 'Gods that Failed' (Atkinson and Elliot 2009). There are other commentators on the social democratic left (Cruddas and Rutherford 2009) who, while trumpeting that the end of the neo-liberal era is nigh, and that the world requires a 'new socialism', argue that we are in a new conjuncture and that reregulated capitalism will have widespread cultural and social effects and consequences for progressive politics. On the other hand, Red Toryism (Blond 2009a and b) sees opportunities for the right to politicise the ongoing crisis in favour of a new civic conservatism, reviving localism and promoting the distributist state. The bigger picture, however, is actually of 'collapse'; as former Conservative partisan and friend of the Tories (Gray and Willetts 1997) John Gray (Gray 2009c: 14) has put it, '[W]e're in the first phase of the collapse of this type of globalisation, or this phase of globalisation, which will have some features in common with the Thirties but will be different in lots of ways.' Moreover, according to some optimistic commentators, we may have to 'go through a global recession before the digital age truly takes off', before there is a 'sustained, technology driven-upturn' (Mason 2009: vii). Globalisation in this sense has all kinds of effects. For example, one instamce of mobile city cultures is that after the Mumbai and Lahore attacks on the sub-continent in late 2008 and early 2009 the global media-driven cricket corporation the Indian Premier League (IPL) relocated the 2009 Twenty20 cricket tournament to South Africa, effectively transporting the eight city cultures around the Delhi, Mumbai, Chennai and other Indian city based teams to South African cities instead. Effectively, the IPL could be held anywhere in the world in the future. The World Cup in soccer in 2022 will take place in Qatar, an emirate with a population of 1.7 million people featuring new stadia to be constructed over the next few years armed with air conditioning technology to combat the extreme summer heat.

The trajectories of collapse are, in my argument, what will constitute the 'new era'. Does all this mean we need a new theory of 'the state we're in' (Hutton 1995, 1997, 2002, 2010) now to make sense of it all? It is most certainly cosmopolitan sociology that has dominated the agenda over the last decade. Cosmopolitan sociology has, oddly, given its left-leaning politics, been the theoretical concomitant of the neo-liberal era. But it is in my view claustropolitanism that is now pervasive. Any new thinking needs to include claustropolitan perspectives as well as cosmopolitan. After the economic deluge, claustropolitanism, too, has the potential to be the new big idea in the social sciences and humanities worldwide over the coming years. In this sense Jean Baudrillard and Paul Virilio remain the most significant theorists of catastrophe, as they have, in certain circles, for the past twenty or thirty years.

Paul Virilio, the French urban theorist of speed and catastrophe, is responsible (Virilio 2007b: 68) for the development of the idea of 'claustropolis' (which in his thinking has replaced cosmopolis). Dromomania is Virilio's term for those obsessed with speed and a society where everyone has to keep moving and accelerating – a fitting label for a global finance capitalism driven twenty-first century descent into world chaos. As has been succinctly pointed out by financial journalists (Bowley 2011) '[I]n many of the world's markets, nearly all stock trading is now conducted by computers talking to other computers at high speeds such that the time it takes to complete a trade on average is ninety eight microseconds – a mind numbing speed equal to ninety eight millionths of a seconds.' 'Flash crashes', catastrophic plunges in share prices on global stock markets, are becoming more and more common as the search for fractions of a second advantage spins out of control. Speed is money, we might conclude, a phrase which sounds like a Virilio aphorism. Paul Virilio, too, spotted what he called the potential future 'integral accident' in globalisation some way ahead of bankers and financial journalists. He envisaged the 'integral accident' as he observed the linking together of the world's stock markets in the 1980s. He told Philippe Petit (Virilio and Petit 1999: 107), prophetically, in interview in 1996, a full twelve years before the 2008 crash:

> The speed of circulation has supplanted money. The production that resulted from this three-dimensional money is itself eliminated in favour of pure speculation, in other words a pure electronic game. The movement of dematerialisation which I analysed in reference to the city and the neighbour reappears in the case of money. The logic is exactly the same, in other words, the aesthetics of disappearance, and what is disappearing now is production and the money referent. We exceeded the limit of the speed of exchange with the Trading programme that combined the stock markets into one. Wall Street, London, Frankfurt and Tokyo are now just one stock market.

Virilio also told Petit in the same interview (Virilio with Petit 1999: 93) that the 1987 stock exchange meltdown was 'an accident' waiting to happen (again):

> With the acceleration following the transportation revolution of the last century, the number of accidents suddenly multiplied and sophisticated procedures had to be invented in order to control air, rail and highway traffic. With the current world-wide revolution in communication and telematics, acceleration has reached its physical limit, the speed of electromagnetic waves. So there is the risk not of a local accident in a particular location, but rather of a global accident that would affect if not the entire planet, then at least the majority of people concerned by these technologies. On this subject, consider the stock market crash of 1987 that resulted from the implementation of the Programme Trading of automatic stock quotations on Wall Street. It is apparent that this new notion of the accident has nothing to do with the Apocalypse, but rather with the imperious necessity to anticipate in a rational way this kind of catastrophe by which the interactivity of telecommunications would reproduce the devastating effects of a poorly managed radioactivity – think about Chernobyl.

For Virilio 'the stock market crash' of 1987 was a 'sign of what's to come' (Virilio with Petit 1999: 91). In June 2007 he predicted that the 'stock market . . . is in danger of crashing far more seriously than it did in 1929, since all the stock markets are now interconnected' (Virilio and Lotringer 2008: 230). Eric Wilson has praised the utility of Virilio's analysis in examining the global economic crash as a 'criminogenic event'

(Wilson 2009b) and Virilio has become increasingly one of the theorists to cite when the 2008 crash is subjected to international theoretical and political scrutiny. For Virilio it was with globalisation, in the 1990s, through the 'new technologies', that we began to inhabit a world that is 'foreclosed' (Virilio and Lotringer 2005: 77):

> Globalisation is a major catastrophe, it is the catastrophe of catastrophes. In the same way that time, like Aristotle said, is the accident of accidents, geographic globalisation is by essence a major catastrophe. Not because of bad capitalists, but because it is the end, the closing of the world on itself through speed, the velocity of images, the rapidity of transportation. We live in a world of forclusion.

Virilio sees the globe as a world closed off and closed in. In his self-conscious reflection he has been 'working for some thirty years' on this condition, 'on the shrinking of the world', that is on what he has called 'the world's old age' (Virilio and Depardon 2008b: 8).

I want to argue that we must move firmly towards an adequate understanding of the 'trajectories of the catastrophic' (Virilio and Lotringer 2005; Redhead 2009) whether or not Virilio or Baudrillard have the answers to the questions we wish to ask, and that any simple return to an already constructed Marxism, or other pre-existing social and cultural theory such as cosmopolitan sociology, will not suffice. The era after the crash *is* a watershed in the trajectories of the catastrophic. The 'catastrophic', or what Paul Virilio calls 'claustropolis' (Virilio and Lotringer 2008), which in his view has replaced 'cosmopolis', is a vital part, conceptually, of what Virilio has to offer a reconstructed social and cultural theory of modernity. In his book *The Original Accident*, Paul Virilio (Virilio 2007b: 68) poses the important, cryptic question: ' CLAUSTROPOLIS or COSMOPOLIS? A society of enforced seclusion, as once upon a time, or a society of forcible control?'

Unfortunately for would-be Virilians it is cosmopolis (Boyne 2001) rather than claustropolis that has proved to be the basis for social and political theory after the 'postmodern' turn. We now have calls for a deployment of a 'cosmopolitan imagination' and a 'critical cosmopolitanism' (Delanty 2006). Further, Ulrich Beck, a leading figure in the movement towards a cosmopolitan sociology, has coined the terms 'cosmopolitan society', 'cosmopolitan state', 'cosmopolitan perspective' and 'cosmopolitan vision' and indeed a whole cosmopolitan sociological research agenda (Beck 2000, 2002, 2006). Rather than the cosmopolitan sociology espoused by Beck, Zygmunt Bauman, John Urry and others it

could be that Paul Virilio's work is the basis, necessary though not sufficient, for a possible claustropolitan sociology and bunker anthropology. A
sociology and anthropology, moreover, that is *after* postmodernity?

Paul Virilio, although no postmodernist, talks of the 'postmodern
period' and the 'atheism of postmodernity' as well as the 'profane art of
modernity' (Virilio 2007a). Followers of Virilio have even suggested a
subsequent displacement, or replacement, of the postmodern condition
(always, already redundant) by a social formation they say is the 'dromocratic condition' based on Virilio's idea of dromocracy; the society of speed
or of the 'race' that requires a 'dromoscopy' to apprehend it (Virilio 2005c;
James 2007a: 29–43). A slogan for the start of the third millennium might
be 'we have never been postmodern'! Just when you thought the 'end-of-
the-century party' (Redhead 1990) was closed and the 'millennial blues'
(Redhead 1997) were over and done with, 'accelerated culture' (Redhead
2004b) makes a slight return, illuminated by 'theory at the speed of light'
(Redhead 2004a) in a century of new modernities – creative, fast, mobile,
modern, original, cold. 'Alternative modernities', as Lawrence Grossberg
has dubbed them, are a product of a contemporary 'struggle over modernity' (Grossberg 2006: 12–19). As the fierce conflict over precisely which
capitalism will take over the globe develops apace (Gray 2009b) it seems
that we are consumed by the question of which modernities we will inhabit
in the near future. A fast modernity for Ben Agger's slow modernity and
'fast capitalism'? A cold modernity for a world in what Paul Virilio calls
a 'cold panic' (Virilio 2005a, 2005b)? A dangerous modernity (Redhead
2004b) to go along with the rise of Naomi Klein's 'disaster capitalism'
(Klein 2007), a sign of the sociologies of the future where 'trajectories of
the catastrophic' will materialise more and more?

For Paul Virilio, a Christian since he was eighteen years old, 'God' and
'spirituality' fill in the gaps. His humanism is a major drawback to his
work being accepted as an answer to the question what is it to be human in
a 'post-human' world? (Gray 2002; Gray 2004: 24–31). For non-believers
modernity is profoundly different – a secular modernity. Jean Baudrillard,
Paul Virilio's much more well known countryman, and often known to
comment on Virilio's religiosity, is a case in point (Redhead 2008). As
the open access online journal, edited by Gerry Coulter, at http://www.
ubishops.ca/BaudrillardStudies shows to any who would search for it
Baudrillard was perhaps the most controversial theorist of all global intellectuals in the past quarter of a century. He was known for his trenchant
analyses of media and technological communication but few commentators have actually read exactly what he wrote and taken into account
when he wrote it. To some extent the conflict over Jean Baudrillard's

legacy stems largely from the fact that a comprehensive selection of his writings had, until recently, to be properly translated from the original French. People tended to read only 'fragments' of his often fragmentary, aphoristic, cryptic work, or else quote his myriad interpreters who usually had a large axe to grind. Belonging to the now passed on generation of radical French thinkers that included Gilles Deleuze, Louis Althusser and Michel Foucault, as well as his long time friend Paul Virilio who survives him, Baudrillard has often been savagely vilified by his detractors, but the lasting influence of his work on critical thought, cultural politics, war studies, media events and pop culture is impossible to deny. Baudrillard's central idea was that 'the real' has become transformed in such a way that as the virtual takes over, the real, in its simulation, has scooped up its own images; for Baudrillard the real can no longer be thought separately from the image. In what might be called a commitment to a critical poetics of the modern object, Jean Baudrillard consistently strived to produce a radically uncertain picture of the modern world. But this is a modernity that has changed over the years he was writing about it, since the early 1950s. A couple of years before he died Baudrillard insisted 'what I am, I don't know. I am the simulacrum of myself.' Jean Baudrillard, the simulacrum, is certainly a singular object. As he himself emphasised 'you must create your underground because now there's no more underground, no more avant-garde, no more marginality. You can create your personal underground, your own black hole, your own singularity' (Redhead 2008: 1). To place Jean Baudrillard in any theoretical or political pigeon hole has always been difficult. It remains so today, even after his death in March 2007 with the tantalising publication of 'very late' Baudrillard texts (Baudrillard 2010a and b). Although Baudrillard was influenced by Marxists like Jean-Paul Sartre, Herbert Marcuse and Henri Lefebvre his work has always born a tangential relationship to any brand of Marxism, neo- or otherwise. Philosophical antecedents of Baudrillard's work are complex and for sure Marx and Engels are present but so too is Mani, the Persian Gnostic prophet who wrote 1,800 years ago. Although slated by many critics for being 'postmodernist' the moral relativism often connected to postmodernism is actually nowhere to be seen in Baudrillard. Nevertheless, from the 1970s onwards Baudrillard became associated with terms like postmodernism, postmodern sociology/art/architecture, and the general issues surrounding media and screen culture and virtual cyberspace which seem, inevitably, to attract the label postmodern. It should be said that this process of linking Baudrillard with the idea of the 'post' was mainly through dubious labelling by others and not through Baudrillard's own words. Partly it has been a consequence of commentators using the

term postmodern to cover anything recent especially in the rapidly changing world of new media. In some ways, in any case, Baudrillard is a quite
perverse choice of theorist of the new media technologies, or commentator
on their future potential. He was stubbornly old media. He admitted, in
1996, that he did:

> not know much about this subject. I haven't gone beyond the fax and the
> automatic answering machine. I have a very hard time getting down to work
> on the screen because all I see there is a text in the form of an image which
> I have a hard time entering. With my typewriter, the text is at a distance.
> With the screen, it's different . . . That scares me a little and cyberspace is
> not of great use to me personally. (Redhead 2008: 9)

Baudrillard also always preferred photography, especially his own still
photographs, to digital video. The idea that Baudrillard was essentially a
'postmodern sociologist' is still pervasive, stemming from orthodox 1970s
and 1980s readings of his work, but it is, in the last instance, an unhelp-
ful notion. Politically as well as intellectually such fixed perspectives have
done no favours to Baudrillard or, ultimately, his readers. For instance,
from the early 1960s Baudrillard and his friend Felix Guattari were
regarded, confusingly, as Maoists. Later Baudrillard himself wrote books
debating strands of Marxist theory in the early 1970s but his relationship to
Marx and Marxism is certainly complex. Further, the period Baudrillard
spent around the influential *Utopie* journal in France beginning in the
mid-1960s and continuing until the late 1970s was undoubtedly evidence
of his involvement in ultra-leftist politics in France. But Baudrillard
clearly broke with much European 'leftism' in the late 1970s and 1980s
for being insufficiently radical. His future thinking was a perspective some
way 'beyond' Marx. Baudrillard was present, as a lecturer, at the Nanterre
university campus in France when it became the spark for May '68.
However, Baudrillard was never a paid up member of left organisations
and ploughed a very individual furrow throughout his life. Still the mis-
labelling persisted. Situationist? Though sympathetic to the Situationists
he was never a member of the Situationist International, or ever even met
Guy Debord. New Philosopher? In the 1970s the Nouveaux Philosophes
movement of Andre Glucksmann and Bernard-Henri Levy (former left-
ists who publicly renounced leftism) left Baudrillard untouched but he
became guilty by association in the minds of some Trotskyists when he
later published with Grasset, Bernard-Henri Levy's publishing house,
and wrote in journals in France in the 1980s that were regarded as on the
'new right'.

There is still, then, a possible position in contemporary social and cultural theory that could claim that there is only modernity, and nothing after it or beyond it, but which reflexively is able to take into account the debates about postmodernism, postmodernity and the 'post' as a cultural condition. Jean-Francois Lyotard (Lyotard 1984) in the 1970s and 1980s promulgated the idea that there had, sometime in the late twentieth century, been taking place a transition to what he labelled a 'postmodern condition'. Many other contemporary social theorists involved in the movement towards a cosmopolitan sociology, however, have turned away from their erstwhile interests in the postmodern in the 1980s and 1990s. Scott Lash, for instance, has acknowledged that he does not 'particularly like the term' postmodern (Gane 2004) and one time guru of postmodernity (Bauman 1991, 1993, 1995) Zygmunt Bauman has conceded that for some time he has been distancing himself from the concept (Blackshaw 2005; Bauman and Tester 2001), preferring his own original idea of 'liquid modernity' (Bauman 2007a; Gane 2004) and committing himself to a thorough going sociological rethinking of the modern (Bauman 2001, 2002, 2004a, 2004b, 2007b). Bauman's 'liquid modernity' is seen to be 'characterised by social forms based on transience, uncertainty, anxieties and insecurity and resulting in new freedoms that come at the price of individual responsibility and without the traditional support of social institutions'. In this sense, for cosmopolitan sociologists such as Bauman, 'postmodernism . . . has not displaced modernity but opens the concept up to cosmopolitan possibilities' (Delanty 2006: 34). Increasingly the term 'late modernity' is fashionable again for those wishing to see a reconstructed critical social theory (Delanty 2006: 27; Young 2007) though the lonely hour of the last instance of 'late modernity' never seems to come. In addition, 'supermodern' (Auge 1995) and 'hypermodern' (Armitage 2000, 2001) have also been offered as alternative terms for those who are not any longer satisfied by the idea of postmodernity just as concepts like 'hypercapitalism' (Rifkin 2000) have displaced the term capitalism, or even 'capitalisms' (Gray 2009b). This reconceptualisation of modernity and modernisation is reflected in contemporary debates about 'what it means to be modern' as has been argued in relation to modern terror groups such as Al Qaeda whose origins are for a writer like John Gray (Gray 2003, 2007) squarely in modernity rather than 'tradition'. Further, the question has become what it is to experience 'demodernisation' (say in post-war Iraq) or how 'remodernisation' can take place in the case of what Francis Fukuyama (Fukuyama 2004, 2006) and other neo-conservatives call state building in so-called 'failed states'.

New modernities spawn new catastrophes. Mobile Accelerated

Nonpostmodern Culture is our new sociological object. Historian Eric Hobsbawm has argued in writing about globalisation, democracy and terrorism that coming after the era he has labelled the 'age of extremes' in 'the short twentieth century' there is a 'new era which has emerged from the old' (Hobsbawm 2007: 1). But what precisely is this 'new era' of modernity and when did it begin? What would a better 'story of these times' look like? Bunker anthropology and claustropolitan sociology are challenged to provide such a story by the lack of fit in cosmopolitan sociology or by unreconstructed thought. That is not to say that cosmopolitan sociology and other perspectives in political and cultural theory have not tried to tell the story of transition, of the theory of a new era. Many attempts have been made at capturing such a story in the last decade or so. In the 1990s Anthony Giddens also claimed that we were in a 'period of evident transition' and offered the view that we were now 'living in a post-traditional society' (Beck, Giddens and Lash 1994: 56–109) a notion embraced by much of cosmopolitan sociology. This new era has also been characterised variously as the 'age of greed' (Mason 2009) and 'the age of uncertainty' (Bauman 2007a), the 'age of insecurity' (Atkinson and Elliot 1998, 2009) and the 'age of turbulence' (Greenspan 2007) and there is no let up today in the rush to characterise the culture of the present before it disappears again – the 'new depression' (Jacques 2009a) being the latest to be posted after the global economic meltdown. Paul Virilio himself has speculated that 'our Age will be looked back on tomorrow as that of subliminal blindness, the "Age of Darkness"' (Virilio and Depardon 2008a). So for some time there has been an urgent need for a rethinking of modernity; and for rethinking the 'future of social theory' (Gane 2004). Notions of conditions after modernity are, however, not ultimately persuasive. What can be argued further, from the perspective of an emerging claustropolitan sociology, is that there are only modernities, conflicting and overlapping. 'New' modernities sit alongside 'old' modernities.

Claustropolitan sociology and bunker anthropology are in no way directly readable from the work of Paul Virilio, or for that matter Jean Baudrillard, but a rigorous theory of claustropolitanism is urgently necessary. I have warned many times elsewhere about the dangers of not contextualising the chronology of what, say, Virilio or Baudrillard (Redhead 2004a, 2004b, 2008) have written and exactly when they wrote it. Virilio, despite his humanistic anarcho-Christianity and all the theoretical problems this engenders, is a useful starting point in producing a claustropolian sociology and bunker anthropology which gives the feel of being from within the claustropolis, a position of 'polar inertia' (Virilio 2000) whilst everything passes by at 'the speed of light' (Virilio 2002b). Virilio has suffered personally from claustrophobia and perhaps that has helped him develop some of the elements of such a perspective, giving the idea of a world foreclosed, closed off and closed in. Uploaded on YouTube there is a freely available 7 minute 48 second video of Paul Virilio giving a lecture in French, in 2007, entitled 'Dromology and Claustrophobia'. This public video lecture was originally for faculty and students in the Department of Media and Communication Studies at the European Graduate School in Switzerland, where Virilio is a visiting professor. Virilio and Baudrillard's countryman Jean-Francois Lyotard, inventor of the term 'the postmodern condition' (Lyotard 1984), was a member in the 1960s of an ultra-leftist group called, in English, Socialism or Barbarism. Lyotard has been described, rather ungenerously, as a 'disillusioned former member of the grouplet *Socialisme ou Barbarie*' (Therborn 2008: 30). Now, today, the rhetorical question has become more a case of Capitalism or Barbarism, even after the Credit Crunch and the global Stock Market Crash. In Jean Baudrillard's case, the work helps us to understand the political importance of the question 'what is to be done?'. With interest in Baudrillard at an all time high, new political and intellectual debates around his work will be provoked in the wake of his death. 'Fragments' is an oft used label for Baudrillard's work, employed twice in English translation of titles of his many books (Redhead 2008). What we are left with in his writings, including several posthumous pieces (Baudrillard 2009, 2010a, 2010b) are fragments for the immediate future. In popular culture his influence is still a nagging presence. In 1996 he and a pick up band, called the Chance Band, played a gig at the Chance Event in Stateline, Nevada, where Baudrillard in a gold lame suit with mirrored lapels, read his song/poem 'Motel Suicide'. In August 2009, as if to repay the compliment a band calling itself Forget Foucault (after Baudrillard's infamous essay which apparently annoyed Michel Foucault when it was published in 1977) released an album entitled *Baudrillard's Perfect Crime* (after Baudrillard's book of the same title) which featured songs like 'A Consumer's System of Objects', 'This is an Illusion of the End' and 'What an Ecstasy of Communication' (plundering Baudrillard's books and essays) to a noise metal soundtrack.

Although pursuing different furrows since the 1950s when they first began to write, Virilio and Baudrillard were friends and colleagues for many years and together have a huge back catalogue which is only now being properly reassessed. This book has attempted to move beyond the much utilised dichotomy of modernist and postmodernist studies and pursue their singularity to its limit. Baudrillard and Virilio have both been regularly categorised as postmodernists by scholars in various different fields, but this labelling is seen here to be fundamentally misconceived, misleading and debilitating. I have suggested in this chapter ways in which the substantial legacies of both Paul Virilio and Jean Baudrillard might be better seen as singular, but related, post-theory. The writings of Virilio and Baudrillard which are useful can be assessed anew and a more balanced conclusion formed about their 'extreme theory' for an even more extreme world. Claustropolitan sociology, if we can call the project outlined in this book by a recognisable name, must not be committed to the linear view of history that cosmopolitan sociology has embraced. The 'story of these times', where accident and catastrophe predominate, can be provided by a focus on Mobile Accelerated Nonpostmodern Culture. Or, in acronym, MANC. Such a focus is a more appropriate resolution to the problems caused by the search for a postmodern sociology which permeated the 1980s, 1990s and 2000s than that offered by cosmopolitan sociology.

CHAPTER 10

Post-Future

It is a time for predictions and forecasts. George Friedman, a private forecaster and intelligence analyst has looked ahead to 'the next one hundred years', forecasting the contours of the whole remainder of the twenty-first century to come (Friedman 2010). In geopolitics Friedman has predicted China's decline, a new US/Russia cold war and, by the end of the century, Mexico graduating to become a new superpower. A conference, LandCorp's C2030 Summit in Perth, Western Australia, has looked at the future of the cityscape in the twenty-first century, right on the Indian Ocean. FuturePerth, an urban planning think tank in the so-called City of Lights, proposed a light rail network, moving people in a sustainable manner, an important element in creating liveable, vibrant cities. A former director of the Art Gallery of WA called for Perth to 'develop the north and south banks of the River Swan foreshore into art and entertainment precincts', create 'massive interactive artworks' and become 'the cultural centre of the Indian Ocean rim'. Others argued more specifically for making Perth 'the biggest university city on the Indian Ocean rim'. For Professor Richard Weller from the School of Architecture at the university of Western Australia the city, which could, it has been forecast, 'in the next forty years rise to a population of four and a quarter million' from a million and a quarter today, needed to 'look around the world at other thriving cities, decide what type of metropolis it wanted to be and follow a design to make it happen'. WA sculptor Ben Juniper even futuristically envisaged:

> Perth becoming an electric city powered by the sun. All the central business district roads would be removed and replaced by textured photo-voltaic cells in an interlocking jigsaw type format, enabling it to become the first city in the world to be entirely powered by renewable energy technologies. The amount of power this electric city could generate could easily drive an elevated, dual use, cycle-sky bridge network high above the city's streets.

Is this vision, the cityscape of Futurism, the ultimate destiny of Perth in Western Australia?

Futurism is as significant today as it ever was; *Futurism*, the catalogue of an exhibition that ran at the Centre Pompidou in Paris between October 2008 and February 2009 and at the Tate Modern in London between June and September 2009, published by Editions de Centre Pompidou, Paris, is just one graphic testament to its importance. But a century on from Filippo Marinetti and the fascist leaning Futurists, things *are* different: we are post-Futurist now. Dream City projects like 'Future Perth' incorporate the future already present. As cyber punk writer William Gibson has written, the future is already here, it is just that it is unevenly distributed. We are all 'post-future' now. Perth in Western Australia has had several periods of global focus. The early 2000s was one such period. Six months before the media piled in with the usual news hyperbole, the premier Dr Geoff Gallop had announced a new taskforce from within the Department of Premier and Cabinet that included advisers from other departments to build on the recommendations of earlier taskforces that had studied specific WA creative industries, namely the Contemporary Music Ministerial Taskforce which reported in September 2002 and, especially, the Premier's Fashion Industry Taskforce. The latter, chaired by Professor Ted Snell (later director of the Cultural Precinct project in Perth) concentrated on designer fashion and published its extensive report in August 2003. It noted the increasing recognition in particular in cities in the UK, Australia and New Zealand of the importance of adopting joined up creative industries strategies across government in order to grow the 'creative economy', or more generally the new knowledge economy, in any city-region around the globe. But there are cycles to culture and regeneration. In Liverpool in the UK regeneration through popular music culture struggles to get 'beyond the Beatles' influence from the 1960s (Cohen 2007). In Vancouver, still seen as 'the postmodern city' of Canada (Delany 1994) the hosting of the 2010 Winter Olympics nearly bankrupted the city. The brief of a subsequent Creative Industries Policy Taskforce in Perth in 2004 was essentially to meet over a six month period in order to consider the possibility of producing a creative industries strategy that would co-ordinate the diverse initiatives in the new knowledge economy of WA. The state government had committed to respond to the recommendations of the Premier's Fashion Industry Taskforce by the end of 2003 and decided that rather than develop an industry specific strategy piecemeal there was a historic opportunity to develop a creative industries policy for WA that would encompass industries already assisted by government and identify others that fitted the creative economy, or knowledge economy, vision. The example of Manchester in the UK, a similar size of city to Perth, was taken as a useful barometer for the taskforce. In Manchester, the Manchester Institute for Popular Culture (MIPC) aided the development of cultural quarters (or precincts or clusters) in the city through its research work and input into policy debates over many years. Drew Hemment, director of the thinktank FutureEverything, which draws together new ideas from both technology and art, has been charged with leading Manchester's drive towards becoming the UK's first 'open data city, making all officially held information available to all' (T. Kirby 2010) and has strongly argued that 'cities are changing, they are being rewired. The opening up of public data and the rollout of a grid of high bandwidth connectivity can transform the public realm and the way we live and interact in urban areas'.

As 'smart cities' emerge throughout the globe the traditional and online worlds will merge. It is the ubiquity of ultra-fast broadband, rather than simply its speed, that will transform tomorrow. We certainly now live in instantaneous culture. More than ever in human history we inhabit the 'now'. But it is an instant present that is catastrophic, claustropolitan, a 'university of disaster' in the words of Paul Virilio. Our accelerated communication of the early twenty-first century such as e-mail, mobile phones, Twitter, Facebook, Google and Academia.edu is, oddly in the case of Virilio himself,, Virilian', truly a world devoid of solids. At the turn of the millennium, theorist John Armitage called Paul Virilio 'perhaps the most provocative French cultural theorist on the contemporary intellectual scene' (Armitage 2001: 1). Armitage was surely right then. It is just as true today. We need to have in our pocket, however problematic it may be in the application, the work of Paul Virilio as our guide to the trajectories of the catastrophic more than at any time since the 1930s, the decade when he was born.

Some of the key concepts created by Paul Virilio, and, to some extent, the milieu of their production, are in some ways part of what I see as 'an archaeology of the post-future'. Paul Virilio's old friend, Jean Baudrillard, wrote a short book in 2000 called *Mots de passe* in which he discussed many of his own concepts – the object, value, symbolic exchange, seduction, the obscene, the transparency of evil, the virtual, the perfect crime, impossible exchange, duality and so on. In English translation (Baudrillard 2003) the book was about Baudrillard's 'passwords', and dictionary type volumes have started to appear on the array of concepts that he developed in his lifetime – for instance, a collective work by numerous Baudrillard scholars called *The Baudrillard Dictionary* (Smith 2010) appeared in the international marketplace in 2010. Paul Virilio's work has not yet been given the same treatment but given time it certainly will. A 'Virilio Studies' is always seemingly on the cards, a complementary discipline to the already established off and online 'Baudrillard Studies' (Bishop 2009; Clarke et al. 2008).

Paul Virilio's work has been seen in recent years to be more relevant to our current condition than ever before, despite the major drawbacks of its roots in French phenomenology (James 2007a, 2007b) and Christian humanism (Kroker 1992). Virilio often speaks of himself, unashamedly, by using the label 'Anarchistic Christian'. He has asserted in interview that he is not pessimistic, not simply the harbinger of 'bad tidings', but that what he is saying 'here isn't negative in a desperate way'. He has also declared: 'I'm Christian, I have hope' (Geisler and Doze 2009: 92). In terms of French phenomenology Virilio was massively influenced by Maurice Merleau-Ponty when he was a student at the Sorbonne in the early 1960s, shortly before Merleau-Ponty died. Merleau-Ponty's Marxism, however, did not rub off on Paul Virilio. Virilio chose Catholicism over communism. But Paul Virilio's concepts are prescient now in a way that could not have been foreseen even a decade ago; the 'catastrophic' condition of the world has seen his work rocket to international celebrity culture fame, albeit late in his life. For instance, a short film featuring Paul Virilio was shown at the climate change summit in Copenhagen in December 2009. A year earlier an international symposium in San Francisco in the autumn of 2008 entitled 'Trajectories of the Catastrophic' (Maravelis 2008) was dedicated to a critical appraisal of the work of Virilio. City Lights Bookshop in San Francisco, which stocks copies of all of Paul Virilio's work, and many commentaries on him, hosted the symposium at the San Francisco Art Institute where Sylvere Lotringer's film on Paul Virilio and the 'itinerary of catastrophe' was shown to the participants. In November 2009 at the School of Visual Arts in New York, Sylvere Lotringer introduced the film to the audience with a lengthy personal overview of Virilio's life and work which was entitled 'The Itinerary of Catastrophe'. Lotringer argued in the lecture that Virilio was the most 'important theorist of technology since Martin Heidegger'. He drew attention to Virilio's experience as a captain in the French army at the time of the war of independence in Algeria and described Virilio as 'a pacifist passionately opposed to war'. Lotringer emphasised that Virilio is neither Marxist nor Nietzschean but influenced by the Italian Futurists – 'from futurism to the financial crisis' as Lotringer put it. Paul Virilio is still producing new and provocative output to add to his large back catalogue and resurrected his interest in Albert Einstein and the physics of black holes by preparing to write a book on the Large Hadron Collider (LHC). The year 2009 saw publica-

tion in the USA of a new edition of *Bunker Archeology* (Virilio 2009b),
a self-illustrated book which Virilio first started writing in 1958 and
eventually published in French in 1975. Virilio's haunting still black and
white photography, snapped between 1958 and 1965, lavishly permeates
the text. In early 2010 Virilio's *The University of Disaster* (Virilio 2010b),
first published in French by Editions Galilee in September 2007, saw the
light of day in English translation and in late 2010 *The Futurism of the
Instant* (Virilio 2010a), comprising texts based on an earlier collaboration
with photographer Raymond Depardon, published the previous year by
Editions Galilee, was put out by Polity. Virilio has commented cryptically
in interview on the idea of 'the university of disaster' (Geisler and Doze
2009: 94):

> I was a child of the war and I have published a book called *The University
> of Disaster* – not the disaster of university. I say that we need a university
> founded on the disaster we're discussing, the progress that turns to catastro-
> phe . . . It's in this area that I find my work on 'negative monuments' – but
> now, rather than a museum, I'm proposing a university.

Increasingly, Paul Virilio's idiosyncratic tracing of the 'trajectories of
the catastrophic' over the last fifty years has chimed with the world we
now inhabit – a 'claustropolitan' world of economic downturn, 'impure
war' in Iraq, Gaza, Lebanon and Afghanistan, 'globalitarian' new depression and apocalyptic predictions of 'accelerated' world climate catastrophe. Claude Parent, his partner in architectural crime in the 1960s when
they were 'hip young gunslingers' of 'post-space', described Paul Virilio
as an 'archaeologist of the future'. Virilio himself has been compared to
Marinetti and the Futurists. The appropriation of aesthetic revolt by the
right has meant that association with Marinetti and the Futurists has often
been lambasted by political progressives but it is worth remembering,
as Owen Hatherley noted (Hatherley 2008: 125) that though the 'most
famous example' of 'appropriation of any aesthetic revolt by the right' is
'the Italian Futurists, the Facist Modernists par excellence' the slightest
'digging in the history of cultural politics' reminds 'us that things could
have been different' and that 'Antonio Gramsci wrote in 1922 "before the
war, Futurism was very popular with the workers"'. This is a project of
an 'archaeology of the post-future' as opposed to an 'archaeology of the
future' which Fredric Jameson envisaged (Jameson 2005). In this context,
Paul Virilio is best labelled as an 'archaeologist of the post-future'. He
himself has noted that 'this isn't tomorrow, but now'. He certainly is
acutely aware of this 'archaeology of the post-future', without necessarily
using the same language in his texts. Virilio instead has commented on

what he sees as the 'futurism of the instant' (Virilio 2010a) or the 'futurism of the moment' (Geizler and Doze 2009: 95):

> Octavio Paz wrote 'The Instant is uninhabitable, like the future'. I'm saying that we live in the futurism of the moment and we live in a habitable world. Marinetti's Futurism was still the futurism of History – the racing car, etc. Russian and Italian Futurism was historic, that of long time periods, of history. What we have here is that of the real instant, the live, and that is unhabitable. A big thought, like Octavio Paz's. Tomorrow this real instant will render the Earth uninhabitable, by its acceleration.

Virilio has also proclaimed the world as too small when faced with power of technoscience and acutely understands why astrophysicists want to discover an exoplanet and create a terrestrial atmosphere outside the earth.

Rapidity is often Virilio's focus, but not for its own sake. Acceleration is on the front line for Virilio because he thinks we are continuing to accelerate in an impossible way, threatening the earth itself. Bob Dylan sang 'the world is old, the world is grey' in a soundtrack song for a film directed by Ron Maxwell called *Gods and Generals* about the American civil war (Heylin 2010: 471–3). Dylan's 2002 song was entitled "Cross the Green Mountain' and Paul Virilio has proposed a 'grey ecology' to investigate our old world. Virilio, in conversation at his home in La Rochelle with photographer Raymond Depardon for the catalogue for their *Native Land/Stop Eject* exhibition in Paris (Virilio and Depardon 2008b: 8), has mused that:

> everyone knows that for some thirty years I've been working on speed, on the shrinking of the world, that is, on what I have called the world's old age . . . and today we can say that what with supersonic transport and the speed of telecommunications, the world operates instantaneously. This is what we call real time.

Virilio has argued for many years that technology, war and culture have been intimately related. He has taken up the 'world is grey' theme further in interview (Geisler and Doze 2009: 94), calling explicitly for a 'grey ecology' (Virilio 2009a):

> The real question is our relationship to speed and the exhaustion of the world. What I call 'grey ecology' has to do with the pollution of distances by speed. Air, water, wildlife, flora, and grey ecology, that of distances, the life-sized, proportions. It's not nature that's polluted, but the lifesized. Miniaturisation – tomorrow, today probably, this dictaphone is a chip and it follows on from ENIAC, the computer that was as big as a house and today

fits into your pocket. Next to the central question of speed, you have to take into account the pollution caused by speed, the problem of pollution spread across the world. Our world!

Jean Baudrillard once said, as Jean Nouvel reminded him in conversation, 'all things are curves . . . there are no end points or the end points connect in a curved mirror, all things, in this sense, fulfil their own cycle' (Baudrillard and Nouvel 2002: 15–16). Paul Hegarty (Hegarty 2004) has argued quite correctly, in an excellent book on the 'live' theory of Baudrillard (though he also pointed out that they differed in quite important ways) that Virilio is the one person Jean Baudrillard engaged with most over the years before his death in March 2007. In a 'dialogue of exiles' first mooted by Jean Baudrillard (via Bertolt Brecht) with his correspondent Enrique Valiente Noailles in *Exiles from Dialogue* (Baudrillard and Noailles 2007) Virilio and Baudrillard were inextricably connected. The posthumous 'last' book by Baudrillard *Why Hasn't Everything Already Disappeared?* (Baudrillard 2009), though other late texts are also continuing to emerge (Baudrillard 2010a and b), is a beautiful elegiac text, almost as short as a 'classic' Paul Virilio! The 'curves' connecting and defining the two theorists of the 'end' (or in Virilio's word 'finitude') are certainly intriguing and surprisingly underexplored, and lead away from, rather than towards, the orthodox but misleading 'postmodernist' connection (Gane 2003; Merrin 2005; Pawlett 2007; Clarke et al. 2008; Redhead 2004a, 2008). Collegial work between the two French intellectuals really did sometimes occur, especially in their middle age, from the mid-1970s onwards. As Mike Gane (Gane 2003) has noted in his forensic analysis of French social theory and its main protagonists, Virilio, for instance, worked with Baudrillard in Paris on the journal *Traverses* between 1975 and 1990 after previously working on the Catholic-inspired journal *Esprit* from 1970. In a time of reflection and sadness Virilio told European Graduate School students at La Rochelle in 2007 (Virilio 2009a: 68–70), a couple of weeks after Baudrillard died, about their long time collaboration and that he saw that:

The big difference between Jean and me is that he worked on simulation and I worked on substitution . . . I would like to relate a small anecdote about Baudrillard and simulation and substitution. When we found ourselves at the *Revue Travers*, I had just finished my photographic campaign, which took ten years, on the wall of the Atlantic. Baudrillard hated photography at the time. I went to the *Revue Travers* because before, in the *Revue de l'esprit*, they didn't have photos or images. At the *Revue Travers*, I could publish my photos and I told the revue, 'I am coming'. When I saw Baudrillard, he said 'Tisk, tisk, tisk'. And now he is dead and I am still alive . . . It's been quite a long time now since I have stopped taking photos, but he, he began taking photos. He even finally became a photographer. This is typical in our movement.

Virilio and Baudrillard were both, separately, at various times in the noughties, professors at the European Graduate School, Saas-Fee, Switzerland, where Sylvere Lotringer, a long time friend, publisher and interlocutor of both theorists became the Jean Baudrillard Professor in 2009. Indeed Virilio's academic designation is Professor of Urban Philosophy at the European Graduate School. YouTube has several minutes of both Virilio and Baudrillard giving their various independent French language lectures for the Swiss based European Graduate School; the video lectures have been uploaded on the internet for free download-ing by anyone, all over the world at the same time – exactly Virilio's imag-ined 'city of the instant' in the 'futurism of the moment'.

A critical comparison of Baudrillard and Virilio and their intertwined histories can undoubtedly be made both within and without French social theory as a specific body of knowledge (Redhead 2004b: 1–9; Redhead 2004a: 119–24; Redhead 2008: 1–13; Gane 2003). Virilio, as well as seeing the simulation/substitution debate as a major dividing line between them, commented on subtle, substantive differences with Baudrillard, after the latter's death. In conversation with Sylvere Lotringer of Semiotext(e) in La Rochelle three months after Baudrillard's passing Virilio (Virilio and Lotringer 2008: 235) emphasised that he and his old friend Baudrillard frequently disagreed and that they actually:

> had a radically different approach to things. For me, things have a purpose, every moment has its purpose. He didn't believe so. That is why we could never discuss certain subjects. On the other hand, we had something in common, which was the uncertainty principle, not believing your own eyes, conscientious objections. That is why he wrote what he did about the Gulf War. There are conscientious objectors who don't want to see the war and those who don't believe in the war, even when it takes place, since the war was created out of its image.

Other commentators have drawn attention to the similarities *and* differ-ences in Baudrillard and Virilio. In 'Elegy for a Dead Friend' in Virilio's book *Grey Ecology* (Virilio 2009a: 19) Drew Burk, Virilio's translator into English from the original European Graduate School French language seminars in Virilio's home town of La Rochelle in April 2007, and an interpreter at the event, commented:

I must say that before meeting and interpreting for Virilio, I had quite a few problems with his writings, especially concerning art. I was more akin to his friend and theoretical antagonist, Jean Baudrillard and while I desperately wanted to enjoy both of these thinkers' philosophical inquiries into the mediated world that we find ourselves immersed in today, Virilio's thought, as opposed to Baudrillard's, at the least seemed too defensive. But as Virilio began to plead his case, his presence gave another quality to his work. I couldn't help but deconstruct the scene. Virilio, in the aftermath of his friend's death (Baudrillard had died two weeks prior) seemed more concerned than ever with maintaining a 'distance' from what Baudrillard would name the hyperreal . . . But something struck me quite curiously here when Virilio proposed his grey ecology and with it a *recoil*, a necessity to take a step back from the instantaneity of what he calls 'cinematic energy' in order to maintain a distance. One started to see a certain difference in the unfolding of Virilio's critique and that of his friend Jean Baudrillard . . . Virilio would call this position of study the University of Disaster.

As ever, though, it is religious belief that most clearly divided Baudrillard and Virilio throughout their long friendship. Burk (Virilio 2009a: 20–1) noted the source of this breach, which has deep theoretical repercussions for the interpretation of their work, as the:

Christian ether surrounding Virilio. When he responded to a question regarding what artists today should do to fight the problem of speed and technology he quoted St Augustine, 'Do whatever you want, but do it with love'. But for Virilio there is an interesting twist that makes all the difference. His idea of revelation is not that of the end, but of a revealing, and this for Virilio is the essence as well of his concept of the integral accident. This leads me to Baudrillard and his relationship to Virilio. Virilio believes the biogenetic bomb is one we must be wary of. He warns against cloning not only of people, but perception itself. Virilio however does not believe that we have already entered the 'hyperreal' of Baudrillard. I asked him the question. He thinks we have yet to move over. Virilio still claims we can gain the necessary distance from the technological speed of the virtual. But Baudrillard obviously thought differently. He states 'Distance is obliterated, both external distance from the real world and the internal distance specific to the sign'. Virilio calls for us to take a step back from the instantaneity of screen technology, but for Baudrillard, it has already burned itself onto our retina. For Baudrillard, the cloning that Virilio speaks of has already taken place, perhaps not physically yet (this is debatable, but at least psychically with the mass popularisation of certain figures, styles, etc.). For Baudrillard, the hyperreal has already taken over, and more to the point, we have entered the realm of the pataphysical, the theatre of cruelty that is the science of imaginary solutions. The 'integral accident' of Virilio, his thought is always/already framed in the theatre of the global. But Baudrillard reminds us of the place to which thought should not be instructed, to an idea which he and his friend Virilio would perhaps have agreed upon. Baudrillard states, 'Thought must refrain from instructing or being instructed by, a future reality, for in that game, it will always fall into the trap of a system that holds the monopoly of reality. And this is not a philosophical choice. It is, for thought, a life-and-death question.' And this brings me to a point on which I think both of these philosophers (one always reminding us of his architectural hauntology, the other of his Jarry nature) can agree. They are both trying to carve out a thought and a mimetic mirror of actuality without coming to a limit, an absolute. When Virilio quotes St Augustine, it is in the same way that Baudrillard makes up a fake quote from Ecclesiastes. It is for a love of existence, even if it is the smallest of things.

Virilio (Virilio 2009a: 42) has stated that 'contrary to my old friend Jean Baudrillard, I have no psychoanalytic culture; zero, it doesn't interest me' and further that:

> concerning Baudrillard, I believe that there wasn't much we agreed on. Like the saying goes, we don't have to agree to get along. Jean was a great friend. On many points we were in complete disagreement. Well, you have understood I am a Christian. That is to say, I don't believe in death. And Baudrillard didn't believe in life, that is the reality of life. This is where one gets the idea of simulations. We were both conscientious objectors. Both atheists, but not the same kind: he didn't believe in reality, in particular in its acceleration, and I don't believe in death, that is to say, in cessation.

Whatever their differences (and I would argue that they are singular voices that should be listened to separately) both Baudrillard and Virilio are essential tools in these 'catastrophic' and 'claustropolitan' times. Baudrillard is dead. Virilio, as he never tires of telling us, is still alive – slowing down but still moving, still seen as 'the prophet of the apocalypse' (Virilio and Dumoucel 2010) by open access magazines and someone who can tell us about the 'age of great terror' that is just around the corner, with Virilio assumed to have the 'tools to understand the modern world' of 'speed accidents' when all around us have given up on understanding anything.

In the post-future we are going to be what is in a new sense 'post war'. No periods without war are likely but always, already war is with us. As Paul Hirst put it in a provocative short book about war and power in the twenty-first century 'it is widely believed that technology, the organisation of the armed forces and the nature and purposes of war are possibly in the process of being rapidly transformed. These changes seem to have come together and to have accelerated since the end of the Cold War' (Hirst 2001: 7). Paul Virilio, strangely not referred to at all in Hirst's compre-hensive account of 'power/war', has had more than most to say about such a 'post war' condition. In Virilio's view we have now moved from 'Pure War' to 'Impure War' (Virilio and Lotringer 2008), and 'war on the cities' is the most likely outcome. Indeed, the militarisation of entertainment, and the entwining of the whole 'military industrial media entertainment' complex (Der Derian 2009), what has been labelled 'militainment' (Stahl 2010), is a new social formation for our catastrophic times. The whole question of the militarisation of culture is an urgent contemporary social and political issue. In an era when war is the pre-eminent media spectacle and war journalism consists of embedded 'conscripts' scribbling letters home on behalf of the military in Iraq and Afghanistan we desperately need critical thinking about war, culture and the media. Virilio helps to provide some of it. Since we are not just watching but *playing* war now (Stahl 2010), the entertainment industry has interpellated citizens as sol-diers in various processes and practices. There is also a story to be told of remasculinisation through the discourse of militainment. Paul Virilio proclaimed the modern turn to what he calls 'endocolonisation' – in other words the colonisation of a country's own population. War of course used to be about the colonisation of *other* countries' populations; militain-ment allows endocolinisation to proceed apace. In today's culture where bunkers have become art galleries and Hummers roam the streets the link between war, culture, art and media is critical (Virilio 2003a; Der Derian 2009; Stahl 2010; Redhead 2010). Virilio has consistently been probing this relationship for fifty years but his archaeology of the post-future actu-ally goes back centuries. As Virilio points out (Geisler and Doze 2009: 93):

> War has acclerated technology, science and industry. You cannot under-stand the world of progress without the world of destruction. The mode of destruction carried progress into the production mode. The military-indus-trial complex began with the Arsenale in Venice, the place where Galileo demonstrated his telescope, not for looking at the moon as is said but to see the enemy as soon as possible: a telescope is a machine of optical speed – by bringing perception closer, it acclerates contact. War is a phenomenon of contact. In love, as in war, to succeed you need contact, as Napoleon said. What accelerated war originally was the training of horses, cavalry, knights, riding – speed. Then came artillery, tanks, planes, missiles etc.

Formerly a Parisian, Virilio has lived in La Rochelle on the west coast of France for a decade and has noted that 'the towers of La Rochelle' which date from the fourteenth century provide 'the legend of the bunker and the shield' (Geisler and Doze 2009: 94; Virilio 2009b). The legend of the bunker has been long lasting, giving rise to Mike Gane's astute conceptualisation 'bunker theorising' to situate the work of Paul Virilio (Armitage 2000: 85–102). As Owen Hatherley (Hatherley 2008: 135) has noted:

> It's arguable that one of the stylistic antecedents of the (British) new brutalism (at least in its late 1960s versions when it became a mannerism of the rough and oblique) was the military architecture necessitated by the fear of German invasion. The pillboxes and bunkers of 1940, with their raw concrete, and angular inscrutability, were more akin to the average brutalist structure than was much classical modernism.

Virilio, online and offline, has an array of concepts for the project of an 'archaeology of the post-future' in a world filled with the 'integral accident' (Virilio 2007b) and the 'city of panic' (Virilio 2005c). Fittingly it is the modern hyper-surveillance twenty- first century city, like New York that shows the 'acceleration of realism' in all its glory for Paul Virilio. Writing in an introduction to a book of the photographs of Manhattan in 1980 by Raymond Depardon (Virilio and Depardon 2008a) Virilio, updating Jeremy Bentham's eighteenth- and ninetheenth-century 'panopticism' (Bentham 1995), a concept that enthralled Michel Foucault in his search for the origins of 'disciplinary power', has glimpsed, prophetically, the globalitarian post-future:

> In the dusk-lit slums of the city, the photographer reveals the embezzlement of 'postmodern' observations signalled by the recent development of CCTV surveillance, with millions of automatic cameras relentlessly focusing on the man in the crowd. A vision with no eye for an eye with no vision. We have come full circle. And the untraceable glaucoma of the perception of rushing passersby goes hand in hand with the compulsory automation of mechanical contemplation, as the camera tracking the crowd never stops . . . while last century's totalitarian societies tried unsuccessfully to enforce a policy of PANOPTIC incarceration, the coming 'globalitarian' society will be fully equipped to achieve this, thanks to the ever *increasing speed of reality*, of which the art of watching our peers is the innocent victim.

Welcome to the post-future! As has been noted in this book, from the 1990s the world experienced more than a decade of globalisation, modernisation and mobility but in the wake of economic, political and environmental crises such processes seem to be on the verge of being reversed and deglobalisation, immobility and demodernisation have become obvious trends. For these new times, with all the fast changing new media technologies that underpin them, this book has offered an outline of a project

of a 'bunker anthropology' and 'claustropolitan sociology' for claustropolitan times, and a slogan – we have never been postmodern. Such a
slogan echoes, ironically, the statement made famous by the French social
theorist Bruno Latour that 'we have never been modern'. Theorists like
Jean-Francois Lyotard and Fredric Jameson became associated in the
1970s, 1980s and 1990s with the idea that there had, sometime in the late
twentieth century, been a period of transition, morphing into a 'postmodern condition' which itself had a long trajectory. Today, it is proclaimed,
such an era, or structure of feeling is well and truly over – we are said to
be living somehow *after* postmodernity, though many international scholars are concerned that the critical theory baby has unceremoniously and
erroneously been thrown out with the postmodern bathwater. Others wish
that the incredulity towards grand and meta narratives had never been
born, with Lyotard's ushering in of a widespread postmodern condition
– and as John Gray has shown (Gray 2011) 'science' as one of the grand
narratives is as strong ideologically in its belief that it can cheat death on
behalf of humanity as ever it was. But the warning in this book is clear.
Neo-liberalism may be in its death throes but that does not mean that an
easy return to the more optimistic discourses of yesteryear is on the cards.
The grand and meta narratives associated with the right (the neo-liberal
belief in the primacy of the free market for instance) are on the wane just as
in an earlier era those associated with the left (Marxism and neo-Marxism)
also collapsed in what Eric Hobsbawm has called 'marxism in recession'
(Hobsbawm 2011). The right arguing that it is 'just capital' (Turner 2001)
and the left arguing that it is 'the limits of capital' (Harvey 1999) or the
'enigma of capital' (Harvey 2010) that we should be concerning ourselves
with, are now two sides of the same redundant coin.

The trilogy of the postmodern, postmodernity and postmodernism
were once seemingly so normalised in cultural and political analysis especially in terms of the influence of Jean-Francois Lyotard in particular
(Readings 1991; Appignanesi 1989). While open to different and competing conceptualisations for the new old world we now inhabit where
populations can seemingly go anywhere fast but will still paradoxically be
subject to immobilisation, this book is not claiming that postmodernism is
dead. Perhaps it will, in the future, be remembered simply as a historical
episode in *debates* about 'literary into cultural studies' (Easthope 1991) or
debates about the correct name for a process of 'change in advanced society'
(Crook, Pakulski and Waters 1992), which became, with the demise of
neo-liberalism, eventually, something more profound. Postmodernism is
not 'dead' as some have argued in their search for better and more exciting
alternatives like 'digimodernism' (A. Kirby 2010); this book has claimed

that there never was an era of postmodernity or the postmodern in the first place, but that the era of debates about the postmodern is well and truly over. As Jean Baudrillard (Baudrillard 2010a: 127), often misleadingly labelled a posmodernist, a description he fundamentally rejected again and again, wrote optimistically before he died: 'maybe a new space–time domain for thought is opening up'. Let us hope, for all our sakes, that he is right.

Bibliography

Adorno, T. (1994), *Quasi una Fantasia: Essays on Modern Music*, London: Verso.

—(1991), *The Culture Industry: Selected Essays on Mass Culture*, London: Routledge.

Agamben, G. (2005), *The State of Exception*, Chicago: University of Chicago.

Ahmed, N. (2006), *The London Bombings: An Independent Inquiry*, London: Duckworth.

Ali, T. (2010), *The Idea of Communism*, London: Seagull.

—(2006), *Conversations with Edward Said*, London: Seagull.

—(2005), *Rough Music: Blair / Bombs / Baghdad / London / Terror*, London: Verso.

Althusser, L. (2006), *Philosophy of the Encounter: Later Writings 1978–1987*, London: Verso.

—(2003), *The Humanist Controversy, and Other Writings*, London: Verso.

—(2001), *Lenin and Philosophy, and Other Essays* (with introduction by Fredric Jameson), New York: Monthly Review Press.

—(1994), *The Future Lasts a Long Time, and the Facts*, London: Vintage.

—(1969), *For Marx*, Harmondsworth: Penguin.

Althusser, L. and Balibar, E. (1970), *Reading Capital*, London: New Left Books.

Andersen, L. and Oakley, K. (eds) (2008), *Making Meaning, Making Money: Directions for the Arts and Cultural Industries in the Creative Age*, Newcastle: Cambridge Scholars.

Anderson, P. (2009), *The New Old World*, London: Verso.

—(2005), *Spectrum: From Right To Left in the World of Ideas*, London: Verso.

—(2000), 'Renewals', *New Left Review*, 2 (1), pp. 5–24.

—(1998), *The Origins of Postmodernity*, London: Verso.

—(1983), *In the Tracks of Historical Materialism*, London: Verso.

—(1977), *Considerations on Western Marxism*, London: New Left Books.

—(1974), 'Lucio Colletti: A Political and Philosophical Interview', *New Left Review*, 1 (86), pp. 3–28.

Andrew, A. (2008), 'Hanif Kureishi: A Chronicler of Pain and Pleasure', *The Observer*, 17 February, p. 14.

Appignanesi, L. (ed.) (1989), *Postmodernism: ICA Documents*, London: Free Association.

Armitage, J. (2006), 'Cosmopolis or Chaosmopolis: Hypermodernismo in Bogota', *Left Curve*, 29, pp. 30–45.

—(2005), 'Escape from *Alphaville*: Introducing Paul Virilio's *City of Panic*', *Cultural Politics*, 1 (3), pp. 331–8.

—(ed.) (2001), *Virilio Live: Selected Interviews*, London: Sage.

—(ed.) (2000), *Paul Virilio: From Modernism to Hypermodernism and Beyond*, London: Sage.

Arthurs, A. (2002), 'Arts and Culture in the New Economy', *Journal of Arts Management, Law and Society*, 32 (2), pp. 83–5.

Atkinson, D. and Elliot, L. (2009), *The Gods that Failed*, London: Vintage.

—(1998), *The Age of Insecurity*, London: Verso.

Auge, M. (1995), *Non-Places: Introduction to an Anthropology of Supermodernity*, London: Verso.

Badiou, A. (2010), *The Communist Hypothesis*, London: Verso.

—(2009), *Pocket Pantheon*, London: Verso.

—(2008), *The Meaning of Sarkozy*, London: Verso.

Badiou, A. and Žižek, S. (2009), *Philosophy in the Present*, Cambridge: Polity.

Bairner, A., Magee, J. and Tomlinson, A. (eds) (2005), *The Bountiful Game?*, Aachen: Meyer and Meyer.

Bale, J. and Vertinsky, P. (eds) (2004), *Sites of Sport: Space, Place, Experience*, London: Routledge.

Balibar, E. (2009), 'Althusser and the Rue d'Ulm', *New Left Review*, 2 (58), pp. 91–107.

Baudrillard, J. (2010a), *The Agony of Power*, Los Angeles: Semiotext(e).

—(2010b), *Carnival and Cannibal, or the Play of Global Antagonism*, London: Seagull.

—(2009), *Why Hasn't Everything Already Disappeared?*, London: Seagull.

—(2006a), *Cool Memories V*, Cambridge: Polity.

—(2006b), *Utopia Deferred*, New York: Semiotext(e).

—(2005a), *The Intelligence of Evil or the Lucidity Pact*, Oxford: Berg.

—(2005b), 'Pornography of War', *Cultural Politics*, 1 (1), pp. 23–6.

—(2005c), *The Conspiracy of Art*, New York and Los Angeles: Semiotext(e).

—(2004a), *Fragments*, London: Routledge.

—(2004b), *The Spirit of Terrorism*, London: Verso.

—(2003), *Passwords*, London: Verso.

—(1997), *The Consumer Society*, London: Sage.

Baudrillard, J. and Guillaume, M. (2008), *Radical Alterity*, Los Angeles: Semiotext(e).

Baudrillard, J. and Noailles, E. (2007), *Exiles from Dialogue*, Cambridge: Polity.

Baudrillard, J. and Nouvel, J. (2002), *The Singular Objects of Architecture*, Minneapolis: University of Minnesota Press.

Bauman, Z. (2010a), *Living on Borrowed Time: Conversations with Citlali Rovirosa-Madrazo*, Cambridge: Polity.

—(2010b), *44 Letters from the Liquid Modern World*, Cambridge: Polity.

—(2008), *The Art of Life*, Cambridge: Polity.

—(2007a), *Liquid Times: Living in an Age of Uncertainty*, Cambridge: Polity.

—(2007b), *Consuming Life*, Cambridge: Polity.

—(2006), *Liquid Fear*, Cambridge: Polity.

—(2005), *Liquid Life*, Cambridge: Polity.

—(2004a), *Wasted Lives: Modernity and its Outcasts*, Cambridge: Polity.

—(2004b), *Identity: Conversations with Benedetto Vecchi*, Cambridge: Polity.

—(2003), *Liquid Love*, Cambridge: Polity.

—(2002), *Society under Siege*, Cambridge: Polity.

—(2001), *Community: Seeking Safety in an Insecure World*, Cambridge: Polity.

—(2000), *Liquid Modernity*, Cambridge: Polity.

—(1999), *In Search of Politics*, Cambridge: Polity.

—(1998), *Globalisation: The Human Consequences*, Cambridge: Polity.

—(1995), *Life in Fragments: Essays in Postmodern Morality*, Oxford: Blackwell.

—(1993), *Postmodern Ethics*, Oxford: Blackwell.

—(1991), *Modernity and Ambivalence*, Cambridge: Polity.

Bauman, Z. and Tester, K. (2001), *Conversations with Zygmunt Bauman*, Cambridge: Polity.

Bayley, S. (1998), *Labour Camp: The Failure of Style over Substance*, London: Batsford.

Beck, U. (2006), *Cosmopolitan Vision*, Cambridge: Polity.

—(2005), *Power in the Global Age*, Cambridge: Polity.

—(2002), 'The Cosmopolitan Society and its Enemies', *Theory, Culture and Society*, 19 (1/2), pp. 17–44.

—(2000), 'The Cosmopolitan Perspective: Sociology of the Second Age of Modernity', *British Journal of Sociology*, 51 (1), pp. 79–105.

—(1999), *World Risk Society*, Cambridge: Polity.

—(1992), *Risk Society: Towards a New Modernity*, London: Sage.

Beck, U. and Beck-Gernsheim, E. (2002), *Individualisation*, London: Sage.

Beck, U., Giddens, A. and Lash, S. (1994), *Reflexive Modernisation: Politics, Tradition and Aesthetics in the Modern Social Order*, Cambridge: Polity.

Beck, U. and Willms, J. (2004), *Conversations with Ulrich Beck*, Cambridge: Polity.

Bentham, J. (1995), *The Panopticon Writings*, London: Verso.

Bergen, P. (2001), *Holy War, Inc: Inside the Secret World of Osama Bin Laden*, London: Weidenfeld and Nicolson.

Berman, M. (2010), *All that is Solid Melts into Air: The Experience of Modernity*, London: Verso.

Best, S. and Kellner, D. (1991), *Postmodern Theory: Critical Interrogations*, Basingstoke: Macmillan.

Bewes, T. and Gilbert, J. (eds) (2001), *Cultural Capitalism: Politics after New Labour*, London: Lawrence and Wishart.

Bideau, A. (2002), 'Claude Parent und die Folgen', *Werk, Bauen und Wohnen*, 11, pp. 2–15.

Bignell, J. (2000), *Postmodern Media Culture*, Edinburgh: Edinburgh University Press.

Bilton, C. (2007), *Management and Creativity: From Creative Industries to Creative Management*, Oxford: Blackwell.

Bishop, R. (2009), *Baudrillard Now: Current Perspectives in Baudrillard Studies*, Cambridge: Polity Press.

Blackshaw, T. (2010), *Leisure*, London: Routledge.

—(2005), *Zygmunt Bauman*, London: Routledge.

—(2003), *Leisure Life: Myth, Masculinity and Modernity*, London: Routledge.

Blackshaw, T. and Crabbe, T. (2004), *New Perspectives on Sport and 'Deviance': Consumption, Performativity and Social Control*, London: Routledge.

Blair, T. (1998), *The Third Way: New Politics for the New Century*, London: Fabian Society.

Blond, P. (2010), *Red Tory*, London: Faber.

—(2009a), 'Red Toryism', *Prospect*, March, p. 10.

—(2009b), 'Rise of the Red Tories', *Prospect*, February, pp. 8–12.

Bongiorno, P. and Ricci, A. (2004), *Lucio Colletti: Tra Scienza e Liberta*, Rome: Ideazione.

Botsman, P. and Latham, M. (eds) (2001), *The Enabling State*, Sydney: Pluto Press.

Boutang, Y. (1992), *Louis Althusser, une biographie. Volume I: la formation du mythe 1918–1945: La Matrice*, Paris; Grasset.

Bowley, G. (2011), 'Speed is Money as Cyber Muscle Overruns Markets', *New York Times*, 23 January, pp. 1–2.

Bowman, P. (2007), *Post-Marxism versus Cultural Studies: Theory, Politics and Intervention*, Edinburgh: Edinburgh University Press.

—(ed.) (2003), *Interrogating Cultural Studies*, London: Pluto Press.

Bowman P. and Stamp R. (eds) (2007), *The Truth of Žižek*, London: Continuum.

Boyle, R. (2010), 'Sport and the Media in the UK: The Long Revolution?' *Sport in Society*, 13 (9), pp. 1300–13.

Boyle, R. and Haynes, R. (2009), *Power Play: Sport, the Media and Popular Culture*, Edinburgh: Edinburgh University Press.

—(2004), *Football in the New Media Age*, London: Routledge.

Boyne, R. (2001), 'Cosmopolis and Risk: A Conversation with Ulrich Beck', *Theory, Culture and Society*, 18 (4), pp. 47–63.

Boyne, R. and Rattansi, A. (eds) (1990), *Postmodernism and Society*, Houndmills: Macmillan.

Brabazon, T. (2006), *Playing on the Periphery: Sport, Identity and Memory*, London: Routledge.

Bracewell, M. (2009), 'Morecambe: The Sunset Coast', in L. Fiegel and A. Harris (eds), *Modernism on Sea: Art and Culture at the British Seaside*, Witney: Peter Lang, pp. 35–43.

—(2007), *Re-Make/Re-Model: Art, Pop, Fashion and the Making of Roxy Music 1953–1972*, London: Faber and Faber.

—(2002a), *Remix: Contemporary Art and Pop*, Liverpool: Tate Gallery.

—(2002b), *The Nineties: When Surface was Depth*, London: Flamingo.

—(2001), *Perfect Tense*, London: Jonathan Cape.

—(1997), *England is Mine*, London: Harper Collins.

—(1995), *Saint Rachel*, London: Jonathan Cape.

—(1992), *The Conclave*, London: Secker and Warburg.

—(1989), *Divine Concepts of Physical Beauty*, London: Secker and Warburg.

—(1988), *The Crypto-Amnesia Club*, London: Serpent's Tail.

Bracewell, M., Watson, D. and Edwards, M. (1988), *The Quick End*, London: Fourth Estate.

Bragg, M. (2003), *Hanef Kureishi: South Bank Show*, Carlton TV.

Bratton, B. (2006), 'Introduction: Logistics of Habitable Circulation', in P. Virilio *Speed and Politics*, Los Angeles: Semiotext(e).

Bray, K. (2006), *How To Score*, London: Granta.

Brennan, M. (2008), *Mourning and Disaster: Finding Meaning in the Mourning for Hillsborough and Diana*, Newcastle: Cambridge Scholars.

Brown, G. (2010), *Beyond the Crash: Overcoming the First Crisis of Globalisation*, London: Simon and Schuster.

Brummer, A. (2008), *The Crunch*, London: Random House.

Buchanan, B. (2007), *Hanif Kureishi*, Houndmills: Palgrave MacMillan.

Burke, J. (2006), *On the Road to Kandahar: Travels through Conflict in the Islamic World*, London: Penguin.

—(2003), *Al Qaeda: Casting a Shadow of Terror*, London: I.B. Tauris.

Burn, G. (2009), *Sex and Violence, Death and Silence: Encounters with Recent Art*, London: Faber.

Burn, G. and Hirst, D. (2001), *On the Way to Work*, London: Faber.

Butler, R. (2005), *Slavoj Žižek : Live Theory*, London: Continuum.

Cable, V. (2009), *The Storm: The World Economic Crisis and What It Means*, London: Atlantic Books.

Callaghan, G. (2010), 'Ahead of the Curve', *The Weekend Australian Magazine*, 10–11 July, pp. 14–15.

Campbell, A. (2011), *The Alastair Campbell Diaries, Volume 2: Power and the People 1997–1999*, London: Hutchinson.

—(2010), *The Alastair Campbell Diaries, Volume 1: Prelude to Power 1994–1997*, London: Hutchinson.

Carter, H. (2005), 'Stacks of Potential', *The Guardian*, 15 June, p. 12.

Cashmore, E. (2006), *Celebrity/Culture*, London: Routledge.

Caves, R. (2000), *Creative Industries: Contracts between Art and Commerce*, Cambridge, MA: Harvard University Press.

Chomsky, N. (2001), *September 11*, Sydney: Allen and Unwin.

Clarke, D., Doel, M., Merrin, W. and Smith, R. (eds) (2008), *Jean Baudrillard: Fatal Theories*, London: Routledge.

Clarke, J. (1991), *New Times and Old Enemies: Essays on Cultural Studies and America*, London: Harper Collins.

Clarke, J. and Newman, J. (1997), *The New Managerial State*, London: Sage.

Cockburn, P. (2008), *Muqtada Al-Sadr and the Fall of Iraq*, London: Faber.

—(2006), *The Occupation: War and Resistance in Iraq*, London: Verso.

Cohen, S. (2007), *Decline, Renewal and the City in Popular Music Culture: Beyond the Beatles*, Aldershot: Ashgate.

Colletti, L. (1992), *La Logica di Benedetto Croce*, Rome: Marco.

—(1985), 'Preface' to K. Marx and F. Engels, *Manifesto del Partito Communista*, Bari: Laterza.

—(1984), *Le Declin du Marxisme*, Paris: Presses Universitaires de France.

—(1980), *Tramonto dell'Ideologia*, Bari: Laterza.

—(1975a), 'Introduction', to K. Marx, *Early Writings*, Harmondsworth: Penguin.

—(1975b), 'Marxism and the Dialectic', *New Left Review*, 1 (93), pp. 3–29.

—(1974), *Intervista Politicao-Filosofica, con un Saggio su Marxismo e Dialettica*, Bari: Laterza.

—(1973), *Marxism and Hegel*, London: Verso.

—(1972), *From Rousseau to Lenin: Studies in Ideology and Society*, London: Verso.

—(1971), 'Antonio Gramsci and the Italian Revolution', *New Left Review*, 1 (65), pp. 87–94.

—(1970), 'The Question of Stalin', *New Left Review*, 1 (61), pp. 61–81.

—(1969a), *Il Marxismo e Hegel*, Bari: Laterza.

—(1969b), *Ideologia e Societa*, Bari: Laterza.

Conley, V. (2005), 'Virilio's Electronic Derive', *Cultural Politics*, 1 (3), pp. 365–78.

Connor, S. (1997), *Postmodernist Culture*, Oxford: Blackwell.

Cott, J. (ed.) (2006), *Dylan on Dylan: The Essential Interviews*, London: Hodder and Stoughton.

Cottee, S. and Cushman, T. (eds) (2007), *Christopher Hitchens and his Critics: Terror, Iraq and the Left*, London: New York University Press.

Crawford, G. (2004), *Consuming Sport*, London: Routledge.

Crook, S., Pakulski, J. and Waters, M. (1992), *Postmodernisation: Change in Advanced Society*, London: Sage.

Cruddas, J. and Rutherford, J. (eds) (2009), *The Crash: A View from the Left*, London: Lawrence and Wishart.

—(2008), *Is the Future Conservative?*, London: Lawrence and Wishart.

Cubitt, S. (2001), *Simulation and Social Theory*, London: Sage

Cummins, K. (2010), *Joy Division*, New York: Rizzoli.

—(2009), *Manchester: Looking for the Light through the Pouring Rain*, London: Faber.

—(2008), *Juvenes*, London: Fuel.

—(2003), *We're Not Really Here: Manchester City's Final Season at Maine Road*, London: Dazed Books.

—(2002), *The Smiths and Beyond*, London: Vision On.

Cunningham, S. (2002a), 'From Cultural to Creative Industries: Theory, Industry and Policy Implications', *Media International Australia incorporating Culture and Policy*, 102, pp. 50–61.

—(2002b), 'Social and Creative Disciplines in Ascent', *The Australian*, 10 July, p. 9.

Delany, P. (1994), *Vancouver: Representing the Postmodern City*, Vancouver: Arsenal Pulp Press.

Delanty, G. (2006), 'The Cosmopolitan Imagination: Critical Cosmopolitanism and Social Theory', *British Journal of Sociology*, 57 (1), pp. 25–47.

Della Volpe, G. (1978), *Critique of Taste*, London: New Left Books.

Deleuze, G. (2006), *Two Regimes of Madness: Texts and Interviews 1975–1995*, Los Angeles and New York: Semiotext(e).

Denzin, N. (1991), *Images of Postmodern Society: Social Theory and Contemporary Cinema*, London: Sage.

Der Derian, J. (2009), *Virtuous War: Mapping the Military-Industrial-Media-Entertainment Complex*, London: Routledge.

Der Derian, J. (ed.) (1998), *The Virilio Reader*, Oxford: Blackwell.

Derrida, J. (2002), *Derrida: A Documentary*, DVD, London: ICA.

Devine, H. (2006), *Looking Back: Playwrights at the Royal Court 1956–2006*, London: Faber.

Diamond, P. and Liddle, R. (eds) (2009), *Beyond New Labour: The Future of Social Democracy in Britain*, London: Politico's.

Doogan, K. (2009), *New Capitalism? The Transformation of Work*, Cambridge: Polity.

Douzinas, C. and Warrington, R., with McVeigh, S. (1991), *Postmodern Jurisprudence: The Law of Text in the Texts of the Law*, London: Routledge.

Draper, D. (1997), *Blair's Hundred Days*, London: Faber.

Driver, S. and Martell, L. (1999), 'New Labour: Culture and Economy', in L. Ray and A. Sayer (eds), *Culture and Economy after the Cultural Turn*, London: Sage, pp. 50–69.

Du Gay, P. and Pryke, M. (eds) (2002), *Cultural Economy: Cultural Analysis and Commercial Life*, London: Sage.

Dylan, B. (2005a), *Chronicles, Volume One*, London: Simon and Schuster.

Dylan, B. (2005b), *Tarantula*, London: Harper Perennial.

Eagleton, T. (2010), *On Evil*, London: Yale University Press.

Easthope, A. (1991), *Literary into Cultural Studies*, London: Routledge.

—(1988), *British Post-Structuralism since 1968*, London: Routledge.

Elliott, A. and Turner, B. (2001), *Profiles in Contemporary Social Theory*, London: Sage.

Elliott, G. (1987), *Althusser: The Detour of Theory*, London: Verso.

Featherstone, M. (2007), *Consumer Culture and Postmodernism*, London: Sage.

Featherstone M. (ed.) (1990), *Global Culture: Nationalism, Globalisation and Modernity*, London: Sage.

Feltham, O. (2008), *Alain Badiou: Live Theory*, London: Continuum.

Ferguson, R. et al. (1990), *Discourses: Considerations in Postmodern Art and Culture*, Cambridge, MA: MIT Press.

Ferretter, L. (2006), *Louis Althusser*, London: Routledge.

Fitzpatrick, P. (2001), *Modernism and the Grounds of Law*, Cambridge: Cambridge University Press.

Flew, T. (2003), 'Creative Industries: From the Chicken Cheer to the Culture of Services', *Continuum: Journal of Media and Cultural Studies*, 17 (1), pp. 89–94.

Florida, R. (2010), *The Great Reset: How New Ways of Living and Working Drive Post-Crash Prosperity*, New York: Harper Collins.

—(2008), *Who's Your City? How the Creative Economy is Making where to Live the Most Important Decision of your Life*, New York: Basic Books.

—(2005a), *The Flight of the Creative Class: The New Global Competition for Talent*, New York: Harper Collins.

—(2005b), *Cities and the Creative Class*, London: Routledge.

—(2002), *The Rise of the Creative Class and How it's Transforming Work, Leisure, Community and Everyday Life*, New York: Basic Books.

Foucault, M. (2009), *Security, Territory, Population: Lectures at the College de France 1977–8*, New York: Palgrave.

—(2008), *The Birth of Biopolitics: Lectures at the College de France 1978–9*, New York: Palgrave.

—(2004), *Society Must Be Defended: Lectures at the College de France 1975–6*, London: Penguin.

Fouda, Y. and Fielding, N. (2003), *Masterminds of Terror: The Truth behind the Most Devastating Terrorist Attack the World has Ever Seen*, London: Penguin.

Friedman, G. (2010), *The Next 100 Years: A Forecast for the Twenty First Century*. New York: Anchor.

Frith, S. and Horne, H. (1987), *Art into Pop*, London: Methuen.

Frug, M. (1992), *Postmodern Legal Feminism*, New York: Routledge.

Fukuyama, F. (2006), *After the Neo-Cons: America at the Crossroads*, London: Profile.

—(2004), *Failed States*, London: Profile.

Gane, M. (2003), *French Social Theory*, London: Sage.

Gane, N. (2004), *The Future of Social Theory*, London: Continuum.

Geisler, T. and Doze, P. (2009), 'Rock around the Bunker: Paul Virilio – Design, War and Society', *DAMn* magazine, 21, March/April, pp. 9–15.

Geraghty, C. (2005), *My Beautiful Laundrette*, London: I.B.Tauris.

Gibson, L. (2001), *The Uses of Art*, Brisbane: University of Queensland Press.

Giddens, A. (2009), *The Politics of Climate Change*, Cambridge: Polity.

—(2007), *Over to You, Mr Brown: How Labour Can Win Again*, Cambridge: Polity.

—(2002), *Where Now For New Labour?*, Cambridge: Polity.

—(2000), *The Third Way and its Critics*, Cambridge: Polity.

—(1999), *Runaway World: How Globalisation is Reshaping our Lives*, London: Profile.

—(1998), *The Third Way: The Renewal of Social Democracy*, Cambridge: Polity.

—(1994), *Beyond Left and Right: The Future of Radical Politics*, Cambridge: Polity.

Giddens, A. (ed.) (2003), *The Progressive Manifesto: New Ideas for the Centre-Left*, Cambridge: Polity.

—(2001), *The Global Third Way Debate*, Cambridge: Polity.

Giddens, A. and Hutton, W. (eds) (2000), *On The Edge: Living with Global Capitalism*, London: Jonathan Cape.

Giddens, A. and Pierson, C. (1998), *Conversations with Anthony Giddens: Making Sense of Modernity*, Cambridge: Polity.

Gilbert, D. (2005), *Forever Young: Photographs of Bob Dylan*, Cambridge, MA: Da Capo.

Gill, A. (2006), 'Meet Bob the Cynic', *The Independent*, 25 August, p. 6.

Gilroy, P. (2004), *After Empire: Melancholia or Convivial Culture?*, London: Routledge.

Giulianotti, R. (2005), *Sport: A Critical Sociology*, Cambridge: Polity.

Giulianotti, R. (ed.) (2004), *Sport and Modern Social Theorists*, Basingstoke: Palgrave.

Gottfried, P. (2005), *The Strange Death of Marxism: The European Left in the New Millennium*, Columbia: University of Missouri Press.

—(1978), 'Marxism Contra Hegel: The World of Lucio Colletti', *Marxist Perspectives*, Fall, pp. 51–63.

Graham, S. (2010), *Cities under Siege: The New Military Urbanism*, London: Verso.

—(2004), 'War in the "Weirdly Pervious World": Infrastructure, Demodernisation and Geopolitics', Durham: University of Durham, pp. 1–40.

Gray, J. (2011), *The Immortalisation Commission*, London: Allen Lane.

—(2009a), *Gray's Anatomy*, London: Allen Lane.

—(2009b), *False Dawn: The Delusions of Global Capitalism*, London: Granta.

—(2009c), 'Interview: The World According to John Gray', *The Independent Magazine*, 11 April 11, pp. 9–14.

—(2007), *Black Mass: Apocalyptic Religion and the Death of Utopia*, London: Allen Lane.

—(2004), *Heresies: Against Progress and Other Illusions*, London: Granta.

—(2003), *Al Qaeda and What it Means to be Modern*, London: Faber and Faber.

—(2002), *Straw Dogs: Thoughts on Humans and Other Animals*, London: Granta.

Gray, J. and Willetts, D. (1997), *Is Conservatism Dead?*, London: Profile/Social Market Foundation.

Gray, M. (2006), *The Bob Dylan Encyclopedia*, London: Continuum.

—(2000), *Song and Dance Man III: The Art of Bob Dylan*, London: Cassell.

Greaves, J. (2005), *The Heart of the Game*, London: Time Warner.

Greenhalgh, L. (1998), 'From Arts Policy to Creative Economy', *Media International Australia incorporating Culture and Policy*, 87, pp. 71–90.

Greenspan, A. (2007), *The Age of Turbulence*, London: Allen Lane.

Griffin, D. (2010), *The Mysterious Collapse of World Trade Center 7: Why the Final Official Report about 9/11 is Unscientific and False*, Moreton: Arris.

—(2009), *Osama Bin Laden: Dead or Alive?*, Moreton: Arris.

—(2008a), *The New Pearl Harbor: 9/11, the Cover-Up and the Expose*, Moreton: Arris.

—(2008b), *9/11 Contradictions*, Moreton: Arris.

—(2007), *Debunking 9/11: An Answer to the Defenders of the Official Conspiracy Theory*, Moreton: Arris.

—(2005), *The 9/11 Commission Report: Omissions and Distortions*, Moreton: Arris.

—(2004), *The New Pearl Harbor: Disturbing Questions about the Bush Administration and 9/11*, Northampton, MA: Olive Branch.

Griffin, D. and Scott, P. (eds) (2007), *9/11 and American Empire: Intellectuals Speak Out*, Moreton: Arris.

Griffin, S. (2007), *Million Dollar Bash: Bob Dylan, the Band and the Basement Tapes*, London: Jawbone.

Grossberg, L. (2006), 'Does Cultural Studies have a Future? Should it? (or What's the Matter with New York?): Cultural Studies, Contexts and Conjunctures', *Cultural Studies*, 20 (1), pp. 1–32.

Gunaratna, R. (2002), *Inside Al Qaeda: Global Network of Terror*, Melbourne: Scribe.

Hall, G. (2002), *Culture in Bits: The Monstrous Future of Theory*, London: Continuum.

Hall, G. and Birchall, C. (2006), *New Cultural Studies: Adventures in Theory*, Edinburgh: Edinburgh University Press.

Hall, S. and Jacques, M. (eds) (1989), *New Times*, London: Lawrence and Wishart.

Halliday, F. (2002), *Two Hours that Shook the World – September 11, 2001: Causes and Consequences*, London: Saqi Books.

—(2001), *The World At 2000: Perils and Promises*, Basingstoke: Palgrave.

Hargreaves, I. and Christie, I. (eds) (1998), *Tomorrow's Politics: The Third Way and Beyond*, London: Demos.

Hargreaves, J. (1994), *Sporting Females: Critical Issues in the History and Sociology of Women's Sports*, London: Routledge.

Harris, J. (2011), 'We're All Right', *The Guardian*, 3 February, pp. 14–15.

—(2003), *The Last Party*, London: Fourth Estate.

Harvey, D. (2010), *The Enigma of Capital and the Crises of Capitalism*, London: Profile.

—(1999), *The Limits of Capital*, London: Verso.

—(1989), *The Condition of Postmodernity*, Oxford: Blackwell.

Hatherley, O. (2008), *Militant Modernism*, Winchester: Zero Books.

Healy, K. (2002), 'What's New for Culture in the New Economy?', *Journal of Arts Management, Law and Society*, 32 (2), pp. 86–103.

Heath, C. (1993), *Pet Shop Boys Versus America*, London: Viking.

—(1991), *Pet Shop Boys, Literally*, London: Penguin.

Heartfield, J. (2000), *Great Expectations: The Creative Industries in the New Economy*, London: Design Agenda.

Hedin, B. (ed.) (2006), *Studio A: The Bob Dylan Reader*, New York: W.W. Norton.

Hegarty, P. (2004), *Jean Baudrillard: Live Theory*, London: Continuum.

Henshall, I. (2007), *9/11: The New Evidence*, London: Constable and Robinson.

Hesmondalgh, D. (2002), *The Cultural Industries: Creativity and Power, Change and Continuity*, London: Sage.

Heylin, C. (2010), *Still on the Road: The Songs of Bob Dylan Volume 2: 1974–2008*, London: Constable.

—(2009), *Revolution in the Air: The Songs of Bob Dylan, Volume 1: 1957–1973*, London: Constable.

—(2000), *Bob Dylan behind the Shades: Take Two*, London: Viking.

Hirst, P. (2005), *Space, Power and Culture*, Cambridge: Polity.

—(2001), *War and Power in the Twenty-First Century*, Cambridge: Polity.

Hirst, P. and Thompson, G. (1996), *Globalisation in Question*, Cambridge: Polity.

Hitchens, C. (2007), *God is not Great: The Case against Religion*, London: Atlantic Books.

Hoare, P. and Heath, C. (2006), *Pet Shop Boys: Catalogue*, London: Thames and Hudson.

Hobsbawm, E. (2011), *How to Change the World: Tales of Marx and Marxism 1840–2011*, London: Little, Brown.

—(2007), *Globalisation, Democracy and Terrorism*, London: Little, Brown.

—(2002), *Interesting Times: A Twentieth Century Life*, London: Penguin.

—(1999), *The New Century: In Conversation with Antonio Polito*, London: Little, Brown.

—(1994), *Age of Extremes: The Short Twentieth Century 1914–1991*, London: Michael Joseph.

Hodsoll, F. (2002), 'Cultural Transactions', *Journal of Arts Management, Law and Society*, 32 (2).

Howkins, J. (2001), *The Creative Economy: How People Make Money from Ideas*, London: Allen Lane.

Hunt, A. (1996a), *Governance of the Consuming Passions: A History of Sumptuary Law*, New York: St Martin's Press.

—(1996b), 'Governing the City: Liberalism and Early Modern Modes of Governance', in A. Barry, T. Osborne and N. Rose (eds), *Foucault and Political Reason: Liberalism, Neo-Liberalism and Rationalities of Governance*, London: UCL Press, pp. 104–24.

Hussey, A. (2001), *The Game of War: The Life and Death of Guy Debord*, London: Jonathan Cape.

Hutcheon, L. (1988), *A Poetics of Postmodernism: History, Theory, Fiction*, London: Routledge.

Hutnyk, J. (2004), *Bad Marxism: Capitalism and Cultural Studies*, London: Pluto.

Hutton, W. (2010), *Them and Us: Changing Britain – Why We Need a Fair Society*, London: Little, Brown.

—(2002), *The World We're In*, London: Little, Brown.

—(1999), *The Stakeholding Society: Writings on Economics and Politics*, Cambridge: Polity Press.

—(1997), *The State to Come*, London: Vintage.

—(1995), *The State We're In*, London: Jonathan Cape.

Invisible Committee (2009), *The Coming Insurrection*, Los Angeles: Semiotext(e).

Jacques, M. (2009a), 'The New Depression', *New Statesman*, 16 February, p. 9.

—(2009b), 'When Blue Turned Red', *New Statesman*, 2 March 2, p. 10.

—(2009c), 'A Tale of Two Depressions', *New Statesman*, 30 July 30, pp. 15–16.

—(2009d), *When China Rules the World: The Rise of the Middle Kingdom and the End of the Western World*, London: Allen Lane.

James, I. (2007a), *Paul Virilio*, London: Routledge.

—(2007b), 'Phenomenology in Diaspora: Paul Virilio and the Question of Technology', *French Cultural Studies*, 17 (3), pp. 319–33.

Jameson, F. (2005), *Archaeologies of the Future*, London: Verso.

—(2001), *A Singular Modernity*, London: Verso.

—(1998), *The Cultural Turn: Selected Writings on the Postmodern 1983–1998*, London: Verso.

—(1991), *Postmodernism, or, the Cultural Logic of Capitalism*, London: Verso.

Janszen, E. (2010), *The Post Catastrophe Economy: Rebuilding America and Avoiding the Next Bubble*, London: Penguin.

Jenkins, I. (1980), *Social Theory and the Limits of Law: A Theoretical Essay*, Princeton: Princeton University Press.

Jenkins, S. (2010), 'Compared to a Lootfest like London or Beijing, Delhi is just an Also-Ran', *The Guardian*, 24 September, p. 25.

Jensen, J. (1990), *Redeeming Modernity: Contradictions in Media Criticism*, London: Sage.

Jones, D. (2008), *Cameron on Cameron*, London: Fourth Estate.

Kaleta, K. (1998), *Hanif Kureishi: Postcolonial Storyteller*, Austin: University of Texas Press.

Kaletsky, A. (2010), *Capitalism 4.0*, London: Bloomsbury.

Kaplan, E. and Sprinker, M. (eds) (1993), *The Althusserian Legacy*, London: Verso.

Kellner, D. (ed.) (1994), *Jean Baudrillard: A Critical Reader*, Oxford: Basil Blackwell.

Kepel, G. (2002), *Jihad: The Trail of Political Islam*, London: I.B. Tauris.

Kettle, M. (2010), 'These Credit Agencies are Leading an Assault on all of us', *The Guardian*, 17 December, p. 21.

—(2008), 'Labour Now Delights in its New Mandelson with a Plan', *The Guardian*, 5 December, p. 20.

Kinsella, J., Cohen, B., White, T., Wark, M. (2002), *Speedfactory*, Fremantle: Fremantle Arts Centre Press.

Kirby, A. (2010), 'Successor States to an Empire in Free Fall', *Times Higher Education*, 27 May, pp. 12–14.

—(2009), *Digimodernism: How New Technologies Dismantle the Postmodern and Reconfigure our Culture*, London: Continuum.

Kirby, T. (2010), 'Transforming Tomorrow', *The Guardian*, 8 September, p. 12.

Klein, N. (2007), *The Shock Doctrine: The Rise of Disaster Capitalism*, London: Penguin.

Kong, L. and O'Connor, J. (eds) (2009), *Creative Economies, Creative Cities: Asian-European Perspectives*, London: Springer.

Kroker, A. (1992), *The Possessed Individual*, Basingstoke: Macmillan.

Kureishi, H. (2010), *Collected Stories*, London: Faber.

—(2008), *Something To Tell You*, London: Faber.

—(2007), *Venus*, London: Faber.

—(2006a), 'Weddings and Beheadings', *Zoetrope*, Winter, pp. 14–19.

—(2006b), 'When Hanif Met Amir', *The Observer Sport Monthly*, 5 February, pp. 16–19.

—(2006c), 'End Notes: Review of Edward Said's On Late Style', *New Statesman*, 29 May, p. 12.

—(2006d), 'Reaping the Harvest of our Self-Disgust', *The Guardian*, 30 September, p. 25.

—(2005), *The Word and the Bomb*, London: Faber.

—(2004), *My Ear at his Heart: Reading my Father*, London: Faber.

—(2003), *The Mother*, London: Faber.

—(2002a), *The Body, and Seven Stories*. London: Faber.

—(2002b), *Dreaming and Scheming: Reflections on Writing and Politics*, London: Faber.

—(2002c), *Collected Screenplays I*, London: Faber.

—(2001), *Gabriel's Gift*, London: Faber.

—(1999), *Midnight All Day*, London: Faber.

—(1998), *Intimacy*, London: Faber.

—(1997a), *Love in a Blue Time*, London: Faber.

—(1997b), *My Son the Fanatic*, London: Faber.

—(1995), *The Black Album*, London: Faber.

—(1992), *Outskirts and Other Plays*, London: Faber.

—(1991), *London Kills Me*, London: Faber.

—(1990), *The Buddha of Suburbia*, London: Faber.

—(1988), *Sammy and Rosie Get Laid*, London: Faber.

—(1986), *My Beautiful Laundrette, and The Rainbow Sign*, London: Faber.

Kureishi, H. and Savage, J. (eds) (1995), *The Faber Book of Pop*, London: Faber.

Lacan, J. (2008a), *La Psychanalyse Reinventee / Lacan Parle*, DVD, Paris: Arte.

—(2008b), *My Teaching*, London: Verso.

Lanfranchi P. and Taylor M. (2001), *Moving with the Ball: The Migration of Professional Footballers*, Oxford: Berg.

Landry, C. (2000), *The Creative City*, London: Comedia.

Lash, S. (2003), 'Reflexivity as Non-Linearity', *Theory Culture and Society*, 20 (2), pp. 49–57.

—(2002), *Critique of Information*, London: Sage.

—(1999), *Another Modernity: A Different Rationality*, Oxford: Blackwell.

—(1995), 'Dead Symbols: An Introduction', *Theory, Culture and Society*, 12 (4), pp. 71–8.

—(1990), *Sociology of Postmodernism*, London: Routledge.

Lash, S. and Friedman, J. (eds) (1992), *Modernity and Identity*, Oxford: Blackwell.

Latour, B. (1993), *We Have Never Been Modern*, Cambridge, MA: Harvard University Press.

Laws, D. (2010), *22 Days in May: The Birth of the Lib Dem-Conservative Coalition*, London: Biteback.

Leadbeater, C. (2008), *We-Think*, London: Profile.

—(2002), *Up the Down Escalator: Why the Global Pessimists are Wrong*, London: Viking.

—(1999), *Living on Thin Air: The New Economy*, London: Viking.

—(1997), *Civic Spirit: The Big Idea for a New Political Era*, London: Demos.

Leadbeater, C. and Oakley, K. (1999), *The Independents: Britain's New Cultural Entrepreneurs*, London: Demos.

Leo, P. and Lee, T. (2004), 'The New Singapore: Mediating Culture and Creativity', *Continuum: Journal of Media and Cultural Studies*, 18 (2), pp. 205–18.

Leonard, J. (ed.) (1995), *Legal Studies as Cultural Studies: A Reader in (Post) Modern Critical Theory*, Albany: SUNY Press.

Lethem, J. (2006), 'Bringing It All Back Home', *The Observer*, 3 September, pp. 12–15.

Levy, B.-H. (2008), *Left in Dark Times: A Stand against the New Barbarism*, New York: Random House.

Lipovetsky, G. (2005), *Hypermodern Times*, Cambridge: Polity.

Lotringer, S. (1989), *Overexposed*, New York: Semiotext(e).

Louppe, L. (ed.) (1994), *Traces of Dance*, Paris: Editions de Voir.

Lynskey, D. (2010), 'Synths of our Fathers', *The Guardian*, 19 November, pp. 4–5.

Lyotard, J.-F. (1991), *The Inhuman: Reflections on Time*, Cambridge: Polity.

—(1988), *The Differend*, Minneapolis: University of Minnesota Press.

—(1984), *The Postmodern Condition: A Report on Knowledge*, Minneapolis: University of Minnesota Press.

Lyotard, J.-F. and Thebaud, J.-L. (1985), *Just Gaming*, Minneapolis: University of Minnesota Press.

McDonough, T. (ed.) (2009), *Situationists and the City*, London: Verso.

McGuigan, J. (2009), *Cool Capitalism*, London: Pluto Press.

—(2002), *Modernity and Postmodern Culture*, Buckingham: Open University Press.

—(1998), 'National Government and the Public Sphere', *Media International Australia incorporating Culture and Policy*, 87, pp. 70–87.

McKinlay, A. and Smith, C. (eds) (2009), *Creative Labour: Working in the Creative Industries*, Houndmills: Palgrave.

McLuhan, M. (2003) *Understanding Media*, Corte Madera: Gingko.

McNamara, A. (2002), 'How "Creative Industries" Evoke the Legacy of Modern Visual Art', *Media International Australia incorporating Culture and Policy*, 102, pp. 90–110.

McQuillan, M. (2000), *Post-Theory: New Directions in Criticism*, Edinburgh: Edinburgh University Press.

Mandelson, P. (2010), *The Third Man: Life at the Heart of New Labour*, London: HarperPress.

Mann, G. (2009), 'Colletti on the Credit Crunch: A Response to Robin Blackburn', *New Left Review*, 2 (56), pp. 119–27.

Maravelis, P. (2008), 'Trajectories of the Catastrophic', City Lights, San Francisco, at http://www.trajectoriesofthecatastrophic.net/

Marcus, G. (2010), *Bob Dylan by Greil Marcus: Writings 1968–2010*, New York: Public Affairs.

—(2005), *Like a Rolling Stone: Bob Dylan at the Crossroads*, London: Faber.

—(2001), *The Old, Weird America: The World of Bob Dylan's Basement Tapes*, London: Picador.

—(1997), *Invisible Republic: Bob Dylan's Basement Tapes*, London: Picador.

Marqusee, M. (2005), *Wicked Messenger: Bob Dylan and the 1960s*, New York: Seven Stories Press.

—(2003), *Chimes of Freedom: The Politics of Bob Dylan's Art*, New York: The New Press.

Marrs, J. (2006), *The Terror Conspiracy: Deception, 9/11 and the Loss of Liberty*, New York: Disinformation.

Martin, J. (ed.) (2008), *The Poulantzas Reader: Marxism, Law and the State*, London: Verso.

Marx, K. and Engels, F. (1998), *The Communist Manifesto* (with introduction by Eric Hobsbawm), London: Verso.

Mason, P. (2009), *Meltdown: The End of the Age of Greed*, London: Verso.

May, C. (2002), 'Trouble in E-topia: Knowledge as Intellectual Property', *Urban Studies*, 39 (5–6), pp. 1037–49.

Merrifield, A. (2005), *Guy Debord*, London: Reaktion.

Merrin, W. (2005), *Baudrillard and the Media: A Critical Introduction*, Cambridge: Polity.

Meyssan, T. (2002a), *9/11: The Big Lie*, London: Carnot.

—(2002b), *Pentagate*, London: Carnot.

Migayou, F. and Rambert, F. (2010), *Claude Parent: L'Oeuvre construite, l'oeuvre graphique*, Paris: Cité de l'Architecture.

Miller, J. and Stone, M., with Mitchell, C. (2002), *The Cell: Inside the 9/11Plot and Why The FBI and CIA Failed to Stop it*, New York: Hyperion Books.

Miller, T. (2001), *Sportsex*, Philadelphia, PA: Temple University Press.

Miller, T., Lawrence, G. McKay, J. and Rowe, D. (2001), *Globalisation and Sport*, London: Sage.

Moore, G. (2005), 'Goalkeepers Grapple with the Art of the Impossible in Beach Ball Era', *The Independent*, 7 June, p. 6.

Moore-Gilbert, B. (2001), *Hanif Kureishi*, Manchester: Manchester University Press.

Morgan, R. (2006), *Flight 93 Revealed: What Really Happened on the 9/11 Let's Roll Flight*, London: Constable and Robinson.

Morrison, W. (1997), *Jurisprudence: From the Greeks to Post-Modernism*, London: Cavendish.

—(1995), *Theoretical Criminology: From Modernity to Post-Modernism*, London: Cavendish.

Moya, E. (2010), 'Over One Hundred American Cities Face Ruin in Third Wave of Global Debt Crisis', *The Guardian*, 21 December, p. 25.

Mulgan, G. (2009), 'After Capitalism', *Prospect*, April, pp. 5–7.

Myers, T. (2003), *Slavoj Žižek*, London: Routledge.

Myerscough, J. (1988), *The Economic Importance of the Arts*, London: Policy Studies Institute.

National Commission on Terrorist Attacks upon the United States (2004), *Final Report*, New York: W.W. Norton.

Naves, M. (2000), *Marxismo E Direito: Um Estudo Sobre Pachukanis*, Sao Paolo: Boitempo Editorial.

Naves, M. (ed.) (2009), *O Discreto Charme Do Direito Burgues: Ensaios Sobre Pachukanis*, Sao Paolo: Instituto de Filosofia e Ciencias Humanas.

Neill, A. and Kent, M. (2007), *Anyway Anyhow Anywhere: The Complete Chronology of The Who 1958–1978*, London: Virgin.

Nice, J. (2010), *Shadowplayers: The Rise and Fall of Factory Records*, London: Aurum.

Nicoletti, M. (1998), *Claude Parent: The Oblique Function*, Turin: Testo and Immagine.

Nozick, R. (2001), *Anarchy, State and Utopia*, Oxford: Wiley.

O'Connor, J. (2004), 'Cities, Culture and Transitional Economies: Developing Cultural Industries in St Petersburg', in D. Power and A. Scott (eds), *Cultural Industries and the Production of Culture*, London: Routledge, pp. 15–30.

—(2002), 'Public and Private in the Cultural Industries', in T. Johansson and O. Sernhede (eds), *Lifestyle, Desire and Politics: Contemporary Identities*, Gothenburg: Daidalos.

O'Farrell, J. (1998), *Things Can Only Get Better*, London: Doubleday.

O'Hara, K. (2007), *After Blair: David Cameron and the Conservative Tradition*, London: Icon.

O'Neill, S. and McGrory, D. (2006), *The Suicide Factory: Abu Hamza and the Finsbury Park Mosque*, London: HarperCollins.

Pareles, J. (1993), 'Review/Pop: Dylan Displays His Staying Power', *New York Times*, 19 November, p. 9.

Parent, C. (2001), 'A Paradox: Limits and Fluidity', in P. Cook, N. Spiller, L.

Allen and P. Rawes (eds), *The Lowe Lectures: The Paradox of Contemporary Architecture*, Chichester: Wiley-Academy, pp. 20–5.

—(1982), *L'Architecte bouffon social*, Paris: Casterman.

—(1981), *Entrelacs de l'oblique*, Paris: Editions de Monieur.

—(1975), *Claude Parent, architecte*, Paris: Robert Laffont.

—(1970), *Vivre a l'oblique*, Paris: L'Aventure Urbaine.

Parent, C. and Virilio, P. (1997), *Architecture principe 1966 and 1996*, Besancon: Les Editions de l'Imprimeur.

Patrick, K. (2003), 'The Century of Fear', *Contemporary*, 47–8, pp. 12–14.

Pawlett, W. (2007), *Jean Baudrillard: Against Banality*, London: Routledge.

Perri 6 (1998), *On the Right Lines: The Next Centre-Right in the British Isles*, London: Demos.

Perryman, M. (ed.) (1996), *The Blair Agenda*, London: Lawrence and Wishart.

—(1994), *Altered States: Postmodernism, Politics, Culture*, London: Lawrence and Wishart.

Perryman, M. and Coddington, A. (eds) (1998), *The Moderniser's Dilemma: Radical Politics in the Age of Blair*, London: Lawrence and Wishart.

Plant, S. (1992), *The Most Radical Gesture: The Situationist International in a Postmodern Age*, London: Routledge.

Porter, M. (2002), *Clusters and the New Economics of Competition*, Cambridge, MA: Harvard Business School Press.

Poster, M. (ed.) (2001), *Jean Baudrillard: Selected Writings*, Cambridge: Polity.

Pronger, B. (1998), 'Post-Sport: Transgressing Boundaries in Physical Culture', in G. Rail (ed.), *Sport and Postmodern Times*, Albany: SUNY Press, pp. 50–75.

Proto, F. (ed.) (2006), *Mass/Identity/Architecture: Architectural Writings of Jean Baudrillard*, Chichester: Wiley-Academy.

Radice, G. (2010), *Trio: Inside the Blair, Brown, Mandelson Project*, London: I.B.Tauris.

—(2004), *Diaries: 1980–2001*, London: Weidenfeld and Nicolson.

Ragon, M. (1982), *Monographie critique d'un architecte*, Paris: Dunod.

Ranasinha, R. (2002), *Hanif Kureishi*, Tavistock: Northcote House.

Ranciere, J. (2009), *The Future of the Image*, London: Verso.

Rashid, A. (2008), *Descent into Chaos: The United States and the Failure of Nation Building in Pakistan, Afghanistan and Central Asia*, New York: Penguin.

—(2002), *Taliban: Islam, Oil and the New Great Game in Central Asia*, London: I.B. Tauris.

Rawnsley, A. (2010), *The End of the Party: The Rise and Fall of New Labour*, London: Viking.

—(2000), *Servants of the People: The Inside Story of New Labour*, London: Hamish Hamilton.

Readings, B. (1991), *Introducing Lyotard: Art and Politics*, London: Routledge.

Redhead, S. (2010), 'Militainment: Review of Roger Stahl's Militainment, Inc', *Times Higher Education*, July 15–21, p. 55.

—(2009), 'Before The Bunker', *Nebula* 6.2, at http://www.nobleworld.biz/images/Redhead.pdf

—(2004b), *Paul Virilio: Theorist for an Accelerated Culture*, Edinburgh: Edinburgh University Press/Toronto and Buffalo: Toronto University Press.

—(2000), *Repetitive Beat Generation*, Edinburgh: Rebel Inc/Canongate.

—(1997a), *Subculture to Clubcultures*, Oxford: Blackwell

—(1997b), *Post-Fandom and the Millennial Blues*, London: Routledge.

—(1995), *Unpopular Cultures: The Birth of Law and Popular Culture*, Manchester: Manchester University Press.

—(1990), *The End-of-the-Century Party* (with photographs by Kevin Cummins), Manchester: Manchester University Press.

Redhead, S. (ed.) (2008), *The Jean Baudrillard Reader*, Edinburgh: Edinburgh University Press/New York: Columbia University Press.

—(2004a), *The Paul Virilio Reader*, Edinburgh: Edinburgh University Press/New York: Columbia University Press.

Reeve, S. (1999), *The New Jackals: Ramzi Yousef, Osama Bin Laden and the Future of Terrorism*, London: Andre Deutsch.

Reisz, M. (2010), 'Two Front Attack on "New Aetheists"', *Times Higher Education*, November 25 – December 1, p. 7.

Rentoul, J. (2001), *Tony Blair: Prime Minister*, London: Little, Brown.

Reynolds, S. (2010), *Whatever it Takes: The Real Story of Gordon Brown and New Labour*, London: Fourth Estate.

—(2009), *Totally Wired: Post-Punk Interviews and Overviews*, London: Faber.

—(2008), *Energy Flash: A Journey through Rave Music and Dance Culture*, London: Picador.

—(2005), *Rip It Up And Start Again: Post-Punk 1978–1984*, London: Faber.

Richards. S. (2010), *Whatever It Takes: The Real Story of Gordon Brown and New Labour*, London: Fourth Estate.

Ridgeway, J. (2005), *The 5 Unanswered Questions About 9/11: What the 9/11 Commisssion Report Failed to Tell Us*, New York: Seven Stories.

Rifkin, J. (2000), *The Age of Access: The New Culture of Hypercapitalism, Where All Life is a Paid-For Experience*, Harmondsworth: Penguin.

Robertson, M. (2006), *Factory Records: The Complete Graphic Album*, London: Thames and Hudson.

Ross, A. (ed.) (1989), *The Politics of Postmodernism*, Edinburgh: Edinburgh University Press.

Rowe, D. (2004), *Sport, Culture and the Media*, Buckingham: Open University Press.

Rutherford, J. (2008), 'The Culture of Capitalism', *Soundings*, 38, pp. 8–18.

Rutherford, J. and Chakraborty, A. (2010), 'Britain's Economy is Broken: This is how to Start Fixing it', *The Guardian*, 22 September, p. 24.

Ruthven, M. (2002), *A Fury for God*, London: Granta.

Said, E. (2006), *On Late Style*, London: Bloomsbury.

—(2005), *Edward Said: The Last Interview*, DVD, London: ICA.

Santelli, R. (2005), *The Bob Dylan Scrapbook: 1956–1966*, London: Simon and Schuster.

Savage, J. (2009), *The England's Dreaming Tapes*, London: Faber.

—(2007), *Teenage: The Creation of Youth Culture 1875–1945*, London: Faber.

—(2004), *England's Dreaming*, London: Faber.

—(1996), *Time Travel: Pop, Media and Sexuality 1977–1996*, London: Faber.

—(1984), *The Kinks*, London: Faber.

Saville, P. (2007), *Estate*, Zurich: JRP Ringier.

—(2003), *Designed by Peter Saville*, London: Frieze.

Scraton, P. (2009), *Hillsborough: The Truth*, Edinburgh: Mainstream.

Seldon, A. (2007), *Blair Unbound*, London: Simon and Schuster.

—(2004), *Blair*, London: Simon and Schuster.

Seldon, A. and Lodge, G. (2010), *Brown at 10*, London: Biteback.

Sherwin, R. (2000), *When Law Goes Pop: The Vanishing Line between Law and Popular Culture*, Chicago: Chicago University Press.

Sim, S. (2010), *The End of Modernity*, Edinburgh: Edinburgh University Press.

Sim, S. (ed.) (2005), *The Routledge Companion to Postmodernism*, London: Routledge.

Smith, A. (1986), 'Hegelianism and Marxism: A Reply to Lucio Colletti', *Science and Society*, 50, pp. 1–7.

Smith, C. (1998), *Creative Britain*, London: Faber and Faber.

Smith, D. (2010), *The Age of Instability*, London: Profile.

Smith, R. (ed.) (2010), *The Baudrillard Dictionary*, Edinburgh: Edinburgh University Press/New York: Columbia University Press.

Sokal, A. and Bricmont, J. (2003), *Intellectual Impostures: Postmodern Philosophers' Abuse of Science*, London: Profile Books.

Soros, G. (2006), *The Age of Fallibility*, London: Weidenfeld and Nicolson.

Sounes, H. (2001), *Down the Highway: The Life of Bob Dylan*, London: Doubleday.

Stachel, J. (1988), 'Contradiction, Contrariety and Colletti', seminar paper to Department of Philosophy, University of Sydney.

Stahl, R. (2010), *Militainment, Inc.: War, Media and Popular Culture*, London: Routledge.

Sugden, J. and Tomlinson, A. (eds) (2002), *Power Games: A Critical Sociology of Sport*, London: Routledge.

Taylor, M. (2010), 'Review: Ivan Todorov's In Defence of the Enlightenment', *New Statesman*, 19 June, p. 12.

Tepper, S. (2002), 'Creative Assets and the Changing Economy', *Journal of Arts Management, Law and Society*, 32 (2), pp. 156–68.

Tester, K. (1993), *Life and Times of Postmodernity*, London: Routledge.

Tett, G. (2009), *Fool's Gold*, London: Little, Brown.

Therborn, G. (2008), *From Marxism to Post-Marxism?*, London: Verso.

Thomas, S. (ed.) (2005), *Hanif Kureishi: A Reader's Guide to Essential Criticism*, Houndmills: Palgrave.

Thrift, N. (2005), 'Panicsville: Paul Virilio and the Aesthetic of Disaster', *Cultural Politics*, 1 (3), pp. 353–63.

Tomlinson, A. (ed.) (2006), *The Sports Studies Reader*, London: Routledge.

Toth, J. (2010), *The Passing of Postmodernism: A Spectroanalysis of the Contemporary*, New York: SUNY Press.

Turner, A. (2001), *Just Capital: The Liberal Economy*, Basingstoke: Macmillan.

Turner, B. (ed.) (1990), *Theories of Modernity and Postmodernity*, London: Sage.

Turner, G. (2008), *The Credit Crunch*, London: Pluto Press.

Tusa, J. (2003), 'Thou Shalt Worship the Arts for what They Are', *Arts Education Policy Review*, 104 (3), pp. 3–7.

Urry, J. (2007), *Mobilities*, Cambridge: Polity.

—(2003), *Global Complexity*, Cambridge: Polity.

—(2002), *The Tourist Gaze*, London: Sage.

—(2000), *Sociology beyond Societies: Mobilities for the Twenty-First Century*, London: Routledge.

Virilio, P. (2010a), *The Futurism of the Instant: Stop-Eject*, Cambridge: Polity.

—(2010b), *The University of Disaster*, Cambridge: Polity.

—(2009a), *Bunker Archeology*, New York: Princeton Architectural Press.

—(2009b), *Grey Ecology*, New York: Atropos.

—(2009c), *The Aesthetics of Disappearance*, Los Angeles: Semiotext(e).

—(2007a), *Art as Far as the Eye can See*, Oxford: Berg.

—(2007b), *The Original Accident*, Cambridge: Polity.

—(2006), *Speed and Politics*, Los Angeles: Semiotext(e).

—(2005a), 'Cold Panic', *Cultural Politics*, 1 (1), pp. 27–30.

—(2005b), *Negative Horizon*, London: Continuum.

—(2005c), *City of Panic*, Oxford: Berg.

—(2005d), 'Democracy of Emotion', *Cultural Politics*, 1 (3), pp. 339–51.

—(2003a), *Unknown Quantity*, London: Thames and Hudson.

—(2003b), *The Art of Fear*, London: Continuum.

—(2002a), *Ground Zero*, London: Verso.

—(2002b), *Desert Screen: War at the Speed of Light*, London: Continuum.

—(2001), *Polar Inertia*, London: Sage.

—(2000), *A Landscape of Events*, Cambridge, MA: MIT Press.

—(1997), *Open Sky*, London: Verso.

—(1996a), 'The Silence of the Lambs: Interview with Paul Virilio by Carlos Oliveira', *Apres Coup*.

Virilio, P. (1996b), *The Function of the Oblique: The Architecture of Claude Parent and Paul Virilio 1963–1969*, London: Architectural Association.

Virilio, P. and Depardon, R. (2008a), *Manhattan Out*, Gottingen: Steidl.

—(2008b), *Native Land / Stop Eject*, Paris: Fondation Pour l'Art Contemporain.

Virilio, P. and Dumoucel, C. (2010), 'Paul Virilio', *Vice Magazine*, at http://www.viceland.com/int/v17n9/htdocs/paul-virilio-506.php

Virilio, P. and Lotringer, S. (2008), *Pure War*, 3rd edn, Los Angeles: Semiotext(e).

—(2005), *The Accident of Art*, New York and Los Angeles: Semiotext(e).

—(2002), *Crepuscular Dawn*, New York and Los Angeles: Semiotext(e).

Virilio, P. and Petit, P. (1999), *Politics of the Very Worst*, New York: Semiotext(e).

Whannel, G. (2002), *Media Sport Stars: Masculinities and Moralities*, London: Routledge.

Wheeler, S. (2002), *Corporations and the Third Way*, Oxford: Hart.

White, S. (2009), 'Thinking The Future', *New Statesman*, 7 September, p. 6.

Wilentz, S. (2010), *Bob Dylan in America*, London: Bodley Head.

Wilkerson, M. (2008), *Who Are You: The Life of Pete Townshend*, London: Omnibus.

Willis, P. (1977), *Learning to Labour: How Working Class Kids Get Working Class Jobs*, Farnborough: Saxon House.

Wilson, E. (ed.) (2009a), *Government of the Shadows: Parapolitics and Criminal Sovereignty*, Sydney: Pluto Press.

—(2009b), 'Speed/Pure War/Power Crime: Paul Virilio on the Criminogenic Accident and the Virtual Disappearance of the Suicidal State', *Crime, Law and Social Change*, 51 (3–4), pp. 413–34.

Winner, D. (2005), *Those Feet: A Sensual History of English Football*, London: Bloomsbury.

Woodiwiss, A. (1990), *Social Theory after Postmodernism: Rethinking Production, Law and Class*, London: Pluto Press.

Wright, L. (2006), *The Looming Tower: Al Qaeda's Road to 9/11*, London: Allen Lane.

Wynne, D. (ed.) (1992), *The Culture Industry*, Aldershot: Avebury.

Young, J. (2007), *The Vertigo of Late Modernity*, London: Sage.

Yousaf, N. (2002), *Hanif Kureishi's The Buddha of Suburbia*, London: Continuum.

Zeitlin, J. and Hirst, P. (eds) (1989), *Reversing Industrial Decline? Industrial Structure and Policy in Britain and her Competitors*, Oxford: Berg.

Žižek, S. (2010), *Living in the End Times*, London: Verso.

—(2009), *First as Tragedy, Then as Farce*, London: Verso.

—(2008a), *Violence*, London: Profile.

—(2008b), *In Defence of Lost Causes*, London: Verso.

—(2007), *Žižek ! The Elvis of Cultural Theory*, DVD, London: ICA.

—(2006a), *The Universal Exception*, London: Continuum.

—(2006b), *The Parallax View*, Cambridge, MA: MIT Press.

—(2005), *Interrogating the Real*, London: Continuum.

—(2004), *Iraq: The Borrowed Kettle*, London: Verso.

—(2002a), *Welcome to the Desert of the Real!*, London: Verso.

—(2002b), *Revolution at the Gates: Žižek on Lenin: The 1917 Writings*, London: Verso.

Žižek, S. and Daly, G. (2004), *Conversations with Slavoj Žižek*, Cambridge: Polity.

Index